C# Programming

Vic Broquard

C# Programming
2nd Edition

©2009, 2014 by Vic Broquard

Published by:
Broquard eBooks
http://Broquard-eBooks.com
author@Broquard-eBooks.com
103 Timberlane
East Peoria, IL 61611

ISBN: 978-1-941415-62-7

Table of Contents

Download the sample programs and test data from http://www.broquard-ebooks.com/pb/csharp and take appropriate link.

Chapter 1—An Introduction

C# (pronounced C-sharp like the musical symbol) could narrowly be thought of as Microsoft's replacement for Java, but it is much more than that.

C# provides the following:
> complete OOP platform
> full capabilities for handling strings and graphics
> complete package of GUI (graphical user interface) components
> exception handling
> multithreading
> complete multimedia processing including audio, video, animations, images
> file processing
> data base programming
> a good set of data structures (containers such as arrays, lists, queues, stacks)
> Internet and Web based client-server processing
> networking support
> distributed processing across several servers to decrease workloads
> seamless integration with all other components
> easy interface to DirectX for games programs
> a program should be deployment independent—whether run on a local PC or run across the Internet

Thus, a C# program is a complete solution. As with C++, all projects are now called solutions with the .sln file extension.

But C# is more than just this. Microsoft is looking for a unified platform across PCs, their Windows operating systems, Networks, and the Internet and Web based processes, to say nothing about new consumer electronic devices such as cell phones and personal assistants and even TV based activities. This is their .NET project in which the focus is shifted to a world in which individual devices, Web sites and services and computers work together to provide the solution. A .NET solution contains the .NET Building Block Services (program access to things like file storage, calendar, Passport.NET for identification verification), a common user interface, and the .NET infrastructure consisting of the .NET Framework, Visual Studio, .NET Enterprise Servers and Windows .NET.

C# has its roots in C++ and Java, combining the best ideas of each into a whole. It is an event-driven, object oriented, visual programming language. It remedies the potential pitfalls inherent in the C++ language so that such errors cannot occur, such as forgetting to delete dynamically allocated memory.

The .NET Framework consists of the **Common Language Runtime** system called the **CLR** to provide this platform and the .NET Framework **Class Libraries** or the Base Class Libraries (**BCL**), the ADO.NET, the ASP.NET, and XML web services. The CLR is a virtual machine that runs a .NET solution on any platform on any hardware. All of the .NET languages have the same Class Libraries available for their use. These libraries are similar to the MFC libraries. The class libs provide support for just about anything you care to do, from file I/O, to data structure containers, to GUI components, to database access, XML and the new SOAP.

A **virtual machine** is a high level operating system abstraction in which other operating systems could function in an encapsulated environment. A program that runs in the CLR runs in a completely encapsulated environment, separated from other application processes on that machine.

The CLR is the core of .NET and is a runtime environment. The tasks which run on the CLR are called components which can include complete programs but does not necessarily have to. A component has **properties** and **methods** and may respond to **events**. A component is also an object. All programs are written as a series of inter-relating components. A complete package of components to solve a problem for a user is called a solution.

Here is a typical "Hello World" program in C++.

```
#include <iostream>
using namespace std;
int main (int argc, char* argv[]) {
 cout << "Hello World\n";
 return 0;
}
```

Here is the same program in C#.

```
using System;
namespace Pgm01aConsole {
 class Program  {
  static void Main(string[] args) {
   Console.WriteLine ("Hello World");
  }
 }
}
```

A C# program has no header files, no idl files, no type libraries. The **using System** is a short cut to the System portion of the Class Libraries so that we do not have to code `System.Console.WriteLine`. The next thing to note is that there are no header files. The third thing to note is that everything must be in a class. There are no standalone, outside of a class, type **main** functions.

Here, the console application is triggered by the presence of a **Main public static** function. When this application is launched, the CLR automatically begins execution with the **public static**

Main function of the class. Finally, note that there are no iostreams. These are replaced with common runtime library routines designed to handle the input and output.

What does the C# and other .NET compilers produce? In essence, the CLR is an interpreter. It interprets and executes **MSIL, Microsoft intermediate language** which is akin to assembler language. The C# compiler translates your source statements into MSIL statements storing them in the .exe file. When the application is actually executed, the CLR must translate the MSIL instructions into the actual machine or assembly language instructions of the particular type processor on which the program is running at the moment. Incidentally, the actual startup code that gets control in a C# application is called _CorExeMain. At this point, the CLR compiles the MSIL into a machine-executable format by using the **JIT** compiler - **Just In Time**. It is called the JITer. It compiles only the immediately executing method. Or it JITers each method as it is called. It then caches the JITered coding on the machine on which the program is running.

Three different JITers can be used. Install-time code generation compiles an entire program into specific CPU machine instructions and is done at install time. The default JIT is called at program run time as each method is invoked—rather a pay as you go type of approach. The EconoJIT is designed for systems with limited resources (hand held devices); here code that has been previously compiled is discarded when memory gets low.

Thus, we can now understand the new concepts of **managed code** and **unmanaged code**. Managed code is that which is running under the control of the CLR and is thus being managed by the CLR. The term unmanaged code refers to executing existing non .NET programs, functions, or components, DLLs and so forth.

Additionally, the exe files contain metadata, which is data that describes data members within the component. These are similar to type libraries of COM components. Thus, within a solution, there is no way to lose track of either the methods or data properties of an object, ever. They form a unified whole. Knowing what data types are needed allows the CLR to more efficiently manage a component. The means by which the metadata is queried is called **reflection**. The CLR has a set of methods that anyone can call to get access to the metadata of a component at runtime. Visual Studio uses these methods to provide its IntelliSense handling as you type.

Basics of C# Programming

Every C# program must have at least one **class**, often called the application class in simpler programs, which must have a public and static member function called **Main**.

However, unlike C++ in which you usually have a class definition (.h) file, a class implementation (.cpp) file, and then an implementation (.cpp) file, in C# there is only one file (.cs). In C#, you must define all member functions **inline** within the class definition. Thus, you end up with a single, highly transportable class since there is only the single file that contains everything.

Recall that **static functions** do not have instance data. They service the entire class. That's the purpose of Main. The Main function can and most certainly does allocate one or more instances of the class and invoke various member functions on those instance data.

A C# program invokes many of the Class Library functions. If we documented all of the functions available for our use in a C# program, the documentation would more than fill a book and we could spend an entire semester just looking at them. This huge pile of functions are grouped into **collections**, such as those that perform system type actions, the **System** group. These functions are organized into logical hierarchies. Thus, within the **System** group or **namespace** is the **Console** class of functions. One of these is the **WriteLine** function that we can call to output a line of text. By using the using statements, we can avoid having to fully qualify classes and methods within those classes.

Of course, these functions must be fully qualified.
```
System.Console.WriteLine (...);
```
Further, since an application may use a number of related functions, by using the **using** directive, we can provide a shortcut. If we code
```
using System;
```
then we can shorten the call to this.
```
Console.WriteLine (...);
```

So one would think that we could code
```
using System.Console; // error
```
then we could shorten it to just
```
WriteLine (...);
```
However, **Console** is a class. And the using must specify a hierarchy (i.e. a namespace) and not a specific class. This hierarchy is called a **namespace**. All of the .NET class libraries are organized into many different namespaces. This eliminates the problem of identifier collisions—when the same identifier is used in two or more different places. We are even allowed to create our own namespaces. Normally, this is only done when we are dealing with a very large application, but if the compiler generates the shell, it installs an application specific namespace.

Getting Started—The Hello World Program

Naturally, to create a new program, we choose File-New Project as you might expect. This is shown in Figure 1. Choose C# and then Console Application. Enter a name.

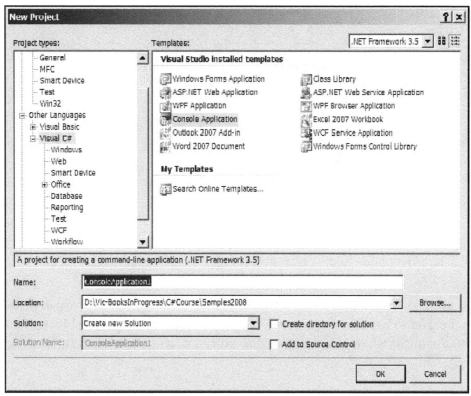

Figure 1.1 Create a New C# Console Project

The New Project dialog appears, as shown in Figure 1.1, you have several choices. For our beginning purposes, two choices are possible: Windows Forms Application or Console Application. If you choose to make a Windows Forms Application, to be useful, you will need some of the more advanced C# features which we will not cover for several weeks. So for now, the best choice is to use Console Application.

Be sure that you enter the Name and Location for the new solution. Leave the checkbox for Create Directory for Solution unchecked. If it is checked, it places the solution or project files in another subfolder from the actual C# files, confusing the issue.

When you click Ok, the IDE creates the project and the basic C# file and opens it for editing as shown in Figure 1.2 below.

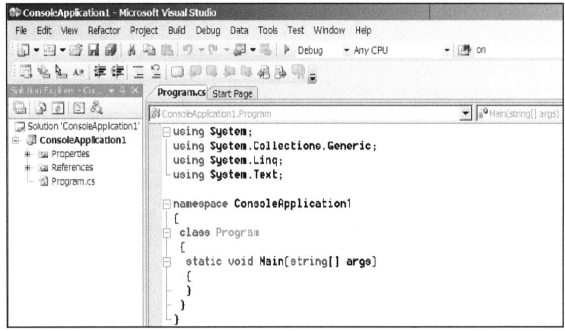

Figure 1.2 The Generated Shell Console Coding

The first thing to notice about this shell is the format of the { } braces. I usually change these as a first action. I prefer to have the begin brace { on the line that launches the block. It also inserts several additional usings that are unneeded at this time. I delete those as well, keeping only the `using System;` line.

The second thing to notice is that the IDE has setup a namespace for the entire application. While this is very useful is the application has a huge number of C# files and/or classes in it, for a beginning program, it is over-kill. I usually remove that block as well.

The third thing to notice is that there is a default class defined, called **Program**, and within it the **Main** member function is defined as a static function. It is this function that is given control first. Remember that a static member function has no instance data. It can, and often does, allocate one or more instances of our class and then perform operations upon those instances.

You probably do not want the default name of the class either. So change it to what is desired. Thus, here is what I have done to the shell program as a first action.

```
using System;
class Hello {
  static void Main(string[] args) {

  }
}
```

The Console class contains a number of functions that we can use to display messages in the DOS window. In the simplest usage, the versatile **WriteLine** function displays a string on the screen and ends it with a new line code, the carraige return and line feed codes. Thus, to display "Hello World," we can code

```
Console.WriteLine ("Hello World");
```

Here is the complete program.

```
using System;
class Hello {
 static void Main(string[] args) {
  Console.WriteLine ("Hello World");
 }
}
```

Next, the solution must be compiled or built. When you look at the Build menu, notice that you have four choices: Build the Solution, Rebuild the Solution, Build the specific application, and Rebuild the specific application.

The difference between Build and Rebuild is the same as it is with C++ programs. Rebuild recompiles all files in the application. Build only compiles those files that have changed since the last build. The difference between building the solution and building the specific application is non-existent at this point. Later on, when a solution can contain several applications, then rebuild solution recompiles the entire collection of application, while rebuild the specific application rebuilds only the currently selected application out of the several that make up the complete solution.

When the program compiles and builds the executable, you can either use the debugger or just execute the program. Figure 1.3 shows the output of the Execute run of the program.

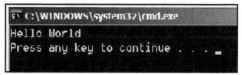

Figure 1.3 Execution of Hello Pgm

The Hello World Program as a Windows Forms Application

Alternatively, you can create a Windows Forms application by choosing File-New Project and selecting Windows Forms Application. Figure 1.4 shows what the default generated application looks like. Note that is the design view, not the actual coding view.

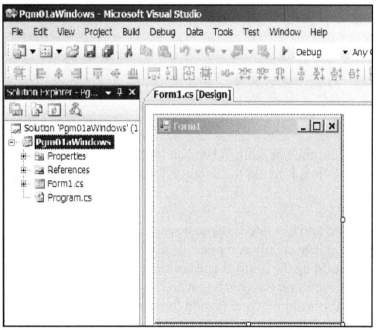

Figure 1.4 Windows Forms New Application

Notice how different this looks. Creating a Windows application is much like creating a FormView or Dialog in C++ Windows programming or like VB or even Access programming.

You next would need to insert some controls onto the blank window form. This is done by dragging the appropriate Toolbox button onto the form. However, if the Toolbox is not visible, as it is not in Figure 1.4, use the View-Toolbox menu item to make it visible, Figure 1.5.

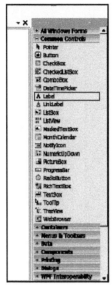

1.5 ToolBox

Notice that there are a large number of categories and controls within those categories. Here, I opened the Common Controls and selected a Label. A label is usually a static control that simply displays some text. In this application, we only want some text to appear. This is done use the Label toolbox item. Drag the label control over the form and drop. This is shown in Figure 1.6.

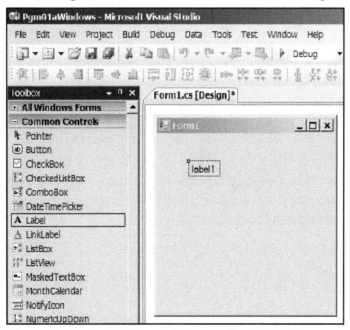

Figure 1.6 A Label Control Dropped onto the Form

Next, one would either enter the text desired into the label by right clicking on it and choose Properties and enter the data there. This is shown in Figure 1.7.

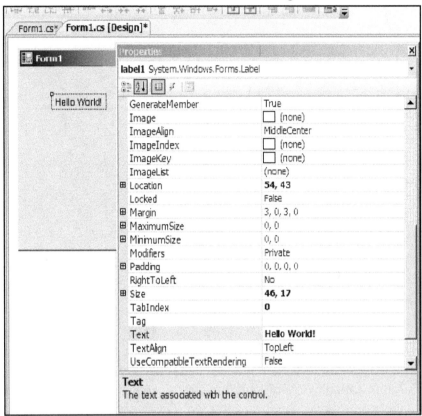

Figure 1.7 Changing the Text to Be Shown in the Label Control

There are a large number of properties that can be set in the label's properties. Experiment with some and see the visual effects they yield.

You can resize and move the label anywhere desired on the form. You can resize the form which represents the size of the window that appears. From the properties, you can alter the font, colors and so on.

By right clicking on the form but not on any control in that form, you can then set the properties of the entire window, specifically the window's caption, which at the moment says "Form1." Figure 1.8 shows what my final form looks like.

Figure 1.8 Hello Program

When you Execute the program, Figure 1.9 shows the window that appears. Notice to terminate the application, you must click on the "X" button.

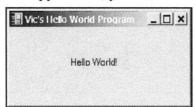

Figure 1.9 Executing Pgm

The reason that we are not beginning the course by using Windows applications is illustrated by using the View-Code menu item, which opens up the C# coding for the program. Here is the C# coding for this trivial program. There are three .cs files that are important. First is the Program.cs file. It contains the Main function which dynamically allocates a new Form1 class and then calls the Run function to execute it, much like a C++ Windows application.

Program.cs

```csharp
using System;
using System.Collections.Generic;
using System.Linq;
using System.Windows.Forms;

namespace Pgm01aWindows
{
 static class Program
 {
  /// <summary>
  /// The main entry point for the application.
  /// </summary>
  [STAThread]
  static void Main()
  {
   Application.EnableVisualStyles();
   Application.SetCompatibleTextRenderingDefault(false);
```

```
  Application.Run(new Form1());
    }
  }
}
```

Second, the Form1 class is divided into two parts. One contains the elements from the Design View and properties. The other contains the run time execution coding that responds to events, such as button clicks. Let's look at the Form1.cs file first.

Form1.cs
```
using System;
using System.Collections.Generic;
using System.ComponentModel;
using System.Data;
using System.Drawing;
using System.Linq;
using System.Text;
using System.Windows.Forms;

namespace Pgm01aWindows
{
 public partial class Form1 : Form
 {
  public Form1()
  {
   InitializeComponent();
  }

  private void label1_Click(object sender, EventArgs e)
  {

  }
 }
}
```

In this application, we are not responding to any events. The framework handles all of the actions a user can perform on the window while it is running, such as clicking on the X button to terminate it. The second file contains all of the initialization code which allocates the new Label control and sets its properties, including our text message.

Form1.Designer.cs
```
namespace Pgm01aWindows
{
 partial class Form1
 {
```

```
/// <summary>
/// Required designer variable.
/// </summary>
private System.ComponentModel.IContainer components = null;

/// <summary>
/// Clean up any resources being used.
/// </summary>
/// <param name="disposing">true if managed resources should be
disposed; otherwise, false.</param>
protected override void Dispose(bool disposing)
{
  if (disposing && (components != null))
  {
   components.Dispose();
  }
  base.Dispose(disposing);
}

#region Windows Form Designer generated code

/// <summary>
/// Required method for Designer support - do not modify
/// the contents of this method with the code editor.
/// </summary>
private void InitializeComponent()
{
  this.label1 = new System.Windows.Forms.Label();
  this.SuspendLayout();
  //
  // label1
  //
  this.label1.AutoSize = true;
  this.label1.Location = new System.Drawing.Point(96, 42);
  this.label1.Name = "label1";
  this.label1.Size = new System.Drawing.Size(84, 17);
  this.label1.TabIndex = 0;
  this.label1.Text = "Hello World!";
 this.label1.Click += new System.EventHandler(this.label1_Click);
  //
  // Form1
  //
  this.AutoScaleDimensions = new System.Drawing.SizeF(8F, 16F);
  this.AutoScaleMode = System.Windows.Forms.AutoScaleMode.Font;
  this.ClientSize = new System.Drawing.Size(292, 114);
  this.Controls.Add(this.label1);
```

13

```
 this.Name = "Form1";
 this.Text = "Vic\'s Hello World Program";
 this.ResumeLayout(false);
 this.PerformLayout();

}

#endregion

private System.Windows.Forms.Label label1;
 }
}
```

This coding uses nearly all of the complexities of the C# language all in one small program! So much for a gradient scale of learning! Thus, we begin our study of C# using Console Applications. Once we have all of the basics of the language learned, then we will return to making Windows Applications. At that point, we will be ready to tackle the coding.

There is yet another cs file that is part of the application, the Assembly.Info.cs file. It contains information about the whole program, including copyright notice, company, and version of the program data. We will later return to these assembly files and make good use of them.

Assembly.Info.cs
```
using System.Reflection;
using System.Runtime.CompilerServices;
using System.Runtime.InteropServices;

// General Information about an assembly is controlled through the
following
// set of attributes. Change these attribute values to modify the
information
// associated with an assembly.
[assembly: AssemblyTitle("Pgm01aWindows")]
[assembly: AssemblyDescription("")]
[assembly: AssemblyConfiguration("")]
[assembly: AssemblyCompany("")]
[assembly: AssemblyProduct("Pgm01aWindows")]
[assembly: AssemblyCopyright("Copyright ©  2009")]
[assembly: AssemblyTrademark("")]
[assembly: AssemblyCulture("")]

// Setting ComVisible to false makes the types in this assembly not
visible
// to COM components.  If you need to access a type in this
assembly from
```

```
// COM, set the ComVisible attribute to true on that type.
[assembly: ComVisible(false)]

// The following GUID is for the ID of the typelib if this project
is exposed to COM
[assembly: Guid("7e9dce30-116f-44bc-a2be-5f8406ecf0db")]

// Version information for an assembly consists of the following
four values:
//
//        Major Version
//        Minor Version
//        Build Number
//        Revision
//
// You can specify all the values or you can default the Build and
Revision Numbers
// by using the '*' as shown below:
// [assembly: AssemblyVersion("1.0.*")]
[assembly: AssemblyVersion("1.0.0.0")]
[assembly: AssemblyFileVersion("1.0.0.0")]
```

Chapter 2—Language Elements

Data Types

The .NET Common Type System (CTS) is at the heart of the .NET framework. The CTS defines all of the data types supported by the basic framework.

Normally a language has two types of data items: intrinsic (primitive) those built into the language and ADTs (abstract data types) created by user classes, such as the BigInt from CS232 class. In such a system, there are many problems, primarily in converting between the two types.

Rule: In C#, all data items are objects.
The rule is simple: everything is an object. Even an integer is an object. All of these are derived from a single base class called **System.Object**.

For speed or efficiency, two types or categories are used: **value types** and **reference types**. A variable of value type is a variable that contains actual data. A variable of reference type contains the memory address of something.

Rule: a variable of value type cannot be null. It must contain a value of some kind.

For example, the class that defines an integer is called **System.Int32**. While one could define an instance this way
```
System.Int32 quantity;
```
Such is cumbersome indeed. Thus, a set of aliases are provided for variable definitions. Table 2.1 shows all of the CTS Types and Aliases.

Table 2.1 The Basic Data Types

CTS Type Name	C# Alias	Description
System.Object	object	base class for all types
System.String	string	character string
System.SByte	sbyte	signed 1-byte integer
System.Byte	byte	unsigned 1-byte integer
System.Int16	short	signed 2-byte integer

CTS Type Name	C# Alias	Description
System.UInt16	ushort	unsigned 2-byte integer
System.Int32	int	signed 4-byte integer
System.UInt32	uint	unsigned 4-byte integer
System.Int64	long	signed 8-byte integer
System.UInt64	ulong	unsigned 8-byte integer
System.Char	char	Unicode 2-byte character
System.Single	float	4-byte floating point number
System.Double	double	8-byte floating point number
System.Boolean	bool	boolean value true or false
System.Decimal	decimal	16-byte data type with 28 digits used in financial applications. The range of values is from 79,228,162,514,264,337,593,543,950,335 to -79,228,162,514,264,337,593,543,950,335

We can also have enums and structures as well. Thus, we can code the following with which we are familiar.

```
int quantity;
double cost;
```

Notice that **char** is very different from **byte**. This is not the case in C++. Recall in C++ we could do any of the following.

```
char x = +65; // C++ only
char y = 'A';
unsigned char z = 65;
```

All of these occupies one byte in C++ and are indistinguishable at run time. In C# numerical values are very different than character data.

Rule: when you pass a variable that is declared to be one of these value types, it is always passed by value, that is its contents are passed, not its memory address.

A reference variable contains the memory address of something. They are fundamentally type-safe pointers. By type-safe, we mean that they can only point to objects of the defined data type.

One of the key reference types is **string** which can only point to a string of characters, null terminated.

Consider these two definitions of a string.
```
string a;
string b = "Hello World";
```
Here, variable a is a reference variable and contains the null value indicating that it points to nothing at the moment. Variable b contains the memory address of the string object containing the indicated series of characters. We will examine strings further when we get to arrays.

Rule: reference variables can be null.

Boxing and Unboxing

Boxing is the conversion of a value type into a reference type.
Unboxing is the conversion of a reference type back into a value type.

An object is only an object when it needs to be. Thus, if we declare our integer **quantity** as above, it is a very efficient 4-byte numerical variable.
```
double total = cost * quantity;
```
However, should we desire to turn it into an object, say to pass a reference to it, we can code the following.
```
int quantity = 42;
object oqty = quantity;        // box quantity
int newquantity = (int) oqty; // unbox oqty
```

Some **System.Object** Functions

The base class of all these types provides some key functions we can use.
bool   Equals () - Compares two objects and returns true if they are the same exact object
Type GetType () - Returns the kind of data this object is
string ToString () - Returns a string that represents the value of the object

For example,
```
  int x = 42;
  Console.WriteLine (x.ToString());
```
Displays the string "42."

```
  int x = 42;
  Console.WriteLine (x.GetType());
```
Displays "System.Int32."

The Inputting and Outputting of Data

Okay, we can define variables pretty much as we are used to doing in C++. But how are we going to input and output them? There are no **cin** or **cout** instructions in C#.

We have already seen one of the output methods, **Console.WriteLine** which outputs a string and the new line code when it is finished. The **Console.Write** method does exactly the same but does **not** output the new line code at the end. However, these functions are more complex than what we have seen thus far. In fact, both take a variable number of arguments, a control string comes first, followed by one or more items to be utilized in the output operation.

If you type in **Console.WriteLine**, highlight it and press F1 for help and look at the methods, you will discover that the **WriteLine** function is highly overloaded. It can be passed no arguments at all. In this case it outputs the new line code only. It can be passed any of the data values from the above table. So one could do the following.

```
int  x = 42;
bool y = true;
Console.WriteLine (x);
Console.WriteLine (y);
```
Incidentally, the output of the boolean **y** variable is the string "True".

Consider this line. Here we want to output some text and the contents of a variable. It is done by using the format specifier, which is enclosed in braces, { }.

```
int x = 42;
Console.WriteLine ("The number is {0}.", x);
```
This usage of the format specifier represents the simplest case. The number within the braces represents the zero-based offset of the subsequent arguments. Offset 0 refers to variable x in this case.

If we coded
```
int x = 42;
int y = 84;
Console.WriteLine ("x is {0} and y is {1}", x, y);
```
Here, {0} refers to x and {1} refers to y.

However, the format specifier can be more complex. In general it is
```
{N, M:formatstring}
```
N refers to the zero-based offset of which argument is to be formatted. M is the total field width occupied. If M is a positive number, then the digits are right aligned within this total field width. As you might expect, if the total field width is too small to hold all of the significant digits or characters, the width is ignored and all the needed digits are shown. If M is negative, the significant digits are left aligned in the total field width. Typically, M is used if we need columnar alignment of output results.

The format string can be used to provide more detailed instructions. In the simplest case, use one of the following codes; they are not case sensitive.

C for currency, adds a $ and comma separators and two decimal digits

D for decimal format and displays it as an integer

E for scientific notation of floating point numbers

F for fixed point format of floating point numbers

G for general format which is the same as E or F

X for hexadecimal format

N for number format.

For example, the following lines produces the following output.
```
int x = 42;
Console.WriteLine ("The number is {0,6:C}", x);
Console.WriteLine ("The number is {0,6:D}", x);
Console.WriteLine ("The number is {0,6:G}", x);
Console.WriteLine ("The number is {0,6:X}", x);
Console.WriteLine ("The number is {0,6:N}", x);


The number is $42.00
The number is     42
The number is     42
The number is     2A
The number is  42.00
```

Further, if the above default formatting is not appropriate, you can define your own formatting specifier. While this can become quite complex, the simplest codes to use are 0 # . and , for doubles. Where there is a 0, this is asking for a digit and will display a 0 if it is a leading 0, but where there is a #, this is asking for a digit and will display a blank if it is a leading 0. The decimal point is where it inserts a decimal point. Likewise, it inserts a comma at the point indicated by the comma.

```
    double x = 4242.50;
    Console.WriteLine ("The number is {0, 12:$##,##0.000}", x);
Produces
    The number is   $4,242.500
```

Thus, there are a wide range of formatting possibilities available for our use. While the above examples use **WriteLine**, they also apply to the **Write** method as well as the **ToString** methods.

When dealing with fancy formatting, sometimes one format needs to be used in several lines of coding. The formatting string can be more conveniently reused this way.
```
string formatSpecial = "{0, 12:$##,##0.00}";
double x = 4242.50;
```

```
Console.WriteLine ("The number is " + formatSpecial, x);
```
or
```
string formatSpecial = "12:$##,##0.00";
double x = 4242.50;
Console.WriteLine ("The number is {0," + formatSpecial + "}", x);
```

The **String** class also supports these same formatting specifications. This is vital if you are making a Windows application. Why? A Windows application does not support the Console methods which are for Console Applications only. In a Windows application, all output must be in the form of strings. Thus, we must convert numbers into strings prior to output operations.

```
double x = 4242.50;
string msg = "The number is ";
string sx =  String.Format ("{0, 12:$##,##0.000}", x);
Console.WriteLine (msg + sx);
```
Notice how the formatting string is passed to the **Format** method. It is the same way as it is passed to **WriteLine**. The above also illustrates that with strings, the + operator is a concatenation operator, joining the **msg** and **sx** strings into a single string for output.

The input of data in a console application comes from the **ReadLine** method. This function inputs the entire line of data into a string. Its basic prototype is

```
string ReadLine ();
```
Thus, we must define a string variable to hold the results and then provide a conversion from string data into numerical values. Remember, when we define a string data variable, it is actually a reference to those characters, that is, its memory location.

```
string s = Console.ReadLine ();
```
The above line inputs the next line of user entered data into a string and copies the address of that data in our variable **s**.

The numerical classes provide static member functions to convert a string into its corresponding numerical value. That method is called **Parse**. Thus, if the string **s** above was supposed to contain the quantity integer value, we could then code

```
int quantity = Int32.Parse (s);
```
to obtain our useable numerical value.

One does not have to define a string variable for the input values. It could also be done this way.

```
int quantity = Int32.Parse (Console.ReadLine());
```
This shorter form is very often used.

Let's put this into practice. Suppose that we wanted to input the quantity ordered and the unit cost so that we could calculate the total cost of an order. We could code it this way.

```
int qty;
double cost;
double total;
Console.Write ("Enter the quantity: ");
qty = Int32.Parse (Console.ReadLine());
Console.Write ("Enter the cost:     ");
cost = Double.Parse (Console.ReadLine ());
total = qty * cost;
Console.WriteLine ("\nThe Total Cost: {0:C}", total);
```

Finally note that you cannot parse out more than one value at a time. So do not try to input two or more numbers on one line at this point.

Strings must be given a value. Both of the following produce the error: Use of unassigned local variable 's'.

```
string s;
Console.WriteLine ("The string contains " + s); // error

static void Main(string[] args) {
    string s;
    Fun (s); // error
}
static void Fun (string s) {
    Console.WriteLine ("The string contains " + s);
}
```

Math and Comparison Operations

The math operators are + − * / and % as you would expect. These operate exactly as they do in C/C++ coding. Parentheses can be used to override the precedence of operators. Remember that multiply and the two divide forms have a higher priority than add and subtract.

The six relational operators are the same as in C++; namely ==, !=, >, >=, <, <=. Similarly the if-then-else structure is exactly the same as in C++.

```
if (test condition) {
   0, 1 or more C# statements to do when true
}
else { // optional
   0, 1 or more C# statements to do when false
}
```
or
```
if (test condition)
   1 C# statement;
else // optional
   1 C# statement;
```
or
```
if (test condition)
   1 C# statement;
```

Likewise, the compound joiner operators are available, the Or and And and Not operators: ||, && and ! Thus, one can code
```
if (count < MAX && value > 0) . . .
```
Remember with these conditional operators, as soon as the compiler can determine the outcome, all further testing is terminated. That is, in the above case, if count equaled MAX, then since the joiner is &&, it is irrelevant what the variable value contains. That test is not done. Rather flow goes immediately to the else clause if present.

On the other hand, the boolean **Or** (|) and **And** (&) work differently. These actually **Or** or **And** the bits together to obtain a final result. So if we wrote
```
if (count < MAX & value > 0) . . .
```
then the compiler must perform both test conditions and then boolean **And** the two results together and finally test the resultant value for not equal to zero. These operators are normally used to test for the presence of a specific bit within a flag integer that could hold many different flags. For example,
```
int flags;
if (flags & 1)
```
tests the rightmost bit in the flags 32 bits to see if it is on.
```
flags = flags | 1;
```
The above turns on the rightmost bit in the flags.

Similarly the **? :** shortcut is available.
```
sales = cost > 0 ? cost * qty : 0;
```

The **inc** and **dec** operators are available and work exactly as in C++, but **only** on the intrinsic types. When we use operator overloaded functions, they do not both work as expected. More on that later on.
```
int x = 42;
int y = 10;
x = y++;
```
yields 10 in x and 11 in y while
```
x = ++y;
```
yields 11 in x and y.

The various **assignment operator** shortcuts are also available in C#. These include +=, -=, *=, /=, and %=.
Thus, we can write
```
total += cost * qty;
```

Looping Instructions

The **while** Statement

C# supports the expected looping instructions as well. The while statement is the workhorse.

```
while (test condition) {
  0, 1 or more statements to do when true
}
```
or
```
while (test condition)
 1 statement to do
```
or
```
while (test condition);
```

However, when making loops involving user entered data via **ReadLine**, some care must be used at this point because **ReadLine** is not an I/O stream and does not have the **good()** function that we so often use in while test conditions. Thus, for now, use a sentinel controlled loop. That is, force the user to input a special value that indicates he or she is finished entering data items.

For example, suppose we wanted to input a series of purchases and then display the order results. We could code the following.

```
using System;

class Hello {
 static void Main(string[] args) {
  int     qty;
  double cost;
  double total = 0;
  Console.Write ("Enter a quantity or -1 to quit: ");
  qty = Int32.Parse (Console.ReadLine());
  while (qty >= 0) {
   Console.Write ("Enter the cost: ");
   cost = Double.Parse (Console.ReadLine ());
   total += cost * qty;
   Console.Write ("Enter a quantity or -1 to quit:");
   qty = Int32.Parse (Console.ReadLine());
  }
  Console.WriteLine(
        "\n\nThe total cost of the order is {0, 12:C}", total);
 }
}
```

The **for** Statement

C# also uses the **for loop** instruction whose syntax is the same as it is in C++.

```
for (0, 1, or more initial statements separated by a comma;
      test condition ;
      0, 1 or more bump expressions, separated by a comma) {
  0, 1 or more statements to do
}
```

For example, the following sums all odd integers from 1 to 100.

```
int sum = 0;
int number;
for (number = 1; number <= 100; number += 2) {
  sum += number;
}
```

The **do until** Statement

C# supports the **do until** structure whose syntax is the same as C++.

```
do {
   0, 1 or more statements to perform
} while (test condition is true);
```

The **break** and **continue** Statements

C# supports the **break** and **continue** statements.

```
char letter;
byte tries = 0;
do {
  Console.Write ("Enter a Y or N: ");
  letter = Char.Parse (Console.ReadLine());
  if (letter == 'y') letter = 'Y';
  if (letter == 'n') letter = 'N';
  tries++;
  if (tries > 5) break;
} while (letter != 'Y' && letter != 'N');
```

This loop attempts to force the user to enter a Y or an N, but after 5 tries, it terminates.

The Do Case Statement

C# supports the Do Case. It behaves just as it does in C++. When a case is finished, the default action it to fall through to the next case unless it encounters a break statement.

```
switch (variable) {
  case value1:
    ...
  case value2:
    ...
  default:
    ...
}
```

The variable can be of any numerical integer type, **char** or even **string**.

For example, the following coding is a portion of a student grade point average calculator program.

```
char grade;
int gpa = 0;
Console.Write ("Enter a letter grade: ");
grade = Char.Parse (Console.ReadLine ());
switch (grade) {
  case 'A':
  case 'a':
   gpa += 4;
   break;
  case 'B':
  case 'b':
   gpa += 3;
   break;
```

Math Functions

The Math class provides many mathematical methods. Among these are the **Pow** function, the **Sqrt** function and the many trigonometry functions. Note that the functions are capitalized over their C++ counterparts.

```
double x;
double y;
double z;
z = Math.Pow (x, y); // x raised to the yth power
z = Math.Sqrt (x);   // square root of x
```

Type in "**Math.**" in a C# source file. In the popup window that appears, examine the functions that are available for your use.

Data Conversions

Data conversions are necessary when the compiler encounters a statement involving different data types. Some conversions are implicitly done by the compiler. Implicit conversions are those that can never have data loss. If there is a possibility of data or precision loss, then you must use an explicit typecast conversion.

The general rule of implicit conversion is similar to that of C++.

All types can be converted implicitly into **object**.

For a **bool**, **decimal**, or **double**, conversion to an **object** is the only implicit conversion possible.

A **float** can also be converted into a **double**.

A **ulong** or **long** can be also converted into a **float**, **double** or a **decimal** without loss of data.

In contrast, an **sbyte** can also be converted into a **short**, **int**, **long**, **float**, double or **decimal** but cannot be converted into an unsigned byte form.

A **byte** (which is unsigned) can be converted into any of the larger unsigned forms, into a **float**, **double**, or **decimal**, and can be converted into a **short**, **int** or **long**. It cannot be converted into a **sbyte**.

Note that none can be converted into a **bool** without the possibility of data loss. Further, notice that type **char** is now *special* as it is a 16-bit Unicode type. Thus, **char** can only be converted into a **ushort** or larger unsigned versions or into an **int** or **long** or the floating point or **decimal** types. Specifically, it cannot be converted into a **short**.

Sometimes, one does need to convert to a smaller type. This is done using the typecast explicitly as it is done in C++.

Suppose that we had calculated a person's grade which is a **double**. We desire to store it as a **sbyte**.

```
double  dgrade;
sbyte   grade = (sbyte) (dgrade + .5);
```

Notice that I added .5 to the double before the conversion to handle rounding. If **dgrade** contained 89.999, without adding +.5 first, the assignment from floating types to integers simple copies the whole number portion, the 89. By adding +.5 first, the resulting double now is 90.4999 which yields 90 in **grade**.

When mixed mode math is done, the compiler converts to the "highest" data type found in the expression. Temporary variables, of course, contain these converted values; the original variables are not altered. Consider the following statement.

```
sbyte   a;
ushort  b;
float   c;
double d = (a + b) / c;
```

Here, **a** is promoted to a **ushort** for the addition. Then, the result of the addition, a **ushort**, is converted into a **float** for the division. Then, the **float** is converted into a **double** for the assignment.

Functions and Passing by Value Versus Passing by Reference

When coding a function or method, values can be passed either by value or by reference, just as in C++. However, with references, C# corrects a defect in the C++ implementation of reference variables.

When we pass by value, the called function cannot alter the caller's data item that was passed. Any attempt alters the function's parameter copy. Suppose that we coded the following. What is the output?

```
using System;

class Hello {
 static void Main(string[] args)      {
  double x = 42;
  double y = FunByValue (x);
  Console.WriteLine (x);
 }

 static double FunByValue (double x) {
  Console.WriteLine (x);
  x = 84;
  Console.WriteLine (x);
  return x;
 }
}
```

In this example, the output is
42
84

42

since the function's parameter x is being altered.

When references are passed, in C++ we could get into trouble. How? Assume that I wrote the following C++ program.

```
#include <iostream>
using namespace std;

double Fun (double& x);

int main () {
  double x;
  double y = Fun (x);
  cout << x << '\n';
}

double Fun (double& x) {
  cout << x << '\n'; // error here
  x = 84;
  cout << x << '\n';
  return x;
}
```

Can you spot what the error is in the above coding? This is a deficiency of the C++ language. The main function's variable x has no initial value and a reference to it is passed to Fun. However, within Fun, the first action is to output its value which is currently non-existent!

The **ref** and **out** Reference Variables

C# totally removes this type of situation by providing two different types of reference variables: **ref** and **out**. Note the symbol used for references in C++, the **&**, is not used in C#, but **ref** or **out** is used ahead of the data type.

```
  static double FunOutOnly (out double x) {
   x = 84;
   Console.WriteLine (x);
   return x;
  }
  static double FunRefOrInOut (ref double x) {
   Console.WriteLine (x);
   x = 84;
   Console.WriteLine (x);
   return x;
  }
```

When the **out** is used, the function cannot use the contents of the reference variable *until* it assigns a value to it. When the **ref** is used, the function can reference its contents at any time, as well as change its value. The compiler catches all violations of this scenario. That is, if a caller's passed reference variable has no value as yet and it is passed as a **ref**, any attempt to access its value creates an error. If a variable is passed as **out** and any attempt is made to access its value prior to assigning it a value generates an error.

This impacts class design as well. Suppose we had a **Point** class setup this way.

```
class Point {
 int x;
 int y;

 public Point (int x, int y) {
  this.x = x;
  this.y = y;
 }

 public void GetPoint (ref int x, ref int y) {// bad one
  x = this.x;
  y = this.y;
 }
}
```

On the surface, this looks just fine. But consider what happens in the client function.

```
static void Main (string[] args) {
 Point p = new Point (10,42);
 int x, y;
 p.GetPoint (x, y); // error
```

Why does this generate an error? Because **Main**'s **x** and **y** variables are uninitialized and they are being passed as a reference **ref** type. Here is another situation where the **out** reference is required. The correct way to code the **GetPoint** method is as follows.

```
 public void GetPoint (out int x, out int y) { // good one
  x = this.x;
  y = this.y;
 }
```

A Beginning Look At Classes

A class begins with the keyword **class** followed by the name of the class which is usually capitalized. The entire definition of the class in enclosed in braces, but there is no ending semicolon as in C++.

```
class Point {
  . . .
}
```

Typically a class has data members and member functions or methods. Each of these items has an access qualifier: **public**, **protected**, **private**. If nothing is said, it is **private**. These three access qualifiers have the same meaning as they do in C++.

Anything made **private** is available only to class methods. This is severely restrictive.

Anything made **public** is available anywhere. Making a data item **public** tends to break down the black box approach or encapsulation and is only done for utility type classes such as a Point, Rectangle, Size. In these classes, it is done for speed and convenience. However, most of the class methods are **public** and form the basis of the user's interface for manipulating the object.

Anything made **protected** is available only to class methods and to derived classes. Thus, if there is any possibility that someone may wish to derive from the class you are creating, consider making the data items **protected** and not **private**.

Now unlike C++, *each* data item and *each* function must have a prefix of **public** or **protected**, otherwise it is **private**. A qualifier applies *only* to the item it prefixes. This is different from C++. In C++ we could code

```
class Point {// C++
 protected:
 int x;
 int y;
```

However, in C# each item must have its own qualifier.

```
class Point { // C#
 protected int x;
 protected int y;
```

Functions can be overloaded just as they are in C++. The same rules apply. The overloaded functions must differ in the number and/or data types of the parameters; return values do not count. Constructors are often overloaded.

For our Point class, we have the following so far. Notice the overloaded constructor.

```
using System;
```

```
class Point {
 protected int x;
 protected int y;

 public Point (int x, int y)  {
  this.x = x;
  this.y = y;
 }

 public Point () {
  x = 0;
  y = 0;
 }

 public void GetPoint (out int x, out int y) {
  x = this.x;
  y = this.y;
 }

 public void SetPoint (int x, int y)  {
  this.x = x;
  this.y = y;
 }

 public void MovePoint (int x, int y)  {
  this.x += x;
  this.y += y;
 }
}
```

However, there is now a difference from C++ in terms of how client programs can create instances.

In C++, we could create instances of our **Point** class in any of these ways:
```
Point p;
Point p ();           // illegal - is a prototype
Point p (10, 10);
Point* ptrp = new Point;
Point* ptrp = new Point (10, 10);
```

However, in C# *all variables* are objects. Any variable other than the value types, such as **sbyte**, **short**, **int**, and **double**, are in fact **reference** variables. That is, such variables are memory addresses of the object. Thus, we have in C# client programs the following available to us.
```
Point p (10, 10);                  // illegal
Point p = new Point;               // illegal
Point P = new Point ();            // valid
```

33

```
Point p = new Point (10, 10); // valid
Point p;  // valid but is only an uninitialized ptr!!
```
In each of the valid C# cases above, variable **p** is a reference to the dynamically allocated **Point** object.

Please note that the last one,
```
Point p;
```
does *not* create a **Point** object but rather is a **reference** to one that is currently uninitialized and does not point to a **Point** object as yet!

Okay, if all instances of objects are dynamically allocated, how are they deleted? The C# runtime environment contains a thread called the **Garbage Collector**. The Garbage Collector automatically deletes all no longer needed objects (and calls their destructors if any). And this immediately raises the question of a variable's lifetime or duration as it is known in C#.

Scope and Duration (Lifetime) of Variables

The scope of a variable is that portion of the program in which that identifier can be accessed. A local variable or reference variable is one that is defined within a block of coding that is not a class member data variable. This is called **block scope**. Local variables can be used from the point of definition to the end of the defining block or nested blocks within the defining block. This is the same as C++ local variable rules.

Members of a class have **class scope** and are available to any member function of that class. This is also the same as in C++.

Local variable of a method or function and the function's parameters have local or block scope. If a local method variable or parameter has the same name as a class member, the class member is hidden but can be accessed using the **this** parameter. This is illustrated in the **GetPoint** and **SetPoint** functions above. Further, if within the function's body there occurs another block of coding that tries to define another local variable with the same name as one in the outer block, an error is generated. For example, the following is illegal.
```
void Fun () {
 int x;
 ...
 while (...) {
  int x; // error
  ...
 }
}
```

The duration of local or block scope variables is the duration of the defining block of coding, just as it is in C++. This is called **automatic duration**. Automatic duration variables are created when the program reaches their definitions. If the programmer initializes them, they are so handled. However, if there is no explicit initialization coded, then the compiler initializes all value types to 0 (or false if it is a bool) and initializes all reference variables to a null pointer. This is exactly what happens when we coded

```
Point p;
```

It is initialized to 0 or the NULL pointer.

Variables of **static duration**, identified by the prefix of **static**, exists for the duration of the program. They exist from the point the class is loaded into memory by the program, usually when the program first begins. However, scope rules apply so that although they continually exist, they might not be directly accessed when out of scope.

So where does this lead us in terms of the destruction of objects? Consider the following coding.

```
static void Main (string[] args) {
 {
  Point p;                    // location A
  p = Fun ();
 }                            // location B
}
static Point Fun () {
 Point pp;                    // location C
 pp = new Point (10, 10);  // location D
 return pp;                   // location E
}                             // location F
```

At location A, variable **p** is created. It is a memory address, currently null. At location C within function **Fun**, variable **pp** is created and is also null. At location D the compiler creates a real **Point** object at some memory address, say 100 and stores it in **pp**. At location E, the memory address 100 is returned to the calling program and is stored in **Main**'s **p** variable. At location F, reference variable **pp** is deleted. However, the memory that it used to point to, address 100, is still in use since **Main**'s **p** contains its address, 100. At location B, **Main**'s **p** goes out of scope and duration. So the compiler deletes the reference variable **p**. At this point, no reference variable in the entire program now points to memory location 100, the real **Point** object. The Garbage Collector now handles the destruction of that **Point** object during some idle time in the background.

We never have to ever concern ourselves with explicitly deleting anything any more, no more memory leaks! (Well, usually. There is more to all this later on.)

This situation is illustrated in the last method of the **Point** class, the **FormatPoint** function.

```
public string FormatPoint () {
```

```
string str;
str = "[" + String.Format ("{0, 5}", x) + ", " +
           String.Format ("{0, 5}", y) + "]";
return str;
}
```

Here I define a string (which is really an array of char as usual) which is a reference variable and is set to null. Next, I construct a string by concatenating a series of strings. Notice that this **String.Format** method allows me to make all of the Point output strings the same length (assuming that no coordinate exceeds 5 digits). Then I return that string, but really it is the address of the concatenated string that is returned. The client then does the following.

```
string msg = p.FormatPoint ();
Console.WriteLine (msg);
```

In the above assignment, msg is assigned the address of the concatenated string.

Here is the complete .cs file for Pgm02aConsole.

```
using System;

// Point class to encapsulate a 2d point
class Point {
 protected int x;
 protected int y;

 public Point(int x, int y) {
  this.x = x;
  this.y = y;
 }

 public Point() {
  x = 0;
  y = 0;
 }

 public void GetPoint(out int x, out int y) {
  x = this.x;
  y = this.y;
 }

 public void SetPoint(int x, int y) {
  this.x = x;
  this.y = y;
 }

 public void MovePoint(int x, int y) {
  this.x += x;
```

```
  this.y += y;
 }

 public string FormatPoint() {
  string str;
  str = "[" + String.Format("{0, 5}", x) + ", " +
                          String.Format("{0, 5}", y) + "]";
  return str;
 }
}
```

Here is the application class to test the Point class.

```
// tester program to validate the Point class
class Application {
 static void Main(string[] args) {
  Point p = new Point(10, 42);
  Point q = new Point(1024, 768);
  Point s = new Point(1, 2);
  Point t = new Point();
  string msg = p.FormatPoint();
  Console.WriteLine(msg);
  msg = q.FormatPoint();
  Console.WriteLine(msg);
  msg = s.FormatPoint();
  Console.WriteLine(msg);
  msg = t.FormatPoint();
  Console.WriteLine(msg);
 }
}
```

Here is the output it gives.

```
[    10,     42]
[  1024,    768]
[     1,      2]
[     0,      0]
```

Programming Problem

Problem 2-1—Temperature Converter

When dealing with temperatures, one common problem is the conversion of a temperature in Fahrenheit degrees into Celsius degrees. The formula is

C = (5/9) (F - 32)

Write a class **Temp** that stores as its only data member the temperature in Fahrenheit as a **double**.

Provide two constructors. The default constructor sets the temperature to 0. An overloaded constructor is passed a Fahrenheit temperature to store.

Provide access functions **GetFTemp** and **SetFTemp** to get and set this **double** Fahrenheit temperature.

Provide a **GetCelsius** function that returns the corresponding Celsius temperature of the stored Fahrenheit temperature.

Finally, provide a **FormatAs** function. The function returns a string (a reference) containing a nicely formatted temperature ready for output. The function is passed a **bool**. When the **bool** is **true**, format the stored temperature as Fahrenheit; when **false**, format the stored temperature as Celsius by converting the stored value into a Celsius temporary temperature and formatting that temporary variable. The formatted strings should look like the following.
    nnn.n F
or
    nnn.n C

Next add a console application class with a **Main** function. The main function prompts the user to enter a Fahrenheit temperature or -999 to quit. Given that temperature, it then outputs a line like this.
    nnn.n F = nnn.n C
Repeat the process until the user enters -999. You may also add in any additional testing code to thoroughly test your **Temp** class.

Chapter 3—Arrays, Strings, and Classes

Single Dimensioned Arrays

The definition of arrays is very different from C++. However, once defined, array processing via subscripts is the same as it is in C++.

> **Rule: All objects must be dynamically allocated with the *new* function.**

Thus, a new style of data definition is used. For a single dimensioned array of double values, we code the following.

```
double[] temps;
```

This is saying that **temps** is a reference variable to an array. The following defines a reference to an array of integer totals.

```
int[] totals;
```

With the reference variable defined, we dynamically allocate the *actual* array and store its address in the reference variable.

```
temps = new double[100];
totals = new int[numTotals];
```

Of course, both could be written shorter this way.

```
double[] temps = new double[100];
int[] totals = new int[numTotals];
```

The array definition syntax is

```
type[] identifier;
```

Arrays can be initialized when they are allocated by placing the series of initial values within a set of braces and separated by commas.

```
int[] storeIds = new int[5] {1, 2, 3, 4, 5};
```

If an array is being allocated and initialized at the same time, it can be shortened to this.

```
int[] storeIds = {1, 2, 3, 4, 5};
```

The compiler counts the number of values provided and allocates an array of integers large enough to hold them all. However, this approach is a bit more error prone; if you omit a value, the array is one element smaller than you intended.

Good programming practice dictates that if an array bounds is actually a constant, a **const int** should be used.

```
const int NUMTEMPS = 100;
double[] temps = new double [NUMTEMPS];
```

Access of the array elements is done by a subscript just as it is in C++ or Java. If we wished to calculate the average temperature and the high and low temperatures from an array that contains **numTemps**, it could be done this way.

```
double[] temps = new double[numTemps];
... fill array
double sum = temps[0];
double high = temps[0];
double low = temps[0];
for (int j=1; j<numTemps; j++) {
  sum += temps[j];
  if (temps[j] > high)
    high = temps[j];
  if (temps[j] < low)
    low = temps[j];
}
double average = sum / numTemps;
```

Passing an array to a function is done similar to C++ and Java. Its data type is **type[]**. Suppose **Main** defined the array of temperatures and passed it to a function **CalcAvg**. It could be coded this way.

```
public static void Main (string[] args) {
  int numTemps;
  ...
  double[] temps = new double[numTemps];
  ...
  double avg = CalcAvg (temps, numTemps);
  ...
public static double CalcAvg (double[] temps,
                              int num) {
  double sum = 0;
  for (int j=0; j<num; j++) {
    sum += temps[j];
  }
  return sum / num;
}
```

However, do to this dynamic memory allocation method for all objects and that the variable containing the object is really a reference variable, we can easily allocate arrays within functions and return them to the caller (really we are returning the memory address of the array).

```
double[] temps;
int numTemps;
temps = LoadArray (numTemps);
```
where the function is defined like this
```
public static double[] LoadArray (out int numTemps) {
 . . .
 numTemps = ...
 double[] temps = new double [numTemps];
 . . .
 return temps;
}
```

Normal operations can be performed on array elements just as in C++ and Java.
```
sum += temps[j];
temps[j]++;
```

Remember that when no reference variable in the entire program points to the array, that's when the Garbage Collector proceeds to delete the array.

All arrays have the **Length** property which contains the number of elements in the array. This can streamline many array processes by eliminating the need to pass the number of elements to functions. We can shorten the **CalcAvg** function this way.
```
public static void Main (string[] args) {
   int numTemps;
   . . .
   double[] temps = new double[numTemps];
   . . .
   double avg = CalcAvg (temps);
   . . .
public static double CalcAvg (double[] temps){
   double sum = 0;
   for (int j=0; j<temps.Length; j++) {
     sum += temps[j];
   }
   return sum / temps.Length;
}
```

In other words, if the array dimension is actually the number of elements that must be processed, you do not need to keep or pass an integer **numElements**. Instead, when the number of elements is needed, as in a **for** loop, just use the **array.Length** property.

There is one major error that you need to be alert for when using C# arrays. Consider the following implementation of **LoadArray**. In **Main** we code the following.
```
double[] temps;
```

```
LoadArray (temps);
```
where the function is defined like this
```
public static void LoadArray (double[] t) {
  ...
  int numTemps = ...
  t = new double [numTemps];
  ...
}
```
This is a disaster in the making and C# will flag this as an error. Let's see why it would be. Let's say that **Main**'s **temps** reference variable is located at memory location 100. **LoadArray's** reference variable **t** is at memory location 200. Initially, **t** is a copy of **Main**'s **temps**, which is **null** since nothing has been allocated as yet. Within **LoadArry**, we allocate the real array of doubles which begins at say memory location 500. Where is the 500 placed? In **t**, or in location 200. What is in **Main**'s temps variable? It is still uninitialized!

In situations such as this, the array should be passed as an **out** reference variable itself. That is, since it has no initial value, it should be an **out** reference variable. Here is the correct way to code **LoadArray**.
```
public static void LoadArray (out double[] t) {
  ...
  int numTemps = ...
  double[] t = new double [numTemps];
  ...
}
```
Here **t** is a reference to **Main**'s **temps** reference variable. The assignment of the real array address of 500 is now stored in **Main**'s **temps** and all is well.

However, the compiler must already have seen the definition of LoadArray before it attempts to make the function call to LoadArray. Assume that we code the class this way.
```
public static void Main (string[] args) {
  double[] temps;
  LoadArray (temps);
}
public static void LoadArray (out double[] t) {
  ...
  int numTemps = ...
  t = new double [numTemps];
  ...
}
```
Then the compiler has not yet seen the definition of LoadArray and does now yet know that it is to pass **temps** as an **out** reference. Hence, it has no choice but to give a compiler error saying that temps needs to be passed as an **out** reference.

We can fix this by coding it this way.

```
public static void Main (string[] args) {
  double[] temps;
  LoadArray (out temps);
```

Alternatively and not necessarily recommended by me, you could code it this way, putting the function physically before the **Main** function.

```
public static void LoadArray (out double[] t) {
  ...
 int numTemps = ...
 t = new double [numTemps];
  ...
}
public static void Main (string[] args) {
  double[] temps;
  LoadArray (temps);
}
```

This is probably the single most confusing aspect of array processing in C#.

The **foreach** Statement

C# introduces a new repetition operator, the **foreach**. In many cases, the **foreach** can simplify iterating sequentially through an array. In the CalcAvg function above, we can use a **foreach** instead of the **for** loop.

```
public static double CalcAvg (double[] temps){
  double sum = 0;
  foreach (double temp in temps) {
    sum += temp;
  }
  return sum / temps.Length;
}
```

The **foreach** begins with element 0. It assigns the array element at subscript 0 to our named variable **temp** and executes the body of the loop. Then, it finds the next element in the array and assigns its value to **temp** and does the body of the loop again. The loop terminates when all elements in the array have been visited.

The **foreach** is available with any array because all arrays in C# are derived from the **Array** class which is providing the **Length** method as well as the **foreach** method.

Here is another example.

```
int[] totals = new int[100];
... fill it up with 100 integers
maxTotal = totals[0]; // initial value
foreach (int value in totals) {
  sum += value;
  if (value > maxTotal)
    maxTotal = value;
}
```

There is a pitfall error that can occur with the **foreach**. If you have allocated an array but not actually allocated all of the element objects, a **foreach** can get you into trouble by attempting to access non-existent element objects. This error will occur at run time.

You can always check for a null object this way and then break out of the loop.

```
if (array[i] == null) { // oops
```

Multiple Dimensioned Arrays

The syntax needed to define and allocate a multiple dimensioned array is very different from C++. To define a reference variable to a 2-dimensional array, the syntax is

```
type[,] identifier;
```

For a 3-d array, it is

```
type[,,] identifier;
```

And so on. A comma indicates that there are two subscripts needed—one on either side of the comma.

The dynamic allocation parallels this syntax.

```
double[,] budget = new double [100, 12];
```

This defines a 2-d array **budget** and allocates space for 100 rows each with 12 columns.

This defines a 3-d array of **totals** and allocates space for 3 stores, each with 4 departments containing 2 cash registers in them.

```
const int STORES = 3;
const int DEPTS = 4;
const int REGS = 2;
long[,,] totals = new long[STORES, DEPTS, REGS];
```

These would be passed to function in a manner similar to that of single dimensioned arrays.

```
CalcBudget (budget);
TallySales (totals);
```

And the functions are defined this way. Of course, if these functions wanted to allocate replacement arrays, then pass them as **ref** or **out**.

```
public void CalcBudget (ref double[,] budget) { }
public void TallySales (ref long[,,] totals) { }
```

When working with multiple dimensioned arrays, the **GetLength** function is very handy. It is passed the 0-based dimension for which you want the current limit. On the totals array above, the following can be coded.

```
totals.GetLength (0); // yields 3 - the leftmost dimension
totals.GetLength (1); // yields 4 - the middle dimension
totals.GetLength (2); // yields 2 - the rightmost dimension
```

Jagged Arrays

Sometimes each row may have a different number of columns. This situation is called a jagged array in which each row may have a different number of elements in it. A jagged array must therefore be allocated differently, as an array of references.

```
double[][] budget = new double[5][];
```

This defines budget as a two dimensional jagged array. Initially, the leftmost subscript refers to an array of 5 row references, each of which must be allocated next. Here I also choose to initialize them as I allocate them.

```
budget[0] = new double [2] {1, 2};
budget[1] = new double [3] {11, 12, 13};
budget[2] = new double [1] {21};
budget[3] = new double [4] {41, 42, 43, 44};
budget[4] = new double [2] {51, 52};
```

Of course, iterating through a jagged array is more complex because each row contains a variable number of columns. Since the budget array itself is a single dimensioned array of references, the Length property assists us. Coding **budget[0].Length** yields the array size of the 0th row, or 2 in the above example. Here is one way one could sum each row of values.

```
double[] sum = new double[5];
for (int row=0; row<5; row++) {
 sum[row] = 0;
 for (int col=0; col< budget[row].Length; col++) {
   sum[row] += budget[row][col];
 }
}
```

The jagged array budget could be defined and implemented in one long statement this way.

```
double[][] budget = {new double [2] {1, 2},
                     new double [3] {11, 12, 13},
                     new double [1] {21},
                     new double [4] {41, 42, 43, 44},
```

```
                    new double [2] {51, 52} };
```

Arrays of Reference Variables

Okay. Here comes the confusing part. Suppose that we have an **Employee** class and want to make an array of Employee objects. One might think the following would work, where the **LoadFromFile** inputs a record with the passed employee id number.

```
Employee[] emps = new Employee [3];
emps[0].LoadFromFile (123456);
emps[1].LoadFromFile (234456);
emps[2].LoadFromFile (244345);
```

The three loads fail at run time with a null object error. Why?

Certainly **emps** is an array of **Employee** objects. However, in fact, it is an array of 3 references to **Employee** objects, three memory addresses. That is, what **new Employee[3]** is allocating, an array of three memory addresses, each of which can point to a real **Employee**, but currently contain null.

There are several ways to correct this situation. One simple way that does not impact the way that **LoadFromFile** operates is to go ahead and allocate the three **Employee** objects.

```
Employee[] emps = new Employee [3];
for (int j=0; j<emps.Length; j++) {
 emps[j] = new Employee;
}
emps[0].LoadFromFile (123456);
emps[1].LoadFromFile (234456);
emps[2].LoadFromFile (244345);
```

Alternatively, one could redesign **LoadFromFile** and make it a static member function that returns a reference to a newly allocated **Employee** object that it allocates and fills from the disk file. This approach would appear as follows.

```
Employee[] emps = new Employee [3];
emps[0] = Employee.LoadFromFile (123456);
emps[1] = Employee.LoadFromFile (234456);
emps[2] = Employee.LoadFromFile (244345);
```

When working with arrays of objects, this is an **extremely** common error. Be alert for it.

Finally, since all arrays are based upon the **Array** class, support is available for several non-traditional array activities. Four of the most useful methods are **Clear**, **Sort**, **Reverse**, and **BinarySearch**. **Array.Clear** sets a range of elements to 0. These can be handy functions.

For example, if we needed to sort the **temps** array into increasing order, we could code the following.

46

```
Array.Sort (temps, 0, 0, temps.Length)
```

The first parameter is the array to be sorted. The second parameter is any parallel array that must be maintained in the same order, here it is 0 meaning none. The third parameter is the starting index because one could sort only a part of the array. The fourth parameter is the number of elements to sort. A fifth parameter (not coded here) is supplied for intrinsic data types and is a compare type function. If you create an array of **Employee** objects, and want to use this method to sort them, you will have to write a compare function to pass to the **Sort** method.

Strings

All strings in C# are instances of **System.String** and are fundamentally an array of Unicode characters.

> **Rule: However, an instance of *string* is an immutable type of data, meaning that none of the characters in the *string* can be modified by the user.**

> **Rule: All operations on a *string* return a modified version of the *string* rather than modifying the existing *string*.**

Thus, when working with strings, extensive use is made of the String methods. The following summarizes some of the more commonly needed functions.

Method	Description
Compare	Compares two strings
CompareTo	Compares the current string instance to another string
EndsWith	Determines if a string ends with a given string
StartsWith	Determines if a string starts with a given string
IndexOf	Returns the position of the first occurrence of a string in another string
LastIndexOf	Returns the position of the last occurrence of a string in another string
Concat	Concatenates two or more strings together. If two objects are passed, it calls the ToString method on them to get them into strings to concatenate; returns the new string
CopyTo	Copies a specified number of characters from a location in this string into another array; returns the new string

47

Method	Description
Insert	Returns a new string with a substring inserted into this string
PadLeft	Right aligns a string in a field; returns the new string
PadRight	Left aligns a string in a field; returns the new string
Remove	Returns a new string with the indicated portion removed
Replace	Returns a new string with all occurrences of a character replaced with another character
Split	Creates an array of strings by splitting a string at any occurrence of one or more characters
Substrng	Extracts a substring from a string returning the new string
ToLower	Returns a new string that is all lowercase
ToUpper	Returns a new string that is all uppercase
Trim	Returns a new string in which all the whitespace has been removed
TrimEnd	Returns a new string which has had a string of characters removed from its end
TrimStart	Returns a new string which has had a string of characters removed from its beginning

Here is an example of using the **Split** method.

```
string msg = "Hello, how are you";
char[] separators = new char[2] {' ', ','};
foreach (string s in msg.Split (separators)) {
  Console.WriteLine ("Word: {0}", s);
}
```

The output would be as follows. Notice that the comma blank series is split twice, once on the comma and then once on the blank.

Word: Hello
Word:
Word: how
Word: are
Word: you

Some Additional Class Features—Properties

Quite commonly, a class will have numerous Access functions to permit the user to get and set various data members of a class. The data members are also called **properties**. However, C# has extended properties to make the Access operations extremely powerful indeed.

A C# **property** appears to the user or client program as if it is a **public data member** of the class and thus they can set or get that **property** directly by using the apparent variable name. However, **properties** in C# use a block of code called an **accessor** to get or set a field. Hence, you can separate the actual member data (which the client cannot get at) with the coding to get or set it. **Properties** are rampantly used within the .NET Framework.

Here is a short example to illustrate the general idea. Then let's look at the specific details.

```csharp
class Employee {
 protected string name;
 public string Name { // the public property
  get {
   return name;
  }
  set {
   name = value;
  }
 }

}
```

And the corresponding client coding is this.

```csharp
Employee e = new Employee;
e.Name = "Fred"; // the set
Console.WriteLine (e.Name); // the get
```

First, one has a protected or private data member for which a get/set is to be provided. Second, one defines a new public **property**, usually with the same name but capitalized to distinguish it from the real member. As part of the body of this **property**, one defines a **get** and **set** operation block of coding. The user's data is called **value** by the system. Third, these blocks to **get** and **set** may perform any needed actions to verify the setting or retrieval of the real data being stored in the private or protected member. One is not limited to just setting the underlying member. Further, the C# compiler actually inlines these trivial **get/set** methods for fast execution.

In the following example, class **Purchase** represents an item that is being purchased. The class **ShoppingCart** contains an array of **Purchase** items and the total cost of the order thus far.

When a **Purchase** has its quantity updated, as part of the set quantity operation, the **ShoppingCart**'s **total** is also updated. (Notice that forward references are not needed.)

Pgm03aConsole.cs

```csharp
using System;
using System.Collections;

class Purchase {

 protected int          quantity;// qty purchased
 protected Decimal       cost;    // cost of one item
 protected ShoppingCart cart;     // reference to the ShoppingCart

 public Purchase (ShoppingCart cart) {
  this.cart = cart;
 }

 public int Quantity {
  get {
   return (quantity);
  }
  set {
   quantity = value;
   cart.UpdateTotal ();
  }
 }

 public Decimal Cost  {
  get {
   return (cost);
  }
  set {
   this.cost = value;
   cart.UpdateTotal ();
  }
 }

 public Decimal Total {
  get {
   return quantity * cost;
  }
 }
}

class ShoppingCart {
```

```
  const int MAXSIZE = 10;
  Purchase[] array = new Purchase[MAXSIZE];

  protected int      numInUse = 0;
  protected Decimal   total;

  public Decimal Total {
   get {
    return total;
   }
  }

  public void UpdateTotal () {
   total = 0;
   for (int i=0; i<numInUse; i++) {
    total += array[i].Total;
   }
  }

  public void AddPurchase (Purchase p) {
   if (numInUse >= MAXSIZE) {
    Console.WriteLine (
                    "Error - shopping cart array size exceeded");
    return;
   }
   array[numInUse] = p;
   numInUse++;
  }

}

class Application {
 static void Main (string[] args) {

   ShoppingCart cart = new ShoppingCart ();

   Purchase p = new Purchase(cart);
   cart.AddPurchase (p);
   p.Cost = 10;
   p.Quantity = 1;
   Console.WriteLine ("Total Order Cost: {0,8:C}", cart.Total);

   p = new Purchase (cart);
   cart.AddPurchase (p);
   p.Cost = 42;
   p.Quantity = 10;
```

```
Console.WriteLine ("Total Order Cost: {0,8:C}", cart.Total);

p = new Purchase (cart);
cart.AddPurchase (p);
p.Cost = 2;
p.Quantity = 100;
Console.WriteLine ("Total Order Cost: {0,8:C}", cart.Total);

  }
}
```

Outputs:
```
Total Order Cost:    $10.00
Total Order Cost:   $430.00
Total Order Cost:   $630.00
```

Constant Data Items

Notice I just inserted a constant item in the above example, the array bounds. C# supports constant data members or static data members. However, they must be assigned their values as they are defined and that value must be therefore known to the compiler.

```
    const public int MAXSIZE = 10;
    const public double PI = 3.1415926;
```

Static Properties—Static Member Functions—Static Constructors—ReadOnly Fields

C# also allows for **static properties** that belong to the whole class rather than to some specific instance. Similarly, **static member functions** operate on static class items, unless a specific class instance is passed to it.

A **static constructor** is a ctor that has the keyword static in front of it and has no parameters. A static ctor will be called sometime **after** the program starts and **before** the first instance of that class is actually allocated. We have **no** control over when it is called by the framework.

One of the more common **static member function** examples is an instance count.
```
class MyClass {
 static int instanceCount = 0;

 public MyClass () {
   instanceCount++;
```

```
  }

  public static GetInstanceCount () {
    return instanceCount;
  }
}
```

Constants must be known at compile time. Sometimes this can create a problem in class design. Suppose that we needed a Color class to encapsulate screen colors. Further, the default colors Red, Green and Blue should be provided. We might begin this way.

```
class Color {
 protected int red;
 protected int green;
 protected int blue;

 public Color (int red, int blue, int green) {
    this.red = red;
    this.blue = blue;
    this.green = green;
 }

 // next three lines fail because constants must be known at
 // compile time.
 public static const Color Red = new Color (255, 0, 0);
 public static const Color Blue = new Color (0,0,255);
 public static const Color Green = new Color (0,255, 0);
```

However, a **static** constructor can be called before any class instances are made that would potentially use these three constant colors. Further, once the **static** ctor has built them, we do not want their values being changed, i.e., the constant idea. This is the purpose of the new **readonly** qualifier. Here is how we can do this.

```
class Color {
 protected int red;
 protected int green;
 protected int blue;

 public Color (int red, int blue, int green) {
    this.red = red;
    this.blue = blue;
    this.green = green;
 }

 public static readonly Color Red;
 public static readonly Color Blue;
```

```
public static readonly Color Green;

public static Color () {
   Red = new Color (255, 0, 0);
   Blue = new Color (0,0,255);
   Green = new Color (0,255, 0);
 }
}


class Application {
 static void Main () {
  Color highlight = Color.Red;
  Color backgrnd = Color.Blue;
```

Thus, there is lot of usage for **readonly** type properties.

Enumerations

Enumerated data types provide an excellent way to assign an easily remembered name to a numerical value. Enums in C# are fully supported and also parallel C++.

```
        public enum PetTypes {Dog, Cat, Pig}
```
Here the public enum data type is PetTypes. Instances of PetType can be created and/or passed and returned from functions. As you would expect, the Dog value, since it is not coded, is 0 and Cat is 1 and so on.

```
        public enum PetTypes {Dog=1, Cat, Pig}
```
Here Dog is 1 and Cat is therefore 2 and so on.

```
        public enum PetTypes {Dog=3, Cat=1, Pig=10}
```
Here each has a unique value.

Since these are class enums, the class qualifier must be used.
```
class Pet {
 public enum PetTypes {Dog, Cat, Pig}

 protected PetTypes type;
 ...
 public void SetPetType (PetType p) {
  type = p;
  switch (p) {
   case PetType.Dog:
     ...
```

```
   case PetType.Cat:
       ...
  }
 }
}
class App {
 static void Main () {
  Pet p = new Pet();
  p.SetPetType (Pet.PetType.Dog);
 }
}
```

Note that one can also typecast to enum values.

```
      p.SetPetType ((Pet.PetType) 42);
```

However, one should always verify that the parameter enum is within the valid range.

Differing from C++, in an enum definition, we are allowed to specify the base data type. In C++ all enums are really of type int. However, in C# we can specify any of the 8 integer types to be the actual base type, such as byte, sbyte, short, int, long. The syntax is

```
      enum type : base {value1=number, value2 = number,...}
```

For example,

```
      enum Letters : byte {A, B, C, D, E};
```

One can define bit flags as well. Usually, hexadecimal notation is used to make unique bit flag values.

```
[Flags]
enum MyFlags : byte {
      None = 0x00,
      One = 0x01,
      Two = 0x02,
      Four = 0x04,
      Eight = 0x08}
```

Notice that each value corresponds to a different bit within a byte. The **[Flags]** is an **attribute** that tells browsers and designers that this item is a flag which whose values can logically be ORed together to make a combined flag setting.

One can typecast to and from an enum value.

```
      Pet.PetType p = (Pet.PetType) 0; // Dog
      int t = (int) p;
```

assuming that the base type is the default of int or that int was specified as a base.

The sole **exception** is the value 0 which does not have to be converted via a typecast. This is done so we may write

```
      if (p == 0)
```

instead of
```
    if (p == (Pet.PetType) 0)
```

Enums are derived from the **System.Enum** type. The **ToString** function of the **Enum** type is rewritten to also provide the textual value of the enum.
```
    Console.WriteLine ("Pet p is {0}", p.type);
    // assuming type is public
```
outputs
```
    Pet p is Dog
```
assuming **p.type** is **Dog** or 0.

There are also the following static methods available using **Enum**.
> **GetName**, **GetNames**, **Parse**, **IsDefined**, and **GetValues**

Indexers—Smart Array Accessors

Sometimes it is far more efficient to access properties of a class as if they were array elements. This is the purpose of an **accessor**—to allow array subscript access to something within a class. The **accessor** works like a property and supports both **get** and **set** and is passed a parameter which is used as the subscript in some manner. Unlike C++, this subscript that is passed can be anything desired, and often is a descriptive string name of the property.

A class can have more than one **accessor** as long as they have different prototypes. The syntax is
```
    accessQualifier returnType this [indexType name1,
                    indexType name2, ...] {
        get {
            // use name1, name2 etc to return a value
        }
        set {
            // use name1, name2 etc to find the index
            // and store passed value here
        }
    }
```

In the following examples of a **Circle** and a **Rectangle**, I chose to store the properties in arrays. For the **Circle**, the three values are **x**, **y** and **radius**. For the **Rectangle**, the four values are **top**, **bottom**, **left**, and **right**. Thus, the user can get at the properties by either providing the integer subscript or the descriptive name of that property. This can be a very handy mechanism and is very versatile. This is Pgm03bConsole.
```
using System;
```

```csharp
class Circle {
 protected string[] names  = {"x", "y", "radius"};
 protected double[] values = new double [3];

 public Circle (double x, double y, double radius) {
  values[0] = x;
  values[1] = y;
  values[2] = radius;
 }

 public double this [int index] {
  get {
   if (index < 0 || index >= values.Length)
    return -1;
   else
    return values[index];
  }
  set {
   if (index < 0 || index >= values.Length) return;
   values[index] = value;
  }
 }

 public double this [string name] {
  get {
   int i = 0;
   while (i < names.Length && name.ToLower() != names[i]) i++;
   if (i == names.Length) return -1;
   return values[i];
  }
  set {
   int i = 0;
   while (i < names.Length && name.ToLower() != names[i]) i++;
   if (i == names.Length) return;
   values[i] = value;
  }
 }
}

class Rectangle {
 protected string[] names  = {"top", "bottom", "left", "right"};
 protected int[]    values = new int [4];

 public Rectangle (int top, int bottom, int left, int right) {
  values[0] = top;
  values[1] = bottom;
```

```
   values[2] = left;
   values[3] = right;
 }

 public int this [int index] {
  get {
   if (index < 0 || index >= values.Length)
    return -1;
   else
    return values[index];
  }
  set {
   if (index < 0 || index >= values.Length) return;
   values[index] = value;
  }
 }

 public int this [string name] {
  get {
   int i = 0;
   while (i < names.Length && name.ToLower() != names[i]) i++;
   if (i == names.Length) return -1;
   return values[i];
  }
  set {
   int i = 0;
   while (i < names.Length && name.ToLower() != names[i]) i++;
   if (i == names.Length) return;
   values[i] = value;
  }
 }
}

class Tester {
 static void Main(string[] args) {
  Circle c = new Circle (1,42,88);
  Rectangle r = new Rectangle (10, 200, 5, 300);

  int i;
  for (i=0; i<3; i++) {
   Console.WriteLine ("Circle c properties from indexer {0}",
                      c[i]);
  }
  Console.WriteLine ("Circle c properties from strings {0}",
                     c["X"]);
  Console.WriteLine ("Circle c properties from strings {0}",
```

```
                        c["Y"]);
    Console.WriteLine ("Circle c properties from strings {0}",
                        c["radius"]);

    for (i=0; i<4; i++) {
     Console.WriteLine ("Rectangle r properties from indexer {0}",
                        r[i]);
    }
    Console.WriteLine ("Rectangle r properties from strings {0}",
                      r["top"]);
    Console.WriteLine ("Rectangle r properties from strings {0}",
                      r["boTTom"]);
    Console.WriteLine ("Rectangle r properties from strings {0}",
                      r["left"]);
    Console.WriteLine ("Rectangle r properties from strings {0}",
                      r["right"]);
  }
}
```

The output is this.
```
Circle c properties from indexer 1
Circle c properties from indexer 42
Circle c properties from indexer 88
Circle c properties from strings 1
Circle c properties from strings 42
Circle c properties from strings 88
Rectangle r properties from indexer 10
Rectangle r properties from indexer 200
Rectangle r properties from indexer 5
Rectangle r properties from indexer 300
Rectangle r properties from strings 10
Rectangle r properties from strings 200
Rectangle r properties from strings 5
Rectangle r properties from strings 300
```

Problems

Problem 3-1—The Square Class

Part A.

Write a class called **Square** that implements the square geometric shape. It should have one data member, the length of a side.

Provide two constructors: a default ctor and one that is passed a side's length.

Provide a **Side** accessor property to allow get/set operations. No side dimension can ever be negative. Handle such errors as you see fit, but you must alert the user to this error in some manner of your choosing.

Provide public GetArea and GetPerimeter functions.

Write a tester program to thoroughly test the class.

Part B.

Next, write a client program that allocates an array of 100 **Square** objects. Then, using conversational I/O, prompt the user to enter as many squares as they desire, subject to the 100 max limit.

When the user has entered all of the squares desired, then print out a report similar to the one below.

```
The Square Report
index    Side Length        Area        Perimeter
  0          10.00         100.00          40.00
  1         100.00       10000.00         400.00
...
```

The report is to be printed twice. The first time, use a **for** loop and the second time use a foreach loop. Be careful with the **foreach** loop. You may need to test for null objects.

Chapter 4 OOP—Inheritance, Polymorphism, and Operator Overloading

Class Accessibility

A class can have two accessibility qualifiers, **internal** and **public**. **Internal** is a way of granting access to a class within a particular assembly without granting access to that class to the outside world. Internal classes are available to all within the assembly that defines that internal class. Usually, these are helper type classes, to which a general user should not have any access.

Thus, we normally begin this way
```
public class MyClass {
```

Principles of Inheritance

In C#, we use the base class-derived class notation. Other languages, such as Java, use superclass-sub-class notation. C# does not support multiple inheritance, that is, having more than one direct base class. However, one can have a hierarchy of classes, each one building upon another.

The first principle of inheritance is, unlike C++, all derived classes are derived publically from the base class. Thus, we have the following inherited characteristics.

```
Item is defined          Becomes in the      Becomes in the
in base class as         derived class       client program

   public                   public            accessible directly
   protected                protected         inaccessible
   private                  inaccessible      inaccessible
   internal accessible if in the same assembly otherwise not
```

The new internal access acts like protected in many ways, but those items are only accessible from locations within the same assembly. This impacts those who create libraries of classes.

Thus, once again, make restricted usage of private data members in the base class. Otherwise, the derived class cannot access them directly without using the get/set methods which adds overhead as well as aggravation. There are only a few items that should be made untouchable by derived classes, such things as reference counting, pointers to lists or chains of data items, and so on.

Similarly, one does not make everything public because that breaks the black box, encapsulation approach and opens up the implementation and, once issued into production, such cannot easily be changed.

Constructions, as in C++, are never inherited. Thus, derived classes are responsible for providing a derived class ctor that also calls the base class ctor. If a derived class ctor fails to call the base class ctor, the compiler automatically calls the base class default ctor.

The other data items and functions of a base class are inherited by the derived class. If an inherited function does not provide proper support for the new derived object, you can override that base class function by redefining it in the derived class.

Some common hierarchies of classes include these:
```
Shape<-Circle
     <-Rectangle
     <-Square
Student<-Undergrad
        <-Graduate
BankAccount<-CheckingAccount<-CheckingWithInterest
            <-SavingsAccount
```

Remember that we typically use the "**is a**" nomenclature with inheritance. A Circle **is a** Shape. A Graduate **is a** Student. A CheckingWithInterest **is a** CheckingAccount **is a** BankAccount. When **has a** is used, it means that it is a data member of the class, as in a Rectangle **has a** length and width.

The syntax to indicate that a class is being derived from a base class is the presence of a : (colon) followed by the base class.
```
class Circle : Shape {
class CheckingAccount : BankAccount {
class CheckingWithInterest : CheckingAccount {
```
Notice that the base class specified is its immediate base class, as with CheckingWithInterest.

Note that every C# class is derived from **Object** implicitly. Thus far, we have said nothing about using a base class notation with the class definitions up to this point. That is because if no base class is coded, the compiler assumes **Object** and handles it accordingly. **Object** gives us the **ToString** method which normally returns a string containing the class name and namespace. We could override it to provide a different string to be used, one that perhaps includes some of the data the instance is storing, such as account number, policy number, item number, and so on.

Let's begin our study of inheritance with a simple **Point** class so that we can easily follow the actions. Here is the base class. Since **Point** is automatically derived from **Object**, I thought it would be nice if the **ToString Object** method returned something like

Point [10, 42]

instead of just the class name

Point

```csharp
using System;

public class Point {
 protected int x;
 protected int y;

 public Point () {
  x = 0;
  y = 0;
 }

 public Point (int x, int y) {
  this.x = x;
  this.y = y;
 }

 public int X {
  get {
   return x;
  }
  set {
   x = value;
  }
 }

 public int Y {
  get {
   return y;
  }
  set {
   y = value;
  }
 }

 public string ToString () {
  return "Point [" + x + ", " + y + "]";
 }
}

class Tester {
 static void Main(string[] args) {
  Point p = new Point (10,42);
  Console.WriteLine (p);
```

```
  Console.WriteLine (p.ToString ());
 }
}
```

Here is the output of the two **WriteLine** instructions. Can you spot the problem?
```
Point
Point [10, 42]
```

When we want to override a base class function, we must add in the keyword **override** to the function definition.
```
 public override string ToString () {
```

Further, the base class must have defined the **ToPoint** function as a **virtual** function, which **Object** does.
```
 public virtual string ToString () {
```

Why do we get the behavior observed in the above example with the **ToString** method? Remember that **WriteLine** is being passed a reference to an **Object** and it then uses that reference to invoke the **ToString** method. Hence, we are in effect using a reference to a base class to invoke the function.

However, the compiler must have a mechanism to determine whether to call **Object**'s **ToString** or **Point**'s **ToString**. Even though the base class has defined the **ToString** as a virtual function, unless the derived class also codes override on that function, the compiler calls the base class **ToString**. In the second call to WriteLine, I explicitly called the derived class's ToString. That works. One can always call directly the derived class's methods. However, more often than not, a reference to the base class is used. So we need to keep the virtual-override mechanism in mind. There are some additional ramifications we will examine shortly.

Now let's make a derived **Circle** class that is a **Point** plus a radius. Consider the following simple **Circle** derivation. The first problem is how to invoke the base class constructor.

If we do not code anything, at block entry to a derived class ctor, the compiler automatically invokes the default ctor of the base class, which usually assigns zeros to everything. This is often just fine when coding the default ctor of the derived class.
```
public class Circle : Point {
 protected double radius;

 public Circle () {
  // implicit call to the base Point default ctor done here
  radius = 0;
 }
```

However, when coding a derived class's constructor that takes parameters, this leads to messy coding since we must also assign all the base class inherited members as well as the new ones in the derived class.

```
public Circle (int x, int y, double radius) {
  // implicit call to the base Point default ctor done here
  this.x = x;
  this.y = y;
  this.radius = radius;
}
```

A better way is to use an explicit call to the base class. This is done using the keyword **: base (parm1, parm2, ...)** as shown below.

```
public Circle (int x, int y, double radius) : base (x, y) {
  this.radius = radius;
}
```

Use a **:** followed by **base()** and then any parameters you want to pass. Note this is different from C++ in which one would code the name of the base class instead of the keyword base.

Similarly we could derive class **Sphere** from a **Circle**. No new data members are needed. Here is what we have going thus far.

```
using System;

public class Point {
 protected int x;
 protected int y;

 public Point () {
  x = 0;
  y = 0;
 }

 public Point (int x, int y) {
  this.x = x;
  this.y = y;
 }

 public int X {
  get {
   return x;
  }
  set {
   x = value;
  }
 }
```

```csharp
 public int Y {
  get {
   return y;
  }
  set {
   y = value;
  }
 }

 public override string ToString () {
  return "Point [" + x + ", " + y + "]";
 }
}

public class Circle : Point {
 protected double radius;

 public double Radius {
  get {
   return radius;
  }
  set {
   if (value >= 0)
    radius = value;
   else
    radius = 0;
  }
 }

 public Circle () { // uses implicit call to Point
  radius = 0;
 }

 public Circle (int x, int y, double radius) : base (x, y) {
  this.radius = radius;
 }

 public override string ToString () {
  return "Circle [" + x + ", " + y + "] of radius " + radius;
 }
}


public class Sphere : Circle {
 public Sphere () {}
 public Sphere (int x, int y, double radius) : base (x, y,
```

```
                                            radius) {}
  public override string ToString () {
   return "Sphere [" + x + ", " + y + "] of radius " + radius;
  }
}

class Tester {
 static void Main(string[] args)    {
  Point p = new Point (10,42);
  Console.WriteLine (p);
  p.X = 42;
  Console.WriteLine (p);
  Circle c = new Circle (2, 5, 10.5);
  Console.WriteLine (c);
  Sphere s = new Sphere (42, 42, 100);
  Console.WriteLine (s);
  s.X = 10;
  Console.WriteLine (s);
  s.Radius = 1;
  Console.WriteLine (s);
 }
}
```

The output is this as expected. This coding is available as Pgm04aConsole.

```
Point [10, 42]
Point [42, 42]
Circle [2, 5] of radius 10.5
Sphere [42, 42] of radius 100
Sphere [10, 42] of radius 100
Sphere [10, 42] of radius 1
```

Inherited Methods and References to Base Class

However, we must look more closely at inherited methods. Let's add a new method to the point class, **OriginDistance**, which calculates the distance from the origin of the point. This method is defined in the **Point** class this way.

```
  public double OriginDistance () {
   return Math.Sqrt (x * x + y * y);
  }
```

This method can be used by **Circle** and **Sphere** since their distances from the origin of the coordinate scheme is figured identically.

67

Typically, a client program is going to allocate an array of base class objects in which to store these shapes. Typical client coding is this.

```
Point[] array = new Point [100];
array[0] = new Point (10,10);
array[1] = new Circle (10, 10, 10);
array[2] = new Sphere (5, 5, 5);
int numItems = 3;
for (int j=0; j<numItems; j++)
  Console.WriteLine ("Origin Distance is {0,6:F}",
                      array[j].OriginDistance ());
```

So far this will work perfectly. But now let's add a **Display** method to the **Point** class that outputs this.

```
Point [42, 42] has an origin distance of 59.40
```

Also, let's do the same thing for the **Circle** and **Sphere** classes. However, their **Display** methods should produce this.

```
Circle [42, 42] of radius 10.00 has an origin distance of 59.40
```

Initially, let's code this in **Point**.

```
public void Display () {
  Console.WriteLine ("Point [" + x + ", " + y +
      "] has an origin distance of {0,6:F}", OriginDistance ());
}
```

And this in **Circle**.

```
public void Display () {
  Console.WriteLine ("Circle [" + x + ", " + y +
  "] of radius " + radius + " has an origin distance of {0,6:F}",
  OriginDistance ());
}
```

And this in **Sphere**.

```
public void Display () {
  Console.WriteLine ("Sphere [" + x + ", " + y +
  "] of radius " + radius + " has an origin distance of {0,6:F}",
  OriginDistance ());
}
```

Now consider what happens in **Main** when we do the following.

```
for (int j=0; j<numItems; j++) {
  array[j].Display ();
}
```

Can you guess what the output is going to be?

```
Point [10, 10] has an origin distance of  14.14
Point [10, 10] has an origin distance of  14.14
Point [5, 5] has an origin distance of   7.07
```

These functions would have worked had we invoked them this way.

```
p.Display ();
c.Display ();
s.Display ();
```

where **p** is a **Point**, **c** is a **Circle**, and **s** is a **Sphere**.

What is lacking is the virtual function mechanism which enables a reference to a base class of a derived class object to invoke overridden methods in the derived class. Remember, that a base class reference only knows about the base class methods unless that function is virtual and is has the override keyword specified in the derived class version. Here is the corrected coding.

In **Point**.

```
public virtual void Display () {
  Console.WriteLine ("Point [" + x + ", " + y +
      "] has an origin distance of {0,6:F}", OriginDistance ());
}
```

And this in **Circle**.

```
public override void Display () {
  Console.WriteLine ("Circle [" + x + ", " + y +
  "] of radius " + radius + " has an origin distance of {0,6:F}",
  OriginDistance ());
}
```

And this in **Sphere**.

```
public override void Display () {
  Console.WriteLine ("Sphere [" + x + ", " + y +
  "] of radius " + radius + " has an origin distance of {0,6:F}",
  OriginDistance ());
}
```

Now we get the correct output from

```
for (int j=0; j<numItems; j++) {
  array[j].Display ();
}
```

as shown below.

```
Point [10, 10] has an origin distance of  14.14
Circle [10, 10] of radius 10 has an origin distance of  14.14
Sphere [5, 5] of radius 5 has an origin distance of   7.07
```

We still have not got a great trio of classes here. Notice the redundant coding extracted from the three classes.

```
Console.WriteLine ("Point [" + x + ", " + y +
"] has an origin distance of {0,6:F}",
OriginDistance ());
```

```
Console.WriteLine ("Circle [" + x + ", " + y +
"] of radius " + radius + " has an origin distance of {0,6:F}",
OriginDistance ());

Console.WriteLine ("Sphere [" + x + ", " + y +
"] of radius " + radius + " has an origin distance of {0,6:F}",
OriginDistance ());
```

And this, too, is redundant.
```
return "Point [" + x + ", " + y + "]";
return "Circle [" + x + ", " + y + "] of radius " + radius;
return "Sphere [" + x + ", " + y + "] of radius " + radius;
```

Remember that we have **GetType** which returns the string class name as well as **ToString** available to us from the **Object** base class. Certainly we can add additional helper functions.

Let's have a **Format** method that handles the creation of the [10, 10] string. And **FormatOriginDistance** creates the " has an origin distance of 14.14" string.

In the **Point** base class we have the following.
```
public virtual string Format () {
  return " [" + x + ", " + y + "]";
}

public virtual string FormatOriginDistance () {
  return String.Format (" has an origin distance of {0,6:F}",
                        OriginDistance ());
}

public override string ToString () {
  return GetType() + Format();
}

public virtual void Display () {
  Console.WriteLine (ToString () + FormatOriginDistance ());
}
```

In the **Circle** class, we now have this.
```
public override string Format () {
  return " [" + x + ", " + y + "]" + " of radius " + radius;
}
```

70

```
public override string ToString () {
 return GetType() + Format();
}

public override void Display () {
 Console.WriteLine (ToString () + FormatOriginDistance());
}
```

And in the **Sphere** class, we have the following.

```
public override string ToString () {
 return GetType() + Format ();
}

public override void Display () {
 Console.WriteLine (ToString () + FormatOriginDistance());
}
```

Thus, we now have an elegant solution. The complete program is Pgm04bConsole.

```
using System;

class Point {
  protected int x;
  protected int y;

  public Point() {
   x = 0;
   y = 0;
  }

  public Point(int x, int y) {
   this.x = x;
   this.y = y;
  }

  public int X {
   get {
    return x;
   }
   set {
    x = value;
   }
  }
```

71

```
public int Y {
  get {
   return y;
  }
  set {
   y = value;
  }
}

public double OriginDistance() {
  return Math.Sqrt(x * x + y * y);
}

public virtual string Format() {
  return " [" + x + ", " + y + "]";
}

public virtual string FormatOriginDistance() {
  return String.Format(" has an origin distance of {0,6:F}",
                     OriginDistance());
}

public override string ToString() {
  return GetType() + Format();
}

public virtual void Display() {
  Console.WriteLine(ToString() + FormatOriginDistance());
}
}

class Circle : Point {
 protected double radius;

 public double Radius {
  get {
   return radius;
  }
  set {
   if (value >= 0)
     radius = value;
   else
     radius = 0;
  }
 }
```

```csharp
public Circle() {
  // uses implicit call to Point
  radius = 0;
}

public Circle(int x, int y, double radius) : base(x, y) {
  this.radius = radius;
}

public override string Format() {
  return " [" + x + ", " + y + "]" + " of radius " + radius;
}

public override string ToString() {
  return GetType() + Format();
}

public override void Display() {
  Console.WriteLine(ToString() + FormatOriginDistance());
}
}

class Sphere : Circle {
  public Sphere() { }
  public Sphere(int x, int y, double radius) : base(x, y, radius)
{ }

  public override string ToString() {
    return GetType() + Format();
  }

  public override void Display() {
    Console.WriteLine(ToString() + FormatOriginDistance());
  }
}

class Tester {
  static void Main(string[] args) {
    Point p = new Point(10, 42);
    Circle c = new Circle(2, 5, 10.5);
    Sphere s = new Sphere(42, 42, 100);
    p.Display();
    c.Display();
    s.Display();
```

```
  Point[] array = new Point[100];
  array[0] = new Point(10, 10);
  array[1] = new Circle(10, 10, 10);
  array[2] = new Sphere(5, 5, 5);
  int numItems = 3;
  for (int j = 0; j < numItems; j++) {
   array[j].Display();
  }
 }
}
```

The output of the program is as follows.

```
Point [10, 42] has an origin distance of  43.17
Circle [2, 5] of radius 10.5 has an origin distance of   5.39
Sphere [42, 42] of radius 100 has an origin distance of  59.40
Point [10, 10] has an origin distance of  14.14
Circle [10, 10] of radius 10 has an origin distance of  14.14
Sphere [5, 5] of radius 5 has an origin distance of   7.07
```

Using base From Other Locations

The base class version of an overridden function can be called from within a derived class overridden function by use of the **base.** qualifier.

Here is another way this same problem could have been solved. In the **Point** class, we now code this, moving the [10, 10] portion into the **ToString** method.

```
public virtual string FormatOriginDistance () {
  return String.Format (" has an origin distance of {0,6:F}",
                        OriginDistance ());
}

public override string ToString () {
  return GetType() + " [" + x + ", " + y + "]";
}

public virtual void Display () {
  Console.WriteLine (ToString () + FormatOriginDistance());
}
```

Now in the **Circle** class, we use the **base** qualifier as follows.

```
public override string ToString () {
  return base.ToString () + " of radius " + radius;
}
public override void Display () {
  Console.WriteLine (ToString () + FormatOriginDistance());
```

74

```
}
```

And then in the **Sphere** class, we do this. Nothing! All of this coding is removed from **Sphere**. It is just

```
public class Sphere : Circle {
  public Sphere () {}
  public Sphere (int x, int y, double radius) : base (x, y,
              radius) {}
}
```

This coding is available in Pgm04cConsole. Follow what happens when the client calls **array[j].Display ()** using a reference to the **Sphere** object. There is no **Display** method overridden in **Sphere**, so it goes to the overridden **Display** of **Circle** which calls **ToString**. However, **Circle**'s **ToString** calls the **Point** base class **ToString**. The **Point** base class first calls **GetType**, but since it is a reference, the function correctly identifies this as a **Sphere**. Next, **Point**'s **ToString** adds on the [n, n] location portion and returns back to **Circle**'s **ToString** which now appends the of radius portion. It returns back to **Circle**'s **Display** which then appends the origin distance. Now we really have an elegant, slick solution!

However, there is one caution when using the **base** qualifier. Consider what would happen if I had accidentally coded the **Circle**'s **ToString** this way.

```
public override string ToString () {
  return ToString () + " of radius " + radius;
        // base.ToString omitted
}
```

It would result in an infinite recursively calling **Circle**'s **ToString**!

Destructors, Object.Finalize, and Garbage Collection

The class destructor is the same name as the class but prefixed with the ~ sign, just as it is done in C++. The destructor function for the **Point** class would be **~Point**.

When derived classes are involved, the compiler knows what the object really is and calls the destructors itself in reverse order. For example, when destroying a **Sphere** object, the compiler first calls **~Sphere** and then **~Circle** and then **~Point** and then **~Object**. If we should implement any of the destructors, it is only necessary to worry about destruction of items within that specific class, since any base class destructors will be called when we return. This is exactly the same as C++.

What actions are commonly found in destructor functions? In C++, the most commonly found coding in a destructor function is deletion of dynamically allocated memory. However, since the C# garbage collector handles all deletions of memory, we never need to worry about it. Thus, at this point, the most likely coding could be decrementing an instance counter or disconnection from a data base. So destructors are not often needed.

Further, we cannot know when exactly the garbage collector will actually delete any given object. It runs in a separate thread and periodically examines memory to find all those objects that are no longer referenced anywhere and then proceeds to delete them. So normally, there is no way to know when an object is actually deleted physically.

However, if your application has just freed up a number of objects, you can notify the garbage collector to take immediate action by coding an explicit call this way.

```
System.GC.Collect ();
```

A great deal of work went into the design of the C# garbage collector. They experimented with a wide variety of approaches before settling on the current implementation. The method in use works as follows.

1. The garbage collector thread keeps track which objects are referenced.
2. The garbage collector always has a low priority thread running scanning its objects looking for those that are no longer referenced anywhere.
3. A second low priority thread is responsible for the actual clean up function calls. This thread calls the **Object.Finalize** method to remove it and handle the destructor calls.

Normally, this is just fine for our applications. However, what if an object has a hold of a system critical resource that really must be given back just as soon as the application no longer needs it? The .NET team suggests the following to handle the freeing up of critical resources.

In a class that allocates a critical resource, provide a public member function called **Dispose**. Instruct the users that they are to call **Dispose** when they want the critical item freed. You implement **Dispose** to actually free that item. In fact, if you look at the actual C# implementation, you will see this function, **Dispose**, being implemented and called within the framework on critical issues.

Conversions From Base Class to Derived Class And Vice Versa

Any instance of a derived class can be treated as an instance of its base class. Of course, the only functions that can be called are base class functions and those that are defined as virtual and which are overridden in the derived class.

However, sometimes there are one or more functions in the derived class that are not present in a base class. Thus, we must have a way to find out if a particular base class reference is actually pointing to a derived class object and then be able to invoke those derived class functions.

To check if a particular reference to an object is actually a specific derived class object, we can use the **is** verb, as in "is an instance of." A type cast is used to assign the reference.

```
Point p = new Circle ();
if (p is Circle) {
  Circle c = (Circle) p;
  c.GetArea (); // and call other functions using c
}
```

If the type cast is invalid, C# throws an **InvalidCastException**. We examine the C# error handling in the next chapter. Thus, it is always wise to first check if an instance actually is of the derived type before attempting the conversion.

Abstract Base Classes

Returning to our **Point-Circle-Sphere** set of classes, when we attempt to add in additional functionality, such as **GetArea**, **GetVolume**, and so on, a new problem arises. Typically, the client programs will be storing arrays of these objects in a base class array and thus using the base class reference to invoke member functions. This presents a new problem. Only those virtual functions in the base class can end up in the appropriate derived class function. What would have to be done to the **Point** class so that the following would work?

```
Point p = new Circle ();
double area = p.GetArea ();
```
where in **Circle** we have
```
public double GetArea () {
  return Math.PI * radius * radius;
}
```

For this to work, the **Point** class must define a **GetArea** virtual function. This yields a design failure on our part. What on earth has a **Point** class got defining **GetArea**? It makes no sense at all.

This is a common OOP design problem, using the wrong base class. A circle and sphere are geometric shapes that have as part of their data the coordinates of their center. A circle is not a point, it is a shape. Thus, we should design a **Shape** base class that utilizes an instance of a **Point** as one of its properties. Then derive **Circle** and **Sphere** from **Shape**. This is done in Pgm04dConsole.

I highlight in bold the major changes. In the **Point** class, there is no need for **virtual** functions any longer, just the **override** for **ToString** of its base **Object** method. For convenience, I added a copy constructor that makes a new **Point** from a parameter **Point** object.

```
using System;

public class Point {
 protected int x;
 protected int y;

 public Point () {
  x = 0;
  y = 0;
 }

 public Point (int x, int y) {
  this.x = x;
  this.y = y;
 }
```

```csharp
public Point (Point p) { // copy ctor
 x = p.x;
 y = p.y;
}

public int X {
 get {
  return x;
 }
 set {
  x = value;
 }
}

public int Y {
 get {
  return y;
 }
 set {
  y = value;
 }
}

public double OriginDistance () {
 return Math.Sqrt (x * x + y * y);
}

public string FormatOriginDistance () {
 return String.Format (" with origin distance {0,1:F}",
                       OriginDistance ());
}

public override string ToString () {
 return " origin at [" + x + ", " + y + "]";
}

public void Display () {
 Console.WriteLine (ToString () + FormatOriginDistance());
 }
}
```

Class **Shape** holds an instance of the **Point** class called **origin**. It has two dimensions defined so that we can easily store two dimensional shapes easily. The ctors must allocate a new **Point** object so that the reference origin has a **Point** object to which to point. The two public dimension properties enforce the rule that a dimension cannot be negative.

When calling the **Point** operations as part of the display operations, notice I use the instance, **origin.ToString()** and **origin.FormatOriginDistance()**. Finally, nothing has to be altered in the **Sphere** class.

```csharp
public class Shape {
 protected Point origin;
 protected double dimension1;
 protected double dimension2;

 public Shape () {
  origin = new Point ();
  dimension1 = dimension2 = 0;
 }

 public double Dimension1 {
  get {
   return dimension1;
  }
  set {
   if (value >= 0) {
    dimension1 = value;
   }
   else {
    Console.WriteLine (
        "Error: Shape Dimension1 cannot be negative");
    dimension1 = 0;
   }
  }
 }

 public double Dimension2 {
  get {
   return dimension2;
  }
  set {
   if (value >= 0) {
    dimension2 = value;
   }
   else {
    Console.WriteLine (
                 "Error: Shape Dimension2 cannot be negative");
```

```csharp
      dimension2 = 0;
    }
  }
}

  public Shape (Point o, double dim1, double dim2) {
   origin = new Point (o);
   Dimension1 = dim1;        // notice negatives are not allowed
   Dimension2 = dim2;
  }

  public override string ToString () {
   return GetType() + origin.ToString();
  }

  public virtual void Display () {
   Console.WriteLine (ToString () +origin.FormatOriginDistance());
  }
}

public class Circle : Shape {

  public double Radius {
   get {
    return dimension1;
   }
   set {
    if (value >= 0)
     dimension1 = value;
    else
     dimension1 = 0;
   }
  }

  public Circle () { // uses implicit call to Shape
  }

  public Circle (int x, int y, double radius) :
                                    base(new Point (x,y),radius,0){
  }

  public override string ToString () {
   return base.ToString () + " and radius of " + dimension1;
```

```
    }

  public override void Display () {
   Console.WriteLine (ToString () +origin.FormatOriginDistance());
  }
}


public class Sphere : Circle {
 public Sphere () {} // implicit call to Circle
 public Sphere (int x, int y, double radius) : base (x, y, radius)
{}
}


class Tester {
 static void Main(string[] args)    {
  Circle c = new Circle ();
  c.Display ();
  Sphere s = new Sphere (20, 20, 20);
  s.Display ();

  Shape[] array = new Shape [100];
  array[0] = new Circle (10, 10, 10);
  array[1] = new Sphere (5, 5, 5);
  int numItems = 2;
  for (int j=0; j<numItems; j++) {
   array[j].Display ();
  }
 }
}
```

The above **Main** produces the following lines.

```
Circle origin at [0, 0] and radius of 0 with origin distance 0.00
Sphere origin at [20, 20] and radius of 20 with origin distance 28.28
Circle origin at [10, 10] and radius of 10 with origin distance 14.14
Sphere origin at [5, 5] and radius of 5 with origin distance 7.07
```

This is our starting point. A **Shape** can easily be thought of as having an "area" so we could provide its definition as follows.

```
    public double GetArea () {
```

However, how do we implement it? Certainly, only the derived classes know how to perform the calculation, not the **Shape** class. Thus, what we want is the base class to provide the virtual function definition only. Of course, if we do not provide any implementation for one or more virtual functions, this makes **Shape** an **abstract** class. No instances of **Shape** can be allocated.

An abstract class is created by using the keyword **abstract** before the class keyword.

```
abstract class Shape {
```

Now there are two ways that the **GetArea** function can be defined in the abstract **Shape** class.

```
public virtual double GetArea () {
    return 0;
}
```

and

```
public abstract double GetArea ();
```

In both cases, the **Circle** class must define **GetArea** the same way.

```
public override double GetArea () {
    return Math.PI * dimension1 * dimension1;
}
```

So what is the difference? If the **Shape** provides a virtual function, then it is possible for **Circle** to not include a **GetArea** at all! In such a case, circle objects always have an area of 0! However, if the **Shape** declares it as abstract and thus provides no implementation, the function is still virtual but the **Circle** class **must** declare and implement it. This makes for far fewer errors. So I recommend using **abstract** and not **virtual** in such cases. In the **Sphere** class, the area is twice that of a circle, so **GetArea** must be further overridden in the **Sphere** class. Notice I again make use of the **base** qualifier.

```
return base.GetArea () * 4;
```

Similarly, we can provide a **GetPerimeter** method because a **Shape** logically has a distance around it. It is implemented in the **Circle** class but not in the **Sphere** class because the formula is the same in both cases.

Okay. But what about functions like **GetVolume**? Here we are facing a common design question. An arbitrary shape is not normally thought of as having a third dimension, so that matters of volume are out of place. Yet the sphere does have a volume. We can create a **GetVolume** function for the **Sphere** class. But how do we get it properly invoked?

If no mention of **GetVolume** is made in the **Shape** class and if the user is using an array of shapes to store the objects, then these **Shape** references cannot be used to directly call **GetVolume**. It is not defined in the **Shape** class in any way. What do we do?

One solution is to put another abstract definition of **GetVolume** into the shape class even though it is out of place there. That would work and is sometimes the easy way out. Perhaps in the entire design if this is the only out of place function that arises, then this would be acceptable. However, in the real world of objects, this out of place function situation occurs frequently. It does not make any sense to load up some abstract base class with numerous functions that have no meaning there. Why? Because all of the other derived classes must implement this function, whether

83

or not it has any meaning to them. In this case, **Circle** would have to implement **GetVolume** which makes no sense at all.

The other approach is to recognize that some of the derived classes will indeed have methods that are not common to the base class hierarchy. These must be called using a proper reference to the proper class to which the base class reference is actually pointing. That is, we need to type cast the base class reference back into an actual derived class reference and use that to invoke these out of place functions.

And this is the approach used here with **GetVolume**, a method unique to the **Sphere** class.

Here is the revised Pgm04eConsole. Nothing was changed in the Point class and it is not shown. I bold faced the changes and omitted the other coding that is the same as the above example.

```csharp
public abstract class Shape {
 protected Point  origin;
 protected double dimension1;
 protected double dimension2;
...
 public abstract double GetArea ();
 public abstract double GetPerimeter ();
}

public class Circle : Shape {
...
 public override double GetArea () {
  return Math.PI * dimension1 * dimension1;
 }

 public override double GetPerimeter () {
  return Math.PI * dimension1 * 2;
 }
}

public class Sphere : Circle {
 public Sphere () {}
 public Sphere (int x, int y, double radius) : base (x, y, radius)
{}

 public override double GetArea () {
  return base.GetArea () * 4;
 }

 public double GetVolume () {
  return 4.0 / 3.0 * Math.PI * Math.Pow (dimension1, 3.0);
```

```
   }
}

class Tester {
 static void Main(string[] args)    {
  Circle c = new Circle ();
  c.Display ();
  Sphere s = new Sphere (20, 20, 20);
  s.Display ();

  Shape[] array = new Shape [100];
  array[0] = new Circle (10, 10, 10);
  array[1] = new Sphere (5, 5, 5);
  int numItems = 2;
  for (int j=0; j<numItems; j++) {
   array[j].Display ();
   Console.WriteLine ("  Area: {0,1:F}", array[j].GetArea ());
   Console.WriteLine ("  Perimeter: {0,1:F}",
                        array[j].GetPerimeter ());
   if (array[j] is Sphere)
     Console.WriteLine ("  Volume: {0,1:F}",
                ((Sphere)(array[j])).GetVolume());
  }
 }
}
```

Here is the **Main** function's output.

```
Circle origin at [0, 0] and radius of 0 with origin distance 0.00
Sphere origin at [20, 20] and radius of 20 with origin distance 28.28
Circle origin at [10, 10] and radius of 10 with origin distance 14.14
  Area: 314.16
  Perimeter: 62.83
Sphere origin at [5, 5] and radius of 5 with origin distance 7.07
  Area: 314.16
  Perimeter: 31.42
  Volume: 523.60
```

Sealed Classes and Methods

When a variable is defined using **const**, it must be initialized when it is defined and cannot thereafter be changed. When a variable is marked **readonly**, it must be initialized in the ctor function and cannot thereafter be changed. Classes and methods can also be marked and unchangeable by additional derived classes. The keyword is **sealed**.

85

If a class or method has the sealed keyword on it, then that class cannot be further derived from or that method cannot be overridden by others. All methods in a sealed class are implicitly sealed as well. One of the benefits of a sealed class is that the compiler can create better execution time performance with those instances.

What types of classes are logical candidates for the sealed option? Certainly one would not expect a derived class to provide an override to the **Sin**, **Sqrt**, **Pow**, and **Cos** functions! Thus, one might expect to find the **Math** set of classes and methods to be sealed. Thus, do not expect to be able to redefine **Math.PI** into some other value. Likewise, the **System.String** class is sealed.

Operator Overloading

Most all of the C# operators are can be overloaded with the exception of function calling, member accessing via the dot operator, the =, &&, ||, ?:, and new. Nor can you overload the compound assignment operators such as +=.

There are two fundamental kinds of operators, unary and binary. The minus operator and the inc and dec operators are unary, meaning that they have only one parameter, the object being modified. The add, multiply, ==, and >= operators are binary, meaning that they have two objects involved.

Rule: All operator overloaded functions must be *static* member functions.

All binary operator overloaded functions have the same general definition.
```
public static returnvalue operatorNN (parm1, parm2) {
```
One of the parameters must be an instance of the class.

All unary operator overloaded functions have this general definition.
```
public static returnvalue operatorNN (parm) {
```
Here the parameter must be an instance of the class.

Rule: There is no way to distinguish between prefix and postfix *inc* and *dec*. Thus, we implement only the before inc or dec operator and the compiler deals with the handling of the after inc or dec by calling the inc or dec after it uses the current value.

Rule: If you overload *operator==*, then you must also overload *operator!=* and *Object.Equals* and *Object.GetHashCode*.

These simplified prototypes greatly reduce the complexity of coding operator overloaded functions, compared to C++.

Returning to our **Point** class, let's add support for the addition operator, the == operator, and the inc operator. Since I am overloading operator==, I must also overload operator!= and the two **Object** functions, **Equals** and **GetHashCode**.

Here is Pgm04fConsole illustrating the operator overloaded functions. I omitted the usual ctor functions that are unchanged from the previous version.

```csharp
using System;

public class Point {
 protected int x;
 protected int y;

 public int X {
   get {    return x;   }
   set {    x = value;   }
 }

 public int Y {
   get {    return y;   }
   set {    y = value;   }
 }

 public double OriginDistance () {
   return Math.Sqrt (x * x + y * y);
 }

 public override string ToString () {
   return "Point [" + x + ", " + y + "]";
 }

 public static Point operator+ (Point p1, int x) {
   return new Point (p1.X + x, p1.Y + x);
 }

 public static Point operator+ (Point p1, Point p2) {
   return new Point (p1.X + p2.X, p1.Y + p2.Y);
 }

 public static Point operator+ (int x, Point p1) {
   return new Point (p1.X + x, p1.Y + x);
 }

 public static bool operator== (Point p1, Point p2) {
   return p1.X == p2.X && p1.Y == p2.Y;
 }
```

```
public static bool operator!= (Point p1, Point p2) {
  return !(p1.X == p2.X && p1.Y == p2.Y);
}

public override bool Equals (Object p1) {
  if (p1 is Point) {
   Point p = (Point) p1;
   return p.X == X && p.Y == Y;
  }
  else return false;
}

public override int GetHashCode () {
  return x.GetHashCode() + y.GetHashCode();
}

public static Point operator++ (Point p) { // before inc
  p.x += 1;
  p.y += 1;
  return p;
 }
}

class Tester {
 static void Main(string[] args)    {
  Point p0 = new Point ();
  Point p1 = new Point (2, 2);
  Point p2 = new Point (42, 42);
  Console.WriteLine ("P0 = " + p0.ToString ());
  p0 = p2 + 1;
  Console.WriteLine ("P0 = " + p0.ToString ());
  p0 = p2 + p1;
  Console.WriteLine ("P0 = " + p0.ToString ());
  p0 = 1 + p2;
  Console.WriteLine ("P0 = " + p0.ToString ());
  if (p0 == p1) Console.WriteLine ("P0 equals p1");
  else Console.WriteLine ("P0 does not equal p1");
  if (p0 != p1) Console.WriteLine ("P0 does not equal p1");
  else Console.WriteLine ("P0 equals p1");
  Console.WriteLine ("Before p2=p0++ P0 = " + p0.ToString ());
  p2 = p0++;
  Console.WriteLine ("After p2=p0++ P0 = " + p0.ToString ());
  Console.WriteLine ("After p2=p0++ P2 = " + p2.ToString ());
  p2 = ++p0;
```

```
  Console.WriteLine ("After p2=++p0 P0 = " + p0.ToString ());
  Console.WriteLine ("After p2=++p0 P2 = " + p2.ToString ());
  int x = 42;
  int y;
  y = x++;
  Console.WriteLine ("x after y=x++; " + x);
  Console.WriteLine ("y after y=x++; " + y);
  y = ++x;
  Console.WriteLine ("x after y=++x; " + x);
  Console.WriteLine ("y after y=++x; " + y);
 }
}
```

The program produces this output:

```
P0 = Point [0, 0]
P0 = Point [43, 43]
P0 = Point [44, 44]
P0 = Point [43, 43]
P0 does not equal p1
P0 does not equal p1
Before p2=p0++ P0 = Point [43, 43]
After p2=p0++ P0 = Point [44, 44]
After p2=p0++ P2 = Point [44, 44]
After p2=++p0 P0 = Point [45, 45]
After p2=++p0 P2 = Point [45, 45]
x after y=x++; 43
y after y=x++; 42
x after y=++x; 44
y after y=++x; 44
```

Experiment with this program and see what happens when you try to implement an after inc.

```
public static Point operator++ (Point p) { // after inc
 point ret(new Point (p));
 p.x += 1;
 p.y += 1;
 return ret;
}
```

Problems

Problem 4-1— Employee Classes

Part A.

Acme wishes a set of classes to encapsulate their employees. They have three types of employees: those that are paid on an hourly basis, those that are paid a flat salary, and those that are paid on piece basis. While their reimbursement is different, all employees share some data items in common: int social security number, first and last name strings.

Create an abstract base class called **Employee** that holds the items all employees hold in common. Provide properties to permit their get/set operations. Next, provide an **Input** method that prompts the user for each of these items and inputs them from the keyboard.

Create an **HourlyEmp** class derived from **Employee**. It adds additional members for hours worked and hourly pay rate along with their properties. Create an **Input** function that first calls the base class to input the basic information and then prompts and inputs from the keyboard the hours worked and hourly pay rate.

Create a **SalariedEmp** class derived from **Employee**. It adds one additional member for the annual pay along with a property to get/set it. Create an **Input** function that first calls the base class to input the basic information and then prompts and inputs from the keyboard the annual pay.

Create a **PieceRateEmp** class derived from **Employee**. These employees are paid a fixed rate for all items produced up to the quota. They are paid a bonus rate for all items produced in excess of that quota. Thus, four additional data members are needed: the fixed rate, the int quota, the bonus rate and the int number they produced this week. Each should have a corresponding property for get/set. Create an **Input** function that first calls the base class to input the basic information and then prompts and inputs from the keyboard these four additional fields.

In the base class, add an abstract function called **WeeklyPay** which returns a double representing this employee's weekly pay. Then, implement this function in the three derived classes. Hourly workers are paid time and a half for all hours worked above 40. The salaried workers are paid their weekly rate so divide their annual pay by 52. Piece rate employees are paid based on the number of items produced this week.

Write a tester program to thoroughly test your program.

Part B.

When you have the classes operational, we want to write a Main function that allocates an array of 100 Employee objects. Then, allocate an instance of the appropriate class using the various values shown below.

The specific objects you are to allocate in this order are as follows.
S for salaried, H for hourly, P for Piece rate employees

Type	SSNO	Last name	First name				
S	333456789	Darnell	Frederick	25000.00			
H	456123456	Nobel	William	12.75	40.0		
H	111223333	Wood	Steven	15.25	45.5		
P	345671234	Nutting	Teresa Elaine	2.50	.50	50	40
S	123456789	Hoop	Jeanette	30000.00			
H	678654321	Bolden	Edward D.	9.09	30.0		
H	555667777	Mc Cleary	Jane	11.11	42.5		
S	004556666	Herlan	William Bart	20000.00			
P	001020003	Anderson	J. Dennis	4.00	1.50	75	100
H	777889999	Hannah	Carol	8.08	40.0		
S	888990000	Raintree	Victoria Lynn	24000.00			
H	467010002	Noncaster	Brenda	6.00	40.0		
S	321456789	Young	Richard	22750.00			
S	333040005	Fresh	Gail	28000.00			
H	234854321	Kingsley	Jackie	10.00	50.0		
P	012998877	Braham	Joseph	2.00	.25	200	250

In the above last column, if this is a salaried worker, the single number is the annual salary. If this is an hourly worker, the first of the two numbers is the hourly rate and the second number is the hours worked. If this is a piece rate worker, then the first number is the base rate, the second number is the bonus for each piece beyond the quota, the third number is the quota, the fourth number is the number they actually made this week.

With the array allocated (this is a substitute for not yet being able to input a file of data), then produce the weekly pay report shown below.

```
                   Acme Manufacturing Weekly Payroll

        ID          Name                        Weekly Pay
    333456789       Darnell, Frederick          $     480.77
    456123456       Nobel, William              $     510.00
    111223333       Wood, Steven                $     735.81
    345671234       Nutting, Teresa Elaine      $     100.00
```

Chapter 5—Exception Handling, Interfaces, Delegates and Event Handling

Exception Handling

C# follows the usual OOP concepts for the handling of errors. That is,

> the callee is responsible for the detection of an error situation and for signaling its presence

> the caller is responsible for attempting the execution of a block of coding that could generate an error and then providing the alternative processing required when an error has been signaled by the callee

The caller wraps the potential problem coding within a **try-catch** block, while the callee uses the **throw** mechanism to signal the presence of an error that it detects. There are four verbs that can be used: **try**, **catch**, **throw**, and **finally**.

All C# error exceptions are derived from the class **Exception**. When the C# environment detects an error situation, such as division by zero, it then creates an instance of the appropriate exception class and throws it into the C# error handling system. That system then looks for the most appropriate **catch** block and invokes it. Since there can be several **catch** blocks specifying different exceptions to be caught by that block, a **catch** block with an exact match wins out over a more general block.

When a divide by zero error occurs, the **DivideByZeroException** is thrown. One can attempt to catch that specific error or just catch anything by using the base class of **Exception**.

```
using System;
class goof {
 static int Zero = 0;
 public static void Main () {
  try {
   int k = 42 / Zero;
   Console.WriteLine ("K = {0}", k); // never executed
  }
  catch (DivideByZeroException e) {
   Console.WriteLine ("Got a divide by 0 error {0}", e);
  }
```

```
catch (Exception e) {
  Console.WriteLine ("Got an error {0}", e);
  }
 }
}
```

In this example, the first **catch** block is used because it is an exact match of the error.

It is important to code the "catch anything" block last. If they were reversed, the **catch** all would end up being called, not the specific divide by zero **catch**!

Suppose that we coded this one. Here function **Fun** raises the division by zero exception. The system looks for a **catch** handler in **Fun** and does not find one. So it looks at the caller of **Fun**, **Main**, and does find one here and executes that **catch** block which is an exact match.

```
using System;
class goof {
 static int Zero = 0;

 public static int Fun () {
  int k = 42 / Zero;
  Console.WriteLine ("K = {0}", k); // never executed
  return k;
 }

 public static void Main () {
  try {
   int k = Fun ();
   Console.WriteLine ("K = {0}", k); // never executed
  }
  catch (DivideByZeroException e) {
   Console.WriteLine ("Got a divide by 0 error {0}", e);
  }
  catch (Exception e) {
   Console.WriteLine ("Got an error {0}", e);
  }
 }
}
```

Many other exceptions that can be thrown. One is an **ArgumentException** which is thrown when an argument is not correct for the situation such as expecting a decimal digit and receiving a letter instead. Here is a list of many of the possibilities.

ArithmeticException	A base class for exceptions that occur during arithmetic operations, such as DivideByZeroException and OverflowException.
ArrayTypeMismatchException	Thrown when a store into an array fails because the

	actual type of the stored element is incompatible with the actual type of the array.
DivideByZeroException	Thrown when an attempt to divide an integral value by zero occurs.
IndexOutOfRangeException	Thrown when an attempt to index an array via an index that is less than zero or outside the bounds of the array.
InvalidCastException	Thrown when an explicit conversion from a base type or interface to a derived types fails at run time.
MulticastNotSupportedException	Thrown when an attempt to combine two non-null delegates fails, because the delegate type does not have a void return type.
NullReferenceException	Thrown when a null reference is used in a way that causes the referenced object to be required.
OutOfMemoryException	Thrown when an attempt to allocate memory (via new) fails.
OverflowException	Thrown when an arithmetic operation in a checked context overflows.
StackOverflowException	Thrown when the execution stack is exhausted by having too many pending method calls; typically indicative of very deep or unbounded recursion.
TypeInitializationException	Thrown when a static constructor throws an exception, and no catch clauses exists to catch it.

Now suppose that the catch blocks do not match the type of exception being thrown.

```
using System;
class goof {
 static int Zero = 0;

 public static int Fun () {
  try {
   int k = 42 / Zero;
   Console.WriteLine ("K = {0}", k); // never executed
   return k;
  }
  catch (NullReferenceException e) {
   Console.WriteLine ("Got a divide by 0 error {0}", e);
  }
 }

 public static void Main () {
```

```
try {
 int k = Fun ();
 Console.WriteLine ("K = {0}", k); // never executed
 }
catch (OverflowException e) {
 Console.WriteLine ("Got a divide by 0 error {0}", e);
 }
 }
}
```

When the divide by zero exception is raised in **Fun**, the system finds no appropriate catch block and so looks next to the immediate called of **Fun**, **Main**. In **Main**, it also finds no appropriate catch block. When it reaches the end of the calling stack at **Main**, and finds no one handling this error, the exception is then caught by the "last chance" handler. Normally, it displays a dialog box outlining the error and then terminates the program.

Our Handling of Exceptions

When a function detects an error has occurred that it cannot fix up at once by alternative coding, then it must let the calling function(s) know about it and let them perform the fix up. There are three ways this is done: Caller Beware, Caller Confuse, Caller Inform.

Caller Beware

The first way is to do nothing at all and not even catch the exception. While sometimes this is the right way to do it, other times, this can leave the object in an invalid state. Suppose the object was trying to load a table of values and it failed to do so. The caller does not know that the object is now invalid and may try to use the non-existent table. It also may give the caller insufficient information about the exact nature of the trouble.

Caller Confuse

The second way is to catch the exception and handle any clean up operations needed and then re-throw the exception. One can re-throw the exception by using **throw** with no operands. Here is an example.

```
using System;
class SummerVacationPay {
 protected int numberOfMonths = 0;
 protected double summerTotalPay = 0;
 protected double monthlyPay;

 public double GetMonthlyPay () {
```

```
 try {
  monthlyPay = summerTotalPay / numberOfMonths;
  return monthlyPay;
 }
 catch (DivideByZeroException e) {
  // do any clean up operations required
  throw;
 }
 }
 }
}

class Application {
 public static void Main () {
  SummerVacationPay p = new SummerVacationPay ();
  try {
   double pay = p.GetMonthlyPay();
   Console.WriteLine ("K = {0}", k); // never executed
  }
  catch (Exception e) {
   Console.WriteLine ("Got some kind of error {0}", e);
  }
 }
}
```

While the **SummerVacationPay** object **p** is now in a valid state, the caller is confused. It has no idea of what the error was, where it was, or how it can be fixed up. This is caller confuse. True, part of the message displayed on the screen will say a division by zero occurred.

Caller Inform

With this approach, additional information is returned to the caller. The caught exception is "wrapped" in an exception that has more information.

```
using System;
class SummerVacationPay {
 protected int numberOfMonths = 0;
 protected double summerTotalPay = 0;
 protected double monthlyPay;

 public double GetMonthlyPay () {
  try {
   monthlyPay = summerTotalPay / numberOfMonths;
  }
  catch (DivideByZeroException e) {
   // do any clean up operations required
   throw (new DivideByZeroException (
```

```
            "numberOfMonths is zero in GetMonthlyPay()", e));
    }
  }
}

class Application {
 public static void Main () {
  SummerVacationPay p = new SummerVacationPay ();
  try {
   double pay = p.GetMonthlyPay();
   Console.WriteLine ("K = {0}", k); // never executed
  }
  catch (Exception e) {
   Console.WriteLine ("Got some kind of error {0}", e);
  }
 }
}
```

Here a new instance of the **DivideByZeroException** is created but with the additional information tying it back to the root cause and where. Notice usually one throws a new instance of the same kind as the original exception, but you do not have to do so.

Notice also that the original exception is passed to the constructor so that the original context data of the original error is maintained in the new instance.

Ideally, each function that wants to re-throw an exception will create a new instance using the old instance's context and append onto it where it is occurring within this function. In such a manner, the user can follow the entire path of how that function was called.

Perhaps even better is to design your own user-defined exception classes. You should derive it from the base class, **ApplicationException** and provide three ctors: a default ctor, a ctor that takes a string message, and a ctor that takes the string message and the previous exception instance.

Here is the most elegant way to handle this situation.

```
using System;
public class NumberOfMonthsIsZeroException :
      ApplicationException {
 public NumberOfMonthsIsZeroException () { }
 public NumberOfMonthsIsZeroException (string msg) :
            base (msg) {}
 public NumberOfMonthsIsZeroException (string msg,
            Exception previous) : base (msg, previous) {}
}
```

```
class SummerVacationPay {
 protected int numberOfMonths = 0;
 protected double summerTotalPay = 0;
 protected double monthlyPay;

 public double GetMonthlyPay () {
  try {
   monthlyPay = summerTotalPay / numberOfMonths;
  }
  catch (DivideByZeroException e) {
   // do any clean up operations required
   throw (new NumberOfMonthsIsZeroException (
        "numberOfMonths is zero in GetMonthlyPay"));
  }
 }
}

class Application {
 public static void Main () {
  SummerVacationPay p = new SummerVacationPay ();
  try {
   double pay = p.GetMonthlyPay();
   Console.WriteLine ("K = {0}", k); // never executed
  }
  catch (NumberOfMonthsIsZeroException e) {
   Console.WriteLine ("Number of months is 0 error {0}", e);
  }
 }
}
```

Since **GetMonthlyPay** is the first to find the error, it creates the first instance of the new type of exception using the string ctor. Now if this function was called by some other function, that other function would use the third ctor to make another new instance, appending the original information from **GetMonthlyPay** to it.

The **finally** clause

Sometimes there is cleanup work that must always be done before the function completes in any manner. One of these is the closing opened files. Although we have not yet discussed files, we can see intuitively how this **finally** clause can be used with files.

Assume that we are in some class.
```
 public int CalcAvg (int count, int sum) {
```

98

```
 ...
 return sum / count;
}

public void ProcessFileData () {
 FileStream file = ...
 try {
  StreamReader = ... opens the file
  ... now process all data in the file
  CalcAvg (...);
 }
 finally {
  file.Close ();
 }
}
```

If **CalcAvg** should throw a divide by zero error, the **finally** clause guarantees that no matter what happens, the **finally** clause is executed and the file closed. Code within a **finally** clause is guaranteed to be executed before the exit of the function, whether it is by normal ending or by an exception being thrown. Without this **finally** clause, if there was an exception, the file would have been left opened!

Use **finally** judiciously!

Please note that constructors often throw exceptions because that is the only effective way they have of notifying the caller that the construction failed!

One member of the **Exception** class is **StackTrace**. This can give useful information when the exception occurred several functions deep. Assuming **e** is an exception instance of some kind, code the following.

```
     Console.WriteLine (e.StackTrace);
```

Design Issues with the **try** Block

Generally speaking, should a try block try to catch every possible exception? No. If a method does not do anything with the error, you would end up with a catch block that does nothing but re-throw. Further, if the type of exceptions being thrown ever changed, you would have to also change these unneeded catch blocks as well.

Design Issues with the **catch** Block

What does one put into a catch block? Generally, you want coding that handles any needed clean up actions, coding that leaves the object in a stable state if possible, display any appropriate error messages, and perhaps re-throw that exception or create a new exception and throw that one.

Quadratic—a Practical Example

Let's illustrate some of the things you can do using try-catch logic. The formula to be solved is the quadratic equation. We must be alert for both division by zero and taking a square root of a negative number. This is Pgm05aConsole.

So I created a **QuadErrorException** class derived from **ApplicationException**. I added a public class enum **ErrorType** and stored an instance in the class. This gives an easy way for the user to determine what kind of error was generated when there are several possibilities.

```
using System;

public class QuadErrorException : ApplicationException {
 public enum ErrorType {DivisionByZero, NegativeDiscriminant}

 private ErrorType errorType;

 public ErrorType GetErrorType () {
  return errorType;
 }

 public QuadErrorException () { }

 public QuadErrorException(string msg, ErrorType t) : base(msg){
  errorType = t;
 }

 public QuadErrorException (string msg, ErrorType t,
                   Exception previous) : base (msg, previous) {
  errorType = t;
 }
}
```

Next, The **QuadraticCalculator** class has a **Quadratric** function that tries to solve the formula. If it finds either of the two error situations, it throws a new instance of the **QuadErrorException** with its values appropriately initialized.

```
public class QuadraticCalculator {
```

```
public double Quadratic (double a, double b, double c) {
  if (a == 0) {
   throw new QuadErrorException ("a is zero",
                 QuadErrorException.ErrorType.DivisionByZero);
  }
  double discriminant= b * b - 4 * a * c;
  if (discriminant < 0) {
   throw new QuadErrorException ("discriminant is negative",
            QuadErrorException.ErrorType.NegativeDiscriminant);
  }
  return (-b - Math.Sqrt (discriminant)) / (2 * a);
 }
}
```

The **Main** function then allocates a new instance of the calculator and proceeds to conversationally ask the user if they wish to input another set of **a**, **b**, **c** values. If so, they are input and the calcualtion tried. If an exception is raised, the catch block tests the instance of **ErrorType** to find out which one it is and then displays a more appropriate error message to the user. I also displayed the default message as well.

Note also how I setup two functions to assist in the data entry operations. **GetYN** and **GetABC**. Notice how the three doubles are passed by reference so that **GetABC** can fill them up with new values.

```
class Application {
 static void Main(string[] args) {
  QuadraticCalculator q = new QuadraticCalculator ();
  double a = 0;
  double b = 0;
  double c = 0;
  char   yn = 'Y';
  while (yn == 'Y') {
   GetABC (out a, out b, out c); // boxes the 3 doubles
   try {
    Console.WriteLine ("Root: {0,1:F}", q.Quadratic (a, b, c));
   }
   catch (QuadErrorException e) {
    if (e.GetErrorType() ==
                 QuadErrorException.ErrorType.DivisionByZero) {
     Console.WriteLine (
                 "a is zero causing a divide by zero error");
     Console.WriteLine (e);
    }
    else {
     Console.WriteLine ("the values ask for taking the square "
```

101

```
                              "root of a negative number");
      Console.WriteLine (e);
    }
  }
  yn = GetYN ();
  }
}

public static void GetABC (out double a, out double b,
                           out double c) {
 bool ok = false;
 double num = 0;
 while (!ok) {
  ok = GetDouble ("Enter a number for a: ", out num);
 }
 a = num;
 ok = false;
 while (!ok) {
  ok = GetDouble ("Enter a number for b: ", out num);
 }
 b = num;
 ok = false;
 while (!ok) {
  ok = GetDouble ("Enter a number for c: ", out num);
 }
 c = num;
}

public static bool GetDouble (string msg, out double num) {
 Console.WriteLine (msg);
 try {
  num = Double.Parse (Console.ReadLine ());
 }
 catch (Exception e) {
  Console.WriteLine (e.Message);
  num = 0;
  return false;
 }
 return true;
}

public static char GetYN () {
 Console.WriteLine ();
 Console.WriteLine ("Do you want to try again?");
 Console.Write ("Enter Y or N: ");
 char c = Char.Parse (Console.ReadLine ());
```

```
  c = Char.ToUpper (c);
  return c;
 }
}
```

Here is a sample run.

```
Enter a number for a:
1
Enter a number for b:
2
Enter a number for c:
3
the values ask for taking the square root of a negative number
QuadErrorException: discriminant is negative
      at QuadraticCalculator.Quadratic(Double  a,  Double  b,  Double  c)  in
D:\Vic-BooksInProgress\C#Course\Samples2008\Pgm05aConsole\Program.cs:line 31
            at      Application.Main(String[]      args)      in
D:\Vic-BooksInProgress\C#Course\Samples2008\Pgm05aConsole\Program.cs:line 47

Do you want to try again?
Enter Y or N: y
Enter a number for a:
0
Enter a number for b:
4
Enter a number for c:
5
a is zero causing a divide by zero error
QuadErrorException: a is zero
      at QuadraticCalculator.Quadratic(Double  a,  Double  b,  Double  c)  in
D:\Vic-BooksInProgress\C#Course\Samples2008\Pgm05aConsole\Program.cs:line 27
            at      Application.Main(String[]      args)      in
D:\Vic-BooksInProgress\C#Course\Samples2008\Pgm05aConsole\Program.cs:line 47

Do you want to try again?
Enter Y or N: y
Enter a number for a:
1
Enter a number for b:
42
Enter a number for c:
1
Root: -41.98

Do you want to try again?
Enter Y or N: y
Enter a number for a:
a
Input string was not in a correct format.
Enter a number for a:
```

Interfaces

Classes are objects that have properties and methods to operate on those properties. That is, a class instance is a **thing** as opposed to a **behavior**. An **interface** is a **behavior**. An interface gives you the ability to define a set of related methods and properties that selected classes can implement regardless of class hierarchy. An interface is a **contract** between two separate pieces of code. Once an interface is defined and a class is defined as implementing that interface, the user of that class is assured that all of the interface methods are indeed implemented and available for his or her use.

There are two terms that are used to describe this action and both are acceptable: **implementing the interface** or **inheriting from the interface**. I personally prefer to call it implementing the interface.

From a C++ point of view an interface is just an abstract class with only pure virtual functions declared in it and perhaps some properties.

It is important to realize that the interface only declares these methods. It does not actually implement them. The implementation is left to the class that is supporting that interface.

C# does not support multiple inheritance, that is, more than one immediate base class. So interfaces offer a way around that barrier.

We are about to get into the graphical user interface side of C# and this is where interfaces begin to appear. Most programmers prefix an interface definition with I for interface. Within the windows gui portion of C# there are a lot of provided interfaces, such as **IDragDrop**, **ISortable**, **ISerialize** (which provides for the object to read or write itself to disk).

Interfaces are created at compile time, not at execution time.

Without going into details, here is an illustration of how this works. Suppose that you wanted to make a new slick tree view control class called TreeView. Since it is a graphical control, its base class is Control. But suppose you also want the user to be able to drag and drop objects into the view. Further, you want a instance to be able to save itself to disk so that when the user returns to this control, it appears with the same contents which it last had. Skeletally, we would do the following.

```
using System;
public class Control {
  ...
}
public interface IDragDrop {
 public void Drag();
 public void Drop();
}
```

```
public interface ISerialize {
 void Serialize ();
}

public interface IGroup : IDragDrop, ISerialize {
 // groups these two interfaces into one
}

public class MyTreeView : Control, IGroup {
 public void Drag () {
  ...
 }
 public void Drop () {
  ...
 }
 public void Serialize () {
  ...
 }
}
...
public static Main () {
 MyTreeView tree = new MyTreeView ();
 tree.Drag ();
 tree.Drop ();
}
```

This is the basic idea. We will be using many of the graphical user interface's interfaces in the next chapter.

Delegates

Delegates are similar to interfaces. A **delegate** defines a contract, a pact, between the caller and the function as it is implemented. However, a **delegate** specifies the form of a single function only. Unlike interfaces, delegates are created at **run time**. They are determined dynamically as the execution situation for their need arises.

Delegates are often used in the graphical windows environment to help in the handling of events that occur, such as a button press or a list box selection. These **events**, as they are called in C#, correspond to "messages" in C++. Indeed the Windows graphical environment is a message driven platform. As things occur, Windows invokes a function designed to handle or process that specific message or event which occurred, such as a button press or a mouse click. The delegate for a specific event defines the prototype of the function that is to handle that message, should it ever occur. It is not the function itself, just the model. We must also create the function with that prototype which is known as the **event handler** function.

Delegates are also known as a safe function pointer because they point to the function that is to handle the event that just occurred.

In order to write a generic sorting algorithm, the sort must be provided a user callback comparison function which is passed two items to be compared and returns an indicator of which is the larger. So another way of thinking about a delegate is that of a callback function.

For example, if we had a **Container** class, it might define the comparison callback delegate this way.

```
public class Container {
 public delegate int CompareCallback (object o1, object o2);
```

Within the **Container**'s **Sort** function, one might expect to find a line such as this.

```
public void Sort (CompareCallback compare) {
 ...
  int retcode = compare (array[i], array[j]);
```

How would it be actually used? Suppose we had a **Car** class. Suppose further that an array of car objects might need to be sorted on Vin numbers or on car makes. The **Car** class would then define two sorting comparison functions this way.

```
public class Car {
 protected string vinNumber;
 protected string make;
 public static int CompareVinNumbers (object o1, object o2) {
  Car c1 = (Car) o1;
  Car c2 = (Car) o2;
```

```
  return String.Compare (c1.vinNumber, c2.vinNumber);
 }
 public static int CompareMakes (object o1, object o2) {
  Car c1 = (Car) o1;
  Car c2 = (Car) o2;
  return String.Compare (c1.make, c2.make);
 }
...
```

The client program would declare an instance of the **Container** and populate it with a number of **Car** objects. When it was time to actually sort the array, the client must create an instance of the desired delegate function and then call the **Sort** function.

```
public static void Main () {
 Container array = new Container ();
 ...
 Container.CompareCallback sortVinNumbers =
      new Container.CompareCallback (Car.CompareVinNumbers);
 array.Sort (sortVinNumbers);
```

With Windows programming it is very common to pass function pointers to the actual function that is to process a given message or event. These C# delegates are often passed static instances instead of member instance functions.

The drawback of the above coding is that the client must allocate a new instance of the callback delegate and then pass it to the **Sort**. We can perform the allocation for them if we create a **public static readonly** instance this way.

```
public class Car {
 protected string vinNumber;
 protected string make;
 public static readonly Container.CompareCallback SortVinNumbers
    = new Container.CompareCallback (CompareVinNumbers);
 public static readonly Container.CompareCallback SortMakes
    = new Container.CompareCallback (CompareMakes);

 public static int CompareVinNumbers (object o1, object o2) {
  Car c1 = (Car) o1;
  Car c2 = (Car) o2;
  return String.Compare (c1.vinNumber, c2.vinNumber);
 }
 public static int CompareMakes (object o1, object o2) {
  Car c1 = (Car) o1;
  Car c2 = (Car) o2;
  return String.Compare (c1.make, c2.make);
```

```
 }
...
```

Now the user can just call the **Sort** function directly, passing the **readonly** instances.
```
public static void Main () {
 Container array = new Container ();
 ...
 array.Sort (Car.SortVinNumbers);
 array.Sort (Car.SortMakes);
```

Multicasting of Delegates

A delegate can refer to more than one function. It can refer to a list of functions to be called in order. This allows a priority pecking order to event handling. That is, if one instance does not want to handle it, the next in the list is given the chance. This is similar to Windows programming in which the Application class is given a chance to process say a mouse click. If it does not want it, the frame window is given a chance, and so on through the components of the program.

There are two ways this can be done. The first approach is to use the **Delegate.Combine** and **Delegate.Remove** functions to join or remove delegate functions from a list of them. However, these functions are not type-safe at compile time, so that there is no way to know if the delegate functions are even compatible at compile time.

The other approach is to use the overloaded += and -= operators, which are type-safe. Without delving into the Windows functions, here is a simple example to illustrate this concept. Suppose we have two classes, **Class1** and **Class2** that each implement a delegate function called **Handler1** and **Handler2** respectively. Further suppose that a class called Test defines a delegate function called **SomeEvent**. We have the following then.
```
public class Class1 {
 public static void Handler1 () {
  // handles the event
 }
}
public class Class2 {
 public static void Handler2 () {
  // handles the event
 }
}
public class Test {
 public delegate void SomeEvent ();
 public static void Main () {
  Class1 c1 = new Class1;
```

```
Class2 c2 = new Class2;

SomeEvent handler = new SomeEvent (c1.Handler1);
handler += new SomeEvent (c2.Handler2);
handler (); // calls both functions in order
```

Delegate functions can even be properties of a class. That is, the get method returns a new instance of the function. There is no set function though.

Events

Delegate functions are used to handle events that occur at run time, such as a button press or mouse click. Let's see how this can be utilized in a rather general way, without getting into Windows specifics.

Suppose that we have displayed a form on which the user is to enter various information. After the user fills in all of the information, they press a button labeled "Do the Calculations." At this point, our Info class gathers the entered user information and does the indicated calculation. So there are two different classes involved here, the **Button** and the **Info** class. Neither knows anything about the other. The **Button** class is only concerned with displaying what looks and operates like a graphical button. The **Info** class only cares about the entered information and doing its calculations.

There must be some mechanism for the general **Button** class to notify the **Info** class that the button has been pressed. This is the delegate process for event handling in action. The **Button** class defines a **ClickHandler** delegate function and implements a function to generically handle a button press. **Info** must then provide a specific **ClickHandler** event function to perform the calculations. The client program then creates a **Button** and **Info** class instances and ties the **ClickHandler** real event function to the **Button** class delegate.

```
public class Button {
 public delegate void ClickHandler (object sender, EventArgs e);
 public ClickHandler Click; // the instance of it

 protected void OnClick () {
  if (Click !- null) Click (this, null);
 }

 public void SimulateClick () {
  OnClick ();
 }
}
```

109

```
public class Info {
 public static void DoCalculations (object sender, EventArgs e) {
  // do the fancy calculations when the button is pressed
 }
...
}

class Tester {
 public static void Main () {
 Button b = new Button ();
 b.Click = new Button.ClickHandler (Info.DoCalculations);
 b.SimulateClick ();
```

Of course, the C# Windows classes own the Button class. So we must know what the delegate functions are so that our Info classes and testers can utilize them.

Now while the delegates and events may seem complex to you at this point, in fact, the C# compiler generates most of the actual coding for you, when we use the fancy design form method of program creation as illustrated in the next chapter. Thus, what we really need is just a basic understanding of what is going on so.

These callback methods are also extensively used in database processing to handle making database connections and so forth.

Chapter 6—The Windows User Interface

The Basics of the Windows User Interface

Let's begin by making a sample Windows C# application, Pgm06aWindows. Choose File-New Project and select Windows Forms Application. In Figure 6.1, I have dragged the Form1 window which represents our application and made it larger. If the toolbox is not visible as in Figure 1, use View-toolbox.

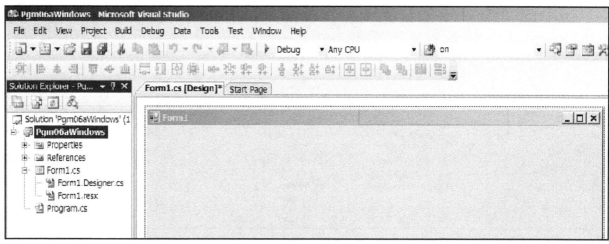

Figure 6.1 Generated Basic Form Resized Larger

The toolbox contains many of the graphical elements that we can add to our program. Essentially, in the graphic design view that we are in, we are building the resources that we need.

The essential process is to drag the desired control from the toolbox and drop it on the form. Then, reposition and resize the control. Then, right click on the control and choose Properties. In the Properties that appear, change those that are desired.

This application allows a user to enter their desires in a used car and then see if we have any that meet their criteria. Thus, the first item is a label saying Enter the Make of the desired car. Beside it is a text control for entering the car make. On the label control, I altered the default text to say "Enter Car Make." In the text control, I need to provide a good programming name for this control instance, not Textbox1 which is the default. Figure 6.2 shows the Properties after these two changes.

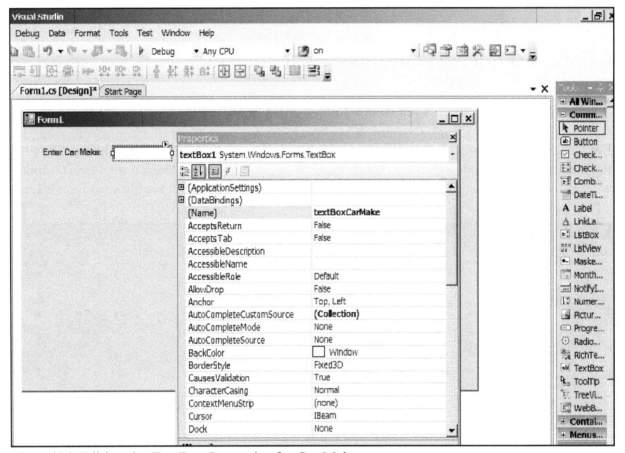

Figure 6.2 Editing the TextBox Properties for Car Make

Next, let's add three radio buttons for the three colors that we carry, Red, White, and Blue. Typically, radio buttons are surrounded by a group box that identifies their purpose. So first I placed a group box whose text was "Choose Color."

Then, I dragged a radio button into the group box. Now the system keeps track of which radio button in a group is selected by the tab index. The first button is 0, the second is 1 and so on. I changed the control's name to be radioButtonRed and the text to say "Red." Then I added the other two buttons in a similar manner.

Figure 6.3 shows what the properties for the red button look like.

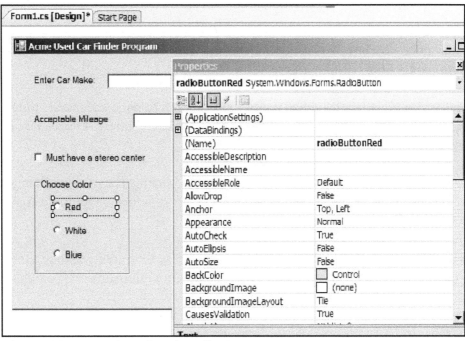

Figure 6.3 Properties of Red Radio Button

The next step is to align all these radio buttons on the left side, make them the same size and space them evenly down. To do these steps, it is necessary to select the three buttons as a group. left click in some area that is beyond the controls and drag the selection rectangle to enclose the three buttons and only the three radio buttons. Figure 6.4 shows what they look like when selected as a group.

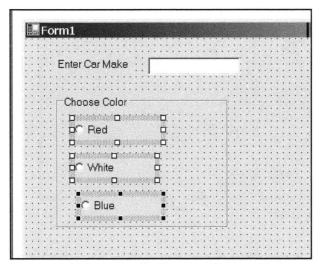

Figure 6.4 Three Radio Buttons Selected

Now use the Format menu. Align Left is useful along with Vertical Spacing—Make Even and Make Same Size—Both dimensions.

Notice that once you have the group nicely laid out, you can move the whole group by dragging the group box.

Then I entered another label and text control pair for entering the acceptable mileage on the used car. A check box is added to control whether or not a stereo is required. A check box only needs its text and name altered.

A button control is added next whose text says "Find Matching Cars." Also change the name of the control to something reasonable other than button1. I also added a Quit button to terminate the program.

Some way must be devised to show the user any matches. One could display a message box containing the results. However, you can also show the results in a multi-line text box that is marked read only. I added another results group box and put in a multi-line text box.

The last step is to adjust the overall form's properties. At the moment, it says Form1. So right click anywhere in the form not occupied by a control and choose properties.

Figure 6.5 shows what the form now looks like.

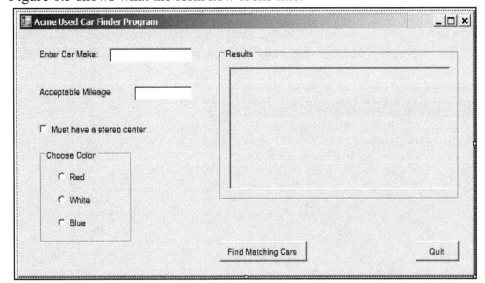

Figure 6.5 Complete Car Finder Form

Before we leave the form, there is one other action you should take: check the tab index order. Click on properties of the first control in which the user could enter data. It should be tab index 0. Usually, we go top-down and left to right. Those thing that you do not want the user tabbing

114

to, such as labels, set their **TabStop** property to false. This way as the user tabs his or her way through the controls, we move sequentially between those in which they must enter data.

I also changed the name from Form1 to FormUsedCarDataEntry. Next, I renamed the actual cs files by right clicking on the Form1.cs in the Solution Explorer and choosing Rename.

Right click on the cs file and choose View Source to examine the source. The whole form coding is split into two parts, the operational coding and the designing coding (...designer.cs). Also there is an application cs file as well.

The Program.cs application file looks like this.

```
using System;
using System.Collections.Generic;
using System.Linq;
using System.Windows.Forms;

namespace Pgm06aWindows
{
  static class Program
  {
   /// <summary>
   /// The main entry point for the application.
   /// </summary>
   [STAThread]
   static void Main()
   {
    Application.EnableVisualStyles();
    Application.SetCompatibleTextRenderingDefault(false);
    Application.Run(new FormUsedCarDataEntry());
   }
  }
}
```

The FormUsedCarDataEntry.cs file, our operations file, looks like this.

```
using System;
using System.Collections.Generic;
using System.ComponentModel;
using System.Data;
using System.Drawing;
using System.Linq;
using System.Text;
using System.Windows.Forms;

namespace Pgm06aWindows
{
```

```
public partial class FormUsedCarDataEntry : Form
 {
  public FormUsedCarDataEntry()
  {
   InitializeComponent();
  }
 }
}
```

The FormUsedCarDataEntry.Designer.cs file contains all of the graphical coding that was done visually thus far.

```
namespace Pgm06aWindows
{
 partial class FormUsedCarDataEntry
 {
  /// <summary>
  /// Required designer variable.
  /// </summary>
  private System.ComponentModel.IContainer components = null;

  /// <summary>
  /// Clean up any resources being used.
  /// </summary>
  /// <param name="disposing">true if managed resources should be disposed;
otherwise, false.</param>
  protected override void Dispose(bool disposing)
  {
   if (disposing && (components != null))
   {
    components.Dispose();
   }
   base.Dispose(disposing);
  }

  #region Windows Form Designer generated code

  /// <summary>
  /// Required method for Designer support - do not modify
  /// the contents of this method with the code editor.
  /// </summary>
  private void InitializeComponent()
  {
   this.labelMake = new System.Windows.Forms.Label();
   this.textBoxCarMake = new System.Windows.Forms.TextBox();
   this.GroupBox1 = new System.Windows.Forms.GroupBox();
   this.textBoxResults = new System.Windows.Forms.TextBox();
   this.label2 = new System.Windows.Forms.Label();
   this.textBoxMileage = new System.Windows.Forms.TextBox();
   this.checkBoxStereo = new System.Windows.Forms.CheckBox();
   this.radioButtonBlue = new System.Windows.Forms.RadioButton();
   this.groupBox2 = new System.Windows.Forms.GroupBox();
   this.radioButtonWhite = new System.Windows.Forms.RadioButton();
   this.radioButtonRed = new System.Windows.Forms.RadioButton();
```

```
this.buttonQuit = new System.Windows.Forms.Button();
this.buttonFindCar = new System.Windows.Forms.Button();
this.GroupBox1.SuspendLayout();
this.groupBox2.SuspendLayout();
this.SuspendLayout();
//
// labelMake
//
this.labelMake.AutoSize = true;
this.labelMake.Location = new System.Drawing.Point(31, 30);
this.labelMake.Name = "labelMake";
this.labelMake.Size = new System.Drawing.Size(110, 17);
this.labelMake.TabIndex = 0;
this.labelMake.Text = "Enter Car Make:";
//
// textBoxCarMake
//
this.textBoxCarMake.Location = new System.Drawing.Point(156, 30);
this.textBoxCarMake.Name = "textBoxCarMake";
this.textBoxCarMake.Size = new System.Drawing.Size(143, 22);
this.textBoxCarMake.TabIndex = 1;
//
// GroupBox1
//
this.GroupBox1.Controls.Add(this.textBoxResults);
this.GroupBox1.Location = new System.Drawing.Point(348, 30);
this.GroupBox1.Name = "GroupBox1";
this.GroupBox1.Size = new System.Drawing.Size(416, 238);
this.GroupBox1.TabIndex = 20;
this.GroupBox1.TabStop = false;
this.GroupBox1.Text = "Results";
//
// textBoxResults
//
this.textBoxResults.Location = new System.Drawing.Point(17, 30);
this.textBoxResults.Multiline = true;
this.textBoxResults.Name = "textBoxResults";
this.textBoxResults.ReadOnly = true;
this.textBoxResults.Size = new System.Drawing.Size(384, 192);
this.textBoxResults.TabIndex = 10;
this.textBoxResults.TabStop = false;
//
// label2
//
this.label2.Location = new System.Drawing.Point(31, 89);
this.label2.Name = "label2";
this.label2.Size = new System.Drawing.Size(136, 23);
this.label2.TabIndex = 9;
this.label2.Text = "Acceptable Mileage";
//
// textBoxMileage
//
this.textBoxMileage.Location = new System.Drawing.Point(199, 90);
this.textBoxMileage.Name = "textBoxMileage";
this.textBoxMileage.Size = new System.Drawing.Size(100, 22);
this.textBoxMileage.TabIndex = 2;
```

117

```
//
// checkBoxStereo
//
this.checkBoxStereo.Location = new System.Drawing.Point(34, 145);
this.checkBoxStereo.Name = "checkBoxStereo";
this.checkBoxStereo.Size = new System.Drawing.Size(200, 24);
this.checkBoxStereo.TabIndex = 3;
this.checkBoxStereo.Text = "Must have a stereo center";
//
// radioButtonBlue
//
this.radioButtonBlue.Location = new System.Drawing.Point(32, 104);
this.radioButtonBlue.Name = "radioButtonBlue";
this.radioButtonBlue.Size = new System.Drawing.Size(104, 24);
this.radioButtonBlue.TabIndex = 6;
this.radioButtonBlue.TabStop = true;
this.radioButtonBlue.Text = "Blue";
//
// groupBox2
//
this.groupBox2.Controls.Add(this.radioButtonBlue);
this.groupBox2.Controls.Add(this.radioButtonWhite);
this.groupBox2.Controls.Add(this.radioButtonRed);
this.groupBox2.Location = new System.Drawing.Point(34, 188);
this.groupBox2.Name = "groupBox2";
this.groupBox2.Size = new System.Drawing.Size(160, 147);
this.groupBox2.TabIndex = 4;
this.groupBox2.TabStop = false;
this.groupBox2.Text = "Choose Color";
//
// radioButtonWhite
//
this.radioButtonWhite.Location = new System.Drawing.Point(32, 68);
this.radioButtonWhite.Name = "radioButtonWhite";
this.radioButtonWhite.Size = new System.Drawing.Size(104, 24);
this.radioButtonWhite.TabIndex = 5;
this.radioButtonWhite.TabStop = true;
this.radioButtonWhite.Text = "White";
//
// radioButtonRed
//
this.radioButtonRed.Location = new System.Drawing.Point(32, 32);
this.radioButtonRed.Name = "radioButtonRed";
this.radioButtonRed.Size = new System.Drawing.Size(104, 24);
this.radioButtonRed.TabIndex = 4;
this.radioButtonRed.TabStop = true;
this.radioButtonRed.Text = "Red";
//
// buttonQuit
//
this.buttonQuit.Location = new System.Drawing.Point(689, 334);
this.buttonQuit.Name = "buttonQuit";
this.buttonQuit.Size = new System.Drawing.Size(75, 31);
this.buttonQuit.TabIndex = 8;
this.buttonQuit.Text = "Quit";
//
```

```
// buttonFindCar
//
this.buttonFindCar.Location = new System.Drawing.Point(348, 334);
this.buttonFindCar.Name = "buttonFindCar";
this.buttonFindCar.Size = new System.Drawing.Size(152, 31);
this.buttonFindCar.TabIndex = 7;
this.buttonFindCar.Text = "Find Matching Cars";
//
// FormUsedCarDataEntry
//
this.AutoScaleDimensions = new System.Drawing.SizeF(8F, 16F);
this.AutoScaleMode = System.Windows.Forms.AutoScaleMode.Font;
this.ClientSize = new System.Drawing.Size(787, 385);
this.Controls.Add(this.buttonQuit);
this.Controls.Add(this.buttonFindCar);
this.Controls.Add(this.groupBox2);
this.Controls.Add(this.checkBoxStereo);
this.Controls.Add(this.textBoxMileage);
this.Controls.Add(this.label2);
this.Controls.Add(this.GroupBox1);
this.Controls.Add(this.textBoxCarMake);
this.Controls.Add(this.labelMake);
this.Name = "FormUsedCarDataEntry";
this.Text = "Acme Used Car Finder Program";
this.GroupBox1.ResumeLayout(false);
this.GroupBox1.PerformLayout();
this.groupBox2.ResumeLayout(false);
this.ResumeLayout(false);
this.PerformLayout();

}

#endregion

private System.Windows.Forms.Label labelMake;
private System.Windows.Forms.TextBox textBoxCarMake;
private System.Windows.Forms.GroupBox GroupBox1;
private System.Windows.Forms.TextBox textBoxResults;
private System.Windows.Forms.Label label2;
private System.Windows.Forms.TextBox textBoxMileage;
private System.Windows.Forms.CheckBox checkBoxStereo;
private System.Windows.Forms.RadioButton radioButtonBlue;
private System.Windows.Forms.GroupBox groupBox2;
private System.Windows.Forms.RadioButton radioButtonWhite;
private System.Windows.Forms.RadioButton radioButtonRed;
private System.Windows.Forms.Button buttonQuit;
private System.Windows.Forms.Button buttonFindCar;
  }
}
```

GUIs are built from components. There are a rather large number of them that are available to use. These components are sometimes called controls or widgets (windows gadgets). The controls must be housed within some kind of container. In this case, the container is a Form. Other forms include dialogs and MDI windows (multiple document interface). A component is a class that

119

implements the **IComponent** interface, which defines the behaviors that components must implement. Specifically, a control is a component with an actual graphical user interface. Thus, controls are visible but components alone are not, for they have no graphical user interface.

Some Windows terminology. The active window is that window that is currently active; its title bar is highlighted. The active window is said to have the input focus which means that any keyboard activity is being routed to that window. A window becomes the active window when the user clicks on it or task switches to it (Alt-Tab, for example).

The form acts as a container for components and controls. These controls must be added to a form via coding. However, when we drag a control onto the form, the compiler automatically inserts the proper coding. It changes that coding as we change a control's properties.

These steps represent the graphical design phase. Now we must add coding to actually do something in response to the events, such as pressing Find Matching Cars.

Event Handling

GUI's are event driven, that is, they generate events when the user interacts with the controls, such as pressing the Find Matching Cars button. The most common events include mouse events, keyboard events, menu events and window action events. Mouse events include moving the mouse, clicking on a control such as a button. Keyboard events usually include typing text into a textbox. Menu events usually include the user making a menu selection. Window events include such things as closing the window by using the X button.

Each control that can generate events has an associated delegate that defines the prototype or signature of a control handler that can process that event. Event delegates are usually multicast which means that a whole series of methods or functions are going to be called, representing various windows or controls and so on.

In most beginning situations, we do not have to create these event handlers ourselves. Most controls already have delegates setup for their normal processing needs. We need only to create our event handlers and register them with the framework. Here the compiler helps us out as well.

To view the Events that are possible for a control, in the properties window, click on the lightening bolt icon.

Figure 6.6 shows the events properties for the **form**. I added an **OnClosing** to be called when the application is attempting to shut down. When you add it, the code window open up and the shell coding is added there for us.

120

```
private void OnClosing(object sender, FormClosingEventArgs e) {

}
```

Here I added a call to the **MessageBox** class to display a simple message box.

```
private void OnClosing(object sender, FormClosingEventArgs e) {
 MessageBox.Show ("Do you really want to quit the application?");
}
```

This function prototype is typical of these event handlers. It is passed a reference to the sender object and some kind of event argument which is specific to the event at hand.

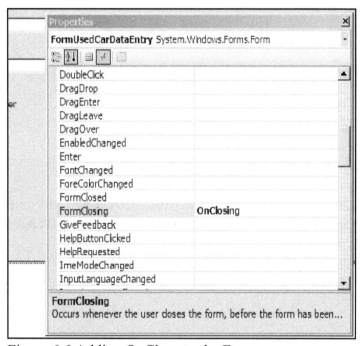

Figure 6.6 Adding OnClose to the Form

Message Boxes

A message box is one of the handiest items in Windows programming. It can be used to display a simple message to the user or it can be used to actually obtain user responses of the Yes or No variety usually. There are five parts to a message box.

First is the caption of the window and second is the text to be displayed in the window. These are passed to the **MessageBox.Show** function as the first two parameters, text comes first and the caption to be used comes second.

```
MessageBox.Show ("This is the text inside the box",
                 "This is the caption");
```

This alone shows a default message box which has an Ok button to enable the user to terminate it.

The third parameter is an identifier to specify which type of buttons should be shown. The possibilities include:

MessageBoxButtons.Ok // the default

MessageBoxButtons.OkCancel

MessageBoxButtons.AbortRetryIgnore

MessageBoxButtons.YesNoCancel

MessageBoxButtons.YesNo

MessageBoxButtons.RetryCancel

The fourth parameter is the icon to be displayed to the left of the message. These include the following.

MessageBoxIcon.Error

MessageBoxIcon.Exclamation

MessageBoxIcon.Information

MessageBoxIcon.Question

Fifth, a message box returns which button was pressed as a **DialogResult** data type (an enumerated data type). Its values which can be used in a **switch** or **if-then-else** statement include these.

DialogResult.Ok

DialogResult.Yes

DialogResult.No

DialogResult.Cancel

DialogResult.Abort

DialogResult.Retry

DialogResult.Ignore

So using these, I altered the coding to this.

```
private      void      OnClosing(object      sender,
System.ComponentModel.CancelEventArgs e) {
 if (MessageBox.Show (
      "Do you really want to quit the application?",
      "Query", MessageBoxButtons.YesNo,
      MessageBoxIcon.Question) != DialogResult.Yes) {
   e.Cancel = true;
  }
 }
```

Figure 6.7 shows what the message box looks like when I press the X button.

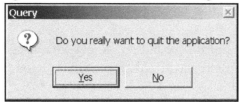

Figure 6.7 The Close Query

To stop the normal closing of the application window, use the passed events argument instance and set its **Cancel** property to **true**. The window will not then be closed.

As you can see, the framework generates the delegates and event functions with empty bodies. We merely need to add the desired coding to respond to the event.

Responding to Button Presses

The next most common event that occurs is a button press. A fast way to generate these event handlers is just to double click on the button in design view. The compiler adds the event handler coding and opens the code view showing that new function ready for your actions.

The event for handling the Find Matching Cars button is this. All buttons pressed events have the same prototype. I simply double clicked the button in the design view and it created the function for me.

```
private void buttonFindCar_Click(object sender, EventArgs e) {

}
```

The event for the Quit button is this.

```
private void buttonQuit_Click(object sender, EventArgs e) {
  this.Close ();
}
```

Notice that I actually implemented it. Any time you want to terminate the program, you call the **Close** method, which in turn calls our **OnClose** query.

Responding to Find Matching Cars presents a major design situation. There are two approaches to processing. One approach is to create member variables to store the various values as entered in the form. Every time a control's value is changed, we code event handlers such as the button press ones and update our member variables accordingly. Then, when Find Matching Car is pressed, we already have all of the current information and so can get right down to the action of looking for a match. This approach is tedious, since it requires a number of member variables and event functions to set them. I tend to try to avoid that situation.

The second approach is, within the event handler for the button, go get what is currently in each of the user entry controls and then do the search for a match. This approach is the one that I am taking here.

So how do we get the text from a text box control? First, we must locate the name the framework created for the object. In this case it is **this.textBoxCarMake**. **Text** is a property of the text box, so we only need to access it like this.

```
string s = this.textBoxCarMake.Text;
```

Of course, if we coded

```
this.CarMake.Text = "Hello";
```

Then the "Hello" will immediately appear in the text box on the form. So here we see the use of properties simplifying our access of the data of a class.

Okay. Text box data acquisition is easy. What about the radio buttons and check box states?

A checkbox has its state stored in a **CheckState** property whose values are **Checked** or **Unchecked**. Thus, we can access it this way.

```
CheckState stereo = this.checkBoxStereo.CheckState;
```

Radio buttons are more problematical. We must respond to each change in a radio button, storing some indicator of which one is now on. I chose to make an int variable color which has the values 0, 1, and 2 for red, white and blue. Of course, one could also use an enum for this.

To implement it, I chose the properties for the red button and for the **CheckChanged** event added **OnColorChange**. The framework then made that function for me. I then selected each of the other radio buttons in the group and set their **CheckChanged** event to this same function, **OnColorChange**. Remember that the first parameter of the event is the sender. I then implemented this function this way.

```
private void OnColorChange(object sender, EventArgs e) {
  if (sender == radioButtonRed) color = 0;
  else if (sender == radioButtonWhite) color = 1;
  else if (sender == radioButtonBlue) color = 2;
  }
```

This also means that I need to add a member int variable color to my form class. Thus, for radio buttons we must manually track the current selection.

The alternative is to check each radio button to see if it is on, which I find worse than this approach.

Okay, so now when the user pressed Find Matching Cars, we have all the information needed to actually perform the search and display the results in the read only edit control. But before we implement that portion, let's look at some of the other things that can be done.

Other Properties and Events

These controls have many properties and events to which you can respond. The compiler displays a short hint about any given item on the bottom of the properties box as it is selected. This is a good way to learn what is available for your use and what events you could respond to if desired.

You can set properties such as **BackColor** and **ForeColor** (the background and foreground colors), the **Font** and even **Visible**.

The **Anchor** property (top, bottom, left, or right) fixes the control to the indicated side of the container. So when the user resizes, this control remains firmly anchored to that side. An anchored control always maintains the same distance from the indicated edge. The **Dock** property does just that, it makes the control firmly affixed to the indicated docking edge. There is no spacing between it and the edge.

Some other useful text box properties include these. **AcceptsReturn**, if true, allows the Enter key to create a new line. **Multiline**, if true, allows imbedded new line codes to operate as new line codes. If you use **Multiline**, you may consider also using **ScrollBars** which automatically add scrollbars when needed. An even lower scale event is **TextChanged** which occurs whenever the user makes any change in the text in the control. If the text box contains a user's password, then use the **PasswordChar** property.

Mouse Events

Mouse events include movement into or out of a control, clicks and even hovering over a control (perhaps one pops up the contents of something or a hint). The events include
MouseEnter and **MouseLeave**
MouseDown, **MouseUp**, **MouseHover**, and **MouseMove**
The argument to the event handler has four useful properties:
X, Y are the coordinates of the event, relative to the control's top left corner
Button contains **left**, **right**, **middle**, or **none**
Clicks contains the number of times the button was clicked

Making the Find Matching Cars Actually Work

To make this into a working application, we must create a **Car** class. Here, I right clicked on the solution and chose Add Class and entered Car.cs. Here is the simple Car class.

```
using System;

namespace Pgm06aWindows
{
 public class Car
 {
  protected string make;
  protected int    mileage;
  protected int    color;
  protected bool   stereo;

  public string Make
  {
   get
   {
    return make;
   }
   set
   {
    make = value;
   }
  }

  public int Mileage
  {
   get
   {
    return mileage;
   }
   set
   {
    mileage = value;
   }
  }

  public int Color
  {
   get
   {
    return color;
   }
```

126

```csharp
  set
  {
   if (value >= 0 && value <= 2)
    color = value;
   else
    color = 0;
  }
}

public bool Stereo
{
 get
 {
  return stereo;
 }
 set
 {
  stereo = value;
 }
}

public Car()
{
 make = "";
 mileage = 0;
 color = 0;
 stereo = true;
}

public Car(string make, int miles, int color, bool stereo)
{
 this.make = make;
 mileage = miles;
 Color = color;
 this.stereo = stereo;
}

public int Match(Car requested)
{
 int count = 0;
 if (make.CompareTo(requested.make) == 0) count++;
 if (requested.stereo && stereo) count++;
 if (mileage <= requested.mileage) count++;
 if (color == requested.color) count++;
 return count;
}
```

```
  }
}
```

Back in our form, since we have not yet addressed using files nor container classes, I'll keep it simple by manually allocating the array items.

Also, when the application starts, it would be nice if one of the color radio buttons was initially selected. So I'll set red. This is done in the constructor after the call to the **InitializeComponent** is finished.

One final aspect. Whenever the user makes any kind of change, the results text box should be cleared. Otherwise, the results that are displayed do not reflect what the user has entered. Thus, I created a single **ClearResults** function.

```
   private void ClearResults(object sender, System.EventArgs e) {
     this.textBoxResults.Text = "";
   }
```

Then, whenever any text is changed in the two text boxes or whenever any of the buttons (check or radio) are clicked, **ClearResults** is invoked.

Here is the operational coding in FormCarFinderDataEntry.

```
using System;
using System.Collections.Generic;
using System.ComponentModel;
using System.Data;
using System.Drawing;
using System.Linq;
using System.Text;
using System.Windows.Forms;

namespace Pgm06aWindows
{
 public partial class FormUsedCarDataEntry : Form
 {
  // my new variables
  private int color;
  private Car[] array;

  public FormUsedCarDataEntry()
  {
   InitializeComponent();
      array = new Car[5];
   array[0] = new Car("Ford", 20000, 0, true);
   array[1] = new Car("Chevy", 70000, 1, true);
   array[2] = new Car("Oldsmobile", 40000, 2, false);
```

128

```csharp
array[3] = new Car("Ford", 50000, 1, true);
array[4] = new Car("Chevy", 60000, 0, true);

// set the red radio button on to begin
this.radioButtonRed.Checked = true;
}

private void OnClosing(object sender, FormClosingEventArgs e) {
 if (MessageBox.Show(
   "Do you really want to quit the application?",
   "Query", MessageBoxButtons.YesNo, MessageBoxIcon.Question) !=
   DialogResult.Yes) {
  e.Cancel = true;
 }
}

private void buttonQuit_Click(object sender, EventArgs e)
{
 this.Close();
}

private void OnColorChange(object sender, EventArgs e)
{
 if (sender == radioButtonRed) color = 0;
 else if (sender == radioButtonWhite) color = 1;
 else if (sender == radioButtonBlue) color = 2;
}

private void ClearResults(object sender, EventArgs e)
{
 this.textBoxResults.Text = "";
}

private void buttonFindCar_Click(object sender, EventArgs e)
{
 Car request = new Car();
 request.Make = this.textBoxCarMake.Text;
 string smiles = this.textBoxMileage.Text;
 try
 {
  request.Mileage = Int32.Parse(smiles);
 }
 catch (Exception ex)
 {
  request.Mileage = 0;
 }
```

```
request.Stereo =
        this.checkBoxStereo.CheckState == CheckState.Checked;
request.Color = color;
int match;
string res = "";
int total = 0;
foreach (Car c in array)
{
 match = c.Match(request);
 if (match > 0)
  {
   total++;
   res += c.Make + "  " + c.Mileage.ToString() + "   ";
   switch (c.Color)
   {
    case 0:
     res += "Red"; break;
    case 1:
     res += "White"; break;
    case 2:
     res += "Blue"; break;
    default:
     res += "Unknown color"; break;
   }
   res += c.Stereo ? "  Stereo" : "  No Stereo";
   res += " Num Matches: " + match + "\r\n";
  }
 }

 if (total == 0) res = "None match";
 this.textBoxResults.Text = res;
 }

 }
}
```

When adding multiple lines to a text box, you must provide both the CR and LF codes. That is "\r\f."

One final note. By keeping the design coding separate from the operational actions coding, a greater simplicity and readability is gained. I find this to be a great benefit.

Problems

Problem 6-1—Temperature Converter Revisited

When dealing with temperatures, one common problem is the conversion of a temperature in Fahrenheit degrees into Celsius degrees. The formula is

$$C = (5/9) (F - 32)$$

Write a Windows GUI application to handle the conversions. The window's caption should read: "your name - Temperature Converter." Provide labels and 2 text boxes for the data entry of a temperature in F or C; one text box for each temperature. Provide a radio button group whose two radio buttons say: "Convert Fahrenheit to Celsius" and "Convert Celsius to Fahrenheit." Provide a button labeled "Do It!" and another labeled "Quit." Establish events according to the following description of its operations.

Whenever a used types anything into a text box, clear the other text box. Initially, the "Convert Fahrenheit to Celsius" radio button is selected.

When the user clicks on Do It!, if the corresponding text box is empty, display an informatory message box explaining that they need to enter a temperature in the indicated box or change their radio button selection. If the corresponding text box contains invalid data, display an appropriate error message box. If the data is okay, then perform the conversion and display the results in the other text box.

When Quit is clicked, display a YesNo query message box and if they select Yes, go ahead and quit. Thoroughly test the application.

You may add other effects and features as you desire for extra credit.

Chapter 7—Files and Container Classes

It's time that we are able to handle file operations. Closely related are the container classes since we need a way to conveniently store the data items. Data stored in files are called **persistent data**.

Console Stream Objects

The runtime environment creates three stream objects for our use: **Console.In**, **Console.Out**, and **Console.Error** which are aliases for the keyboard and the screen. These are analogous to **cin**, **cout**, and **cerr** of C++. The first two are used by Console.WriteLine and Console.Read.

File Objects

However, files are handles by the **System.IO** namespace, which provides a wealth of actions one can perform on files and directories, including the normal File-Open and File-Save common dialogs. There is even a memory mapped file class for blazing I/O operations. Both text and binary files are supported. C# borrows terminology from Windows programming. An object can be written in binary format to a file; this is called **serialization**. However, they invented a new term for reading it back in, **deserialization**.

The key classes are **StreamReader**, **StreamWriter**, **FileStream** (update files), **BinaryFormatter**, and **MemoryStream**.

The File and Directory classes have a number of handy static methods for our use. Table 7.1 shows some of these key functions.

File Class Functions	Description
AppendText	Returns a StreamWriter ready to append new data on to the end of another or a new file, if it does not exist
Copy	Copies the file to the destination
Create	Creates the file and returns a FileStream ready for operations
CreateText	Creates the file and returns a StreamWriter ready for text type operations

File Class Functions	Description
Delete	Deletes the specified file
Exists	Returns true if the file exists
Move	Moves a file to the desired location
Open	Returns a FileStream ready for I/O per your options
OpenRead	Returns a FileStream ready to read only
OpenWrite	Returns a FileStream ready to write
OpenText	Returns a StreamReader ready to read the stream
Directory Class Functions	
CreateDirectory	Builds a new folder and returns its information in a DirectoryInfo instance
Delete	Removes the specified directory
Exists	Returns true if the directory exists
GetDirectories	Returns a string array of all subdirectories in this dir
GetFiles	Returns a string array of all files in this folder
Move	Moves this directory to another location

Let's look at some of the directory functions' usage.

```
using System.IO;
...
string filename;
string dirname;
...
if (File.Exists (filename)) { // do something with file
if (Directory.Exists (dirname)) { // do something

string[] dirlist = Directory.GetDirectories (dirname);
for (int j=0; j<dirlist.Length; j++) {
 string dir = dirlist[j]; // do something with this dir
}

string[] filelist = Directory.GetFiles (dirname);
```

133

```
for (int j=0; j<filelist.Length; j++) {
 string item = filelist[j]; // do something with this file
}
Directory.Delete (dirname);
```

Of course, it is file operations that most concern us. File I/O is handled in three basic ways: **text**, **binary**, and **serialization**. Each has pros and cons and uses. Text file operations are slow because of the constant data conversion that must be done and the incredible awkwardness of the inputting process needed to extract variables. Binary files incur no data conversion overhead and the actual process to input or output variables is easy. However, you must know the order of the fields in the file in order to read them back. Serialization, in which data is also saved in binary format, allows entire classes to be input or output with a single I/O statement is the simplest to code. However, the actual resulting binary file is quite bloated with extra information required for the input or deserialization process.

For this example, I created a one line text file containing an item number, description, quantity and cost. Here is the entire contents of the 31-byte text file.
```
12345 "Pots and Pans" 1 14.99
```
It looks just like an ordinary C++ style text file. The binary file version of this data has a size of 30 bytes. The serialized binary file size is 211 bytes! So the price we pay for this serialization convenience is a much larger file size.

Pgm07aWindows illustrates both input and output in these three schemes.

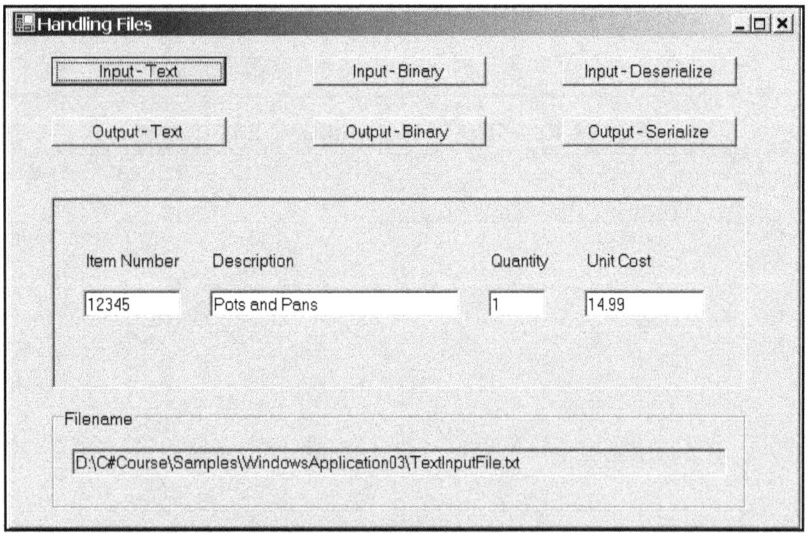

Figure 7.1 Pgm07aWindows — File Handling

When you click on any of the six buttons, either the **OpenFileDialog** or **SaveFileDialog** is run. These are the Win32 common dialogs that appear. The provided system dialog classes permit

134

us to set the initial folder to use, the file filter to use, such as *.txt files, initial filenames, and the setting of commonly used flags like ensuring the file or folder chosen actually exists.

Let's begin by examining how to use the common file dialogs.

The Common File Dialogs

To being up the file open dialog, one constructs an instance of the **OpenFileDialog** class. The class has implemented numerous properties that you can set before you actually run the dialog. **CheckFileExists** and **CheckPathExists** boolean properties guarantee that the user is actually choosing a file that does in fact exist, so you can expect no surprises when you try to open the chosen file later on. The string property **InitialDirectory** can be set to point to the desired initial folder of your choice.

```
OpenFileDialog dlg = new OpenFileDialog ();
dlg.CheckFileExists = true;
dlg.CheckPathExists = true;
dlg.Filter = "Serialized Binary Files (*.bin)|*.bin";
dlg.InitialDirectory =
              "D:\\C#Course\\Samples\\WindowsApplication03";

if (dlg.ShowDialog () == DialogResult.Cancel) return;
filename = dlg.FileName;
this.fileName.Text = filename;
```

However, if you are not familiar with Windows C++ programming, the file filter needs some explanation. The file filter defines which files extension are to be shown in the Files of Type combo box. Each file filter is composed to two portions: the text to be shown in the combo box and the actual DOS file filter. The two items are separated by a vertical bar |. The same | separates each filter pair, if you have more than one.

The combo box text should contain a descriptive name of this file type along with the actual DOS filter to be used in parentheses. Here I used the string: "Serialized Binary Files (*.bin)". The actual DOS filter is "*.bin". For example, the string of:

```
"C# Files (*.cs)|*.cs|Java Files (*.js)|*.js|C++ Files (*.cpp)|*.cpp"
```
Requests that files of extensions *.cs, *.js, *.cpp be available in the combo box for the user to choose between.

With the dialog instance allocated and its initial properties set, the dialog is executed by calling the **ShowDialog** method. The system then shows and operates the dialog automatically. The user can click either Ok or Cancel. Thus, when the dialog terminates, it must return which button was pressed. The return type is **DialogResult.Cancel** or **DialogResult.Ok**. In this example, if the user chose Cancel, I just return from the function inputting or saving nothing.

The dialog property **FileName** contains the full path and filename ready for an open statement. Usually, this is copied from the dialog property into another local string.

For the **SaveFileDialog**, the principle is the same.

```
SaveFileDialog dlg = new SaveFileDialog ();
dlg.CheckPathExists = true;
dlg.Filter = "Serialized Binary Files (*.bin)|*.bin";
dlg.InitialDirectory = "D:";
if (dlg.ShowDialog () == DialogResult.Cancel) return;
filename = dlg.FileName;
this.fileName.Text = filename;
```

For only a little coding, we gain a rather lot of functionality.

Defining the File Stream—For All Three Methods

No matter which method of file I/O you intend to use, a new **FileStream** object must be allocated. The constructor is passed the filename to use and the open flags. The two most common flags are **FileMode.Open** which opens an existing file for input operations. If the file does not exist, an exception is thrown. For output files, **FileMode.Create** is used which creates a new file if the file does not yet exists. If the file does exist, its contents are cleared and set to an empty file ready for the first output operation.

```
FileStream file;
try {
 file = new FileStream (filename, FileMode.Open);
}
catch (FileNotFoundException) {
 MessageBox.Show ("File " + filename + "does not exist",
         "Error", MessageBoxButtons.OK, MessageBoxIcon.Error);
 return;
}
```

Typically, try-catch logic surrounds the attempted open in case it should fail.

For the output files, we have this.

```
FileStream file;
try {
 file = new FileStream (filename, FileMode.Create);
}
catch (FileNotFoundException) {
 MessageBox.Show ("File " + filename + "does not exist",
         "Error", MessageBoxButtons.OK, MessageBoxIcon.Error);
 return;
}
```

There are additional parameters and options that can be used. One can specify that this file is to be read only, for example.

```
file = new FileStream (filename, FileMode.Open, FileAccess.Read);
```

However, for most operations, the defaults are fine.

In Pgm07aWindows, all six functions that respond to button presses have this same coding, differing only in whether it is opened or created, input or output.

Text I/O Operations

To handle a text file, one uses an instance of the **StreamReader** or **StreamWriter** classes. For the input operation I coded this.

```
StreamReader stream = new StreamReader (file);
string buf = stream.ReadLine ();
ParseTextLine (buf);
stream.Close ();
file.Close ();
```

The problem is unraveling the line which contains four fields. Because we cannot perform direct operations on individual characters within a string, we must use the string functions, all of which return a new result string or an index of the desired location within the constant passed string. Hence, you must develop some kind of string parsing methods that emulate the extraction operator of C++. I created the ParseTextLine function to do this.

Note that if you intend to do much text file processing, then it would be wise to create some utility static functions to extract the data type from a string, giving you back the extracted string and the remainder of the string.

Here is the function. Now let's examine how it works.

```
private void ParseTextLine (string buf) {
 char[] trim = new Char[] {' '};
 buf = buf.TrimStart (trim);
 buf = buf.TrimEnd (trim);
 int i = buf.IndexOf (" ", 0);
 string item = buf.Substring (0, i);
 buf = buf.Substring (i+1);
 purchase.ItemNumber = Int32.Parse (item);
 this.itemNumber.Text = purchase.ItemNumber.ToString ();
 buf = buf.TrimStart (trim);
 buf = buf.Substring (1);
 i = buf.IndexOf ("\"",0);
 item = buf.Substring (0, i);
```

137

```
purchase.Description = item;
this.description.Text = purchase.Description;
buf = buf.Substring (i+1);
buf = buf.TrimStart (trim);
i = buf.IndexOf (" ", 0);
item = buf.Substring (0, i);
purchase.Quantity = Int32.Parse (item);
this.quantity.Text = purchase.Quantity.ToString ();
buf = buf.Substring (i+1);
buf = buf.TrimStart (trim);
item = buf;
purchase.UnitCost = Double.Parse (item);
this.unitCost.Text = purchase.UnitCost.ToString();
}
```

The first action I did was to trim off all leading and trailing blanks. To do so, you need an array of characters that you wished trimmed. In this case the array contains only one char, the blank. One could also use this operation to remove leading 0 digits as well.

```
char[] trim = new Char[] {' '};
buf = buf.TrimStart (trim);
buf = buf.TrimEnd (trim);
```

The string function **TrimStart** removes all of the trim characters that lie at the beginning of the string, while **TrimEnd** removes them from the end of the string. Both functions return a new string with the blanks removed. Notice how I reassigned the new cleaned up string back to the initial **buf** string reference variable.

Next, the first field is the integer item number. So one begins by extracting out just that string of digits. We know that numbers are separated by blanks, usually, so I use the **IndexOf** function to find the first blank beginning at the start of the string. **IndexOf** returns the subscript of the first blank which is the end of the integer field. The **Substring** function is then used to make a new string consisting of just these first digits.

```
int i = buf.IndexOf (" ", 0);
string item = buf.Substring (0, i);
buf = buf.Substring (i+1);
purchase.ItemNumber = Int32.Parse (item);
this.itemNumber.Text = purchase.ItemNumber.ToString ();
```

Once this is done, I again use **Substring** to make a new string with everything up to and including this found blank removed and again store this remainder string in **buf**. Next, with the string item containing the digits that make up the item number, it is converted from string form into an actual integer using **Int32.Parse**. I store the new item number in the purchase class instance's itemNumber as well as directly into the text box on screen.

The next field is the double quote delimited description string. So we must extract the leading double quote mark and then extract all characters to the trailing double quote mark. The first step is to skip over blanks, so again I used **TrimStart**. A better method would be to add all of the other white space characters to this trim array, such as the tab, CR, and LF codes. Since the first non-white space character is the double quote, I skip over it. Notice that I did not check to make sure that there is a double quote here, for simplicity.

```
buf = buf.TrimStart (trim);
buf = buf.Substring (1);
i = buf.IndexOf ("\"",0);
item = buf.Substring (0, i);
purchase.Description = item;
this.description.Text = purchase.Description;
```

The remaining extractions parallel that of the first integer.

I think you can see that if you needed to so a lot of text file inputting, you would be wise to create some generalized extraction parsing methods, one for each data type you needed to extract.

The Purchase Class

Since I am storing the data into a purchase instance, let's see what that class looks like. In fact, it is very simple and is a good guideline for creating a serializable class. Please note, that the **[Serializable]** attribute **must** precede the class definition. This notifies the compiler that this class can be so handled. The class itself just contains the four data items and their get-set properties along with rudimentary ctor functions.

```
[Serializable]
public class Purchase {
 protected int itemNumber;
 public int ItemNumber {
  get {
   return itemNumber;
  }
  set {
   itemNumber = value;
  }
 }

 protected string description;
 public string Description {
  get {
   return description;
  }
  set {
   description = value;
```

139

```
    }
  }

  protected int quantity;
  public int Quantity {
   get {
     return quantity;
   }
   set {
     quantity = value;
   }
  }

  protected double unitCost;
  public double UnitCost {
   get {
     return unitCost;
   }
   set {
     unitCost = value;
   }
  }

  public Purchase () : this (0, "", 0, 0.0) {}
  public Purchase (int inum, string desc, int qty, double cost) {
   itemNumber = inum;
   description = desc;
   quantity = qty;
   unitCost = cost;
  }
 }
```

Text output operations, in contrast, are very easy. One only needs to output a string. One begins by making an instance of the **StreamWriter** class. Next, build the output string that represents the data to be written. **WriteLine** is used to write the string to the text file. Other functions are available as well, but this is the simplest.

```
StreamWriter stream = new StreamWriter (file);
string buf = purchase.ItemNumber.ToString() + " \"" +
             purchase.Description + "\" " +
             purchase.Quantity + " " + purchase.UnitCost;
stream.WriteLine ("{0}",buf);
stream.Close ();
file.Close ();
```

Binary File I/O

In contrast to the tedious text file input and output operations, binary I/O is easy. This time we construct an instance of the **BinaryReader** class on the file. This class has methods to input all the basic data types. Thus, to input a field, you just call the appropriate method for its data type.

```
BinaryReader stream = new BinaryReader (file);
purchase.ItemNumber = stream.ReadInt32 ();
purchase.Description = stream.ReadString ();
purchase.Quantity = stream.ReadInt32 ();
purchase.UnitCost = stream.ReadDouble ();
this.itemNumber.Text = purchase.ItemNumber.ToString();
this.description.Text = purchase.Description;
this.quantity.Text = purchase.Quantity.ToString();
this.unitCost.Text = purchase.UnitCost.ToString();
stream.Close ();
file.Close ();
```

Output is similarly done using an instance of **BinaryWriter**.

```
BinaryWriter stream = new BinaryWriter (file);
stream.Write (purchase.ItemNumber);
stream.Write (purchase.Description);
stream.Write (purchase.Quantity);
stream.Write (purchase.UnitCost);
stream.Close ();
file.Close ();
```

Binary I/O is an easy, effective, and fast method indeed.

Serialization/Deserialization of a Class

Any class can be serialized (written to disk) and deserialized (read back in from disk). The class definition is preceded with the **[Serializable]** attribute shown above. If all data members are to be read or written, nothing else must be done. However, if some data items are not to be I/Oed, then you can insert customized serialization routines within the class. For convenience, we add two more usings.

```
using System.Runtime.Serialization;
using System.Runtime.Serialization.Formatters.Binary;
```

Only two lines of code, in bold, are needed to input the entire class instance from disk. We construct an instance of the **BinaryFormatter** this time.

```
BinaryFormatter reader = new BinaryFormatter ();
try {
 purchase = (Purchase) reader.Deserialize (file);
 this.itemNumber.Text = purchase.ItemNumber.ToString();
 this.description.Text = purchase.Description;
 this.quantity.Text = purchase.Quantity.ToString();
 this.unitCost.Text = purchase.UnitCost.ToString();
}
catch (SerializationException) {
 // eof
 file.Close ();
}
file.Close ();
```

The try-catch logic shows how to detect eof as well.

For output, it is just this.

```
BinaryFormatter writer = new BinaryFormatter ();
writer.Serialize (file, purchase);
file.Close ();
```

This is super convenient, easy I/O, to say the least.

The Window's Programming Techniques of Data Transfer To Controls

This application also demonstrates some needed techniques when events can trigger changes in a window's controls. Two scenarios arise.

The first occurs whenever the user presses any of the save buttons. Notice that there is a memory instance of **Purchase**, here called **purchase**. The visible text box controls are displaying data items. However, the user could very well have made changes to those text box items, and those changes are not yet stored in the **purchase** instance. That is, the memory **purchase** and the text boxes are potentially **out of synch** with each other. Thus, the very first action that all save functions must to is to ensure that the memory **purchase** instance accurately reflects what is now in the user's text box controls.

(For those of you who have been through C++ Windows programming, this is the old UpdateData function.) Thus, the first line in the three save functions is as follows.

```
UpdatePurchaseFields ();
```

This function must acquire the current contents of each text box and store it in **purchase**.

```
private void UpdatePurchaseFields () {
  purchase.ItemNumber = Int32.Parse (this.itemNumber.Text);
  purchase.Description = this.description.Text;
  purchase.Quantity = Int32.Parse (this.quantity.Text);
  purchase.UnitCost = Double.Parse (this.unitCost.Text);
}
```

When an input button is pressed, a similar situation occurs. However, in these three input functions, I stored the purchase data items directly into the corresponding text boxes. I did it for ease of understanding. In the real world, one would make another function to store all of the purchase fields into their corresponding text boxes. However, an even better encapsulation of these processed is to make one update function that is passed a bool indicating the direction of data travel.

```
private void UpdatePurchaseData (bool saveIntoTextboxes) {
  if (saveIntoTextboxes) {
    this.itemNumber.Text = purchase.ItemNumber.ToString();
    this.description.Text = purchase.Description;
    this.quantity.Text = purchase.Quantity.ToString();
    this.unitCost.Text = purchase.UnitCost.ToString();
  }
  else {
    purchase.ItemNumber = Int32.Parse (this.itemNumber.Text);
    purchase.Description = this.description.Text;
    purchase.Quantity = Int32.Parse (this.quantity.Text);
    purchase.UnitCost = Double.Parse (this.unitCost.Text);
  }
```

```
}
```

This becomes a much more elegant and versatile method of handling both problems. Another technique is to use an array of strings to update all the text boxes.

For your easy reference, here is the complete Form1.cs operational coding.

```csharp
using System;
using System.Collections.Generic;
using System.ComponentModel;
using System.Data;
using System.Drawing;
using System.Linq;
using System.Text;
using System.Windows.Forms;
using System.IO;
using System.Runtime.Serialization;
using System.Runtime.Serialization.Formatters.Binary;

namespace Pgm07aWindows
{
 public partial class Form1 : Form
 {
  public Form1()
  {
   InitializeComponent();
  }

  protected string filename;
  Purchase purchase = new Purchase();

  private void ClearTextBoxes()
  {
   this.itemNumber.Text = "";
   this.description.Text = "";
   this.quantity.Text = "";
   this.unitCost.Text = "";
  }

  private void UpdatePurchaseFields()
  {
   purchase.ItemNumber = Int32.Parse(this.itemNumber.Text);
   purchase.Description = this.description.Text;
   purchase.Quantity = Int32.Parse(this.quantity.Text);
   purchase.UnitCost = Double.Parse(this.unitCost.Text);
  }

  private void OnInputText(object sender, EventArgs e)
```

```
{
 ClearTextBoxes();
 OpenFileDialog dlg = new OpenFileDialog();
 dlg.CheckFileExists = true;
 dlg.CheckPathExists = true;
 dlg.Filter = "Text Files (*.txt)|*.txt";
 dlg.InitialDirectory = "D:";

 if (dlg.ShowDialog() == DialogResult.Cancel) return;
 filename = dlg.FileName;
 this.fileName.Text = filename;
 FileStream file;
 try
 {
  file = new FileStream(filename, FileMode.Open);
 }
 catch (FileNotFoundException)
 {
  MessageBox.Show("File " + filename + "does not exist",
          "Error", MessageBoxButtons.OK, MessageBoxIcon.Error);
  return;
 }
 StreamReader stream = new StreamReader(file);
 string buf = stream.ReadLine();
 ParseTextLine(buf);
 stream.Close();
 file.Close();
}

private void ParseTextLine(string buf)
{
 char[] trim = new Char[] { ' ' };
 buf = buf.TrimStart(trim);
 buf = buf.TrimEnd(trim);
 int i = buf.IndexOf(" ", 0);
 string item = buf.Substring(0, i);
 buf = buf.Substring(i + 1);
 purchase.ItemNumber = Int32.Parse(item);
 this.itemNumber.Text = purchase.ItemNumber.ToString();
 buf = buf.TrimStart(trim);
 buf = buf.Substring(1);
 i = buf.IndexOf("\"", 0);
 item = buf.Substring(0, i);
 purchase.Description = item;
 this.description.Text = purchase.Description;
 buf = buf.Substring(i + 1);
```

```csharp
 buf = buf.TrimStart(trim);
 i = buf.IndexOf(" ", 0);
 item = buf.Substring(0, i);
 purchase.Quantity = Int32.Parse(item);
 this.quantity.Text = purchase.Quantity.ToString();
 buf = buf.Substring(i + 1);
 buf = buf.TrimStart(trim);
 item = buf;
 purchase.UnitCost = Double.Parse(item);
 this.unitCost.Text = purchase.UnitCost.ToString();
}

private void OnOutputText(object sender, EventArgs e)
{
 UpdatePurchaseFields();
 SaveFileDialog dlg = new SaveFileDialog();
 dlg.CheckPathExists = true;
 dlg.Filter = "Text Files (*.txt)|*.txt";
 dlg.InitialDirectory = "D:";

 if (dlg.ShowDialog() == DialogResult.Cancel) return;
 filename = dlg.FileName;
 this.fileName.Text = filename;
 FileStream file;
 try
 {
  file = new FileStream(filename, FileMode.Create);
 }
 catch (FileNotFoundException)
 {
  MessageBox.Show("File " + filename + "does not exist",
          "Error", MessageBoxButtons.OK, MessageBoxIcon.Error);
  return;
 }
 StreamWriter stream = new StreamWriter(file);
 string buf = purchase.ItemNumber.ToString() + " \"" +
              purchase.Description + "\" " +
              purchase.Quantity + " " + purchase.UnitCost;
 stream.WriteLine("{0}", buf);
 stream.Close();
 file.Close();
}

private void OnInputBinary(object sender, EventArgs e)
{
 ClearTextBoxes();
```

```csharp
OpenFileDialog dlg = new OpenFileDialog();
dlg.CheckFileExists = true;
dlg.CheckPathExists = true;
dlg.Filter = "Binary Files (*.dat)|*.dat";
dlg.InitialDirectory = "D:";

if (dlg.ShowDialog() == DialogResult.Cancel) return;
filename = dlg.FileName;
this.fileName.Text = filename;

FileStream file;
try
{
 file = new FileStream(filename, FileMode.Open);
}
catch (FileNotFoundException)
{
 MessageBox.Show("File " + filename + "does not exist",
         "Error", MessageBoxButtons.OK, MessageBoxIcon.Error);
 return;
}
BinaryReader stream = new BinaryReader(file);
purchase.ItemNumber = stream.ReadInt32();
purchase.Description = stream.ReadString();
purchase.Quantity = stream.ReadInt32();
purchase.UnitCost = stream.ReadDouble();
this.itemNumber.Text = purchase.ItemNumber.ToString();
this.description.Text = purchase.Description;
this.quantity.Text = purchase.Quantity.ToString();
this.unitCost.Text = purchase.UnitCost.ToString();
stream.Close();
file.Close();
}

private void OnOutputBinary(object sender, EventArgs e)
{
 UpdatePurchaseFields();
 SaveFileDialog dlg = new SaveFileDialog();
 dlg.CheckPathExists = true;
 dlg.Filter = "Binary Files (*.dat)|*.dat";
 dlg.InitialDirectory = "D:";

 if (dlg.ShowDialog() == DialogResult.Cancel) return;
 filename = dlg.FileName;
 this.fileName.Text = filename;
 FileStream file;
```

```
try
{
  file = new FileStream(filename, FileMode.Create);
}
catch (FileNotFoundException)
{
  MessageBox.Show("File " + filename + "does not exist",
          "Error", MessageBoxButtons.OK, MessageBoxIcon.Error);
  return;
}
BinaryWriter stream = new BinaryWriter(file);
stream.Write(purchase.ItemNumber);
stream.Write(purchase.Description);
stream.Write(purchase.Quantity);
stream.Write(purchase.UnitCost);
stream.Close();
file.Close();
}

private void OnInputDeserialize(object sender, EventArgs e)
{
ClearTextBoxes();
OpenFileDialog dlg = new OpenFileDialog();
dlg.CheckFileExists = true;
dlg.CheckPathExists = true;
dlg.Filter = "Serialized Binary Files (*.bin)|*.bin";
dlg.InitialDirectory = "D:";

if (dlg.ShowDialog() == DialogResult.Cancel) return;
filename = dlg.FileName;
this.fileName.Text = filename;
FileStream file;
try
{
  file = new FileStream(filename, FileMode.Open,
                        FileAccess.Read);
}
catch (FileNotFoundException)
{
  MessageBox.Show("File " + filename + "does not exist",
          "Error", MessageBoxButtons.OK, MessageBoxIcon.Error);
  return;
}
BinaryFormatter reader = new BinaryFormatter();
try
{
```

```
        purchase = (Purchase) reader.Deserialize (file);
        this.itemNumber.Text = purchase.ItemNumber.ToString();
        this.description.Text = purchase.Description;
        this.quantity.Text = purchase.Quantity.ToString();
        this.unitCost.Text = purchase.UnitCost.ToString();
      }
    catch (SerializationException)
    {
      // eof
      file.Close();
    }
    file.Close();
  }

  private void OnOutputSerialize(object sender, EventArgs e)
  {
    UpdatePurchaseFields ();
    SaveFileDialog dlg = new SaveFileDialog ();
    dlg.CheckPathExists = true;
    dlg.Filter = "Serialized Binary Files (*.bin)|*.bin";
    dlg.InitialDirectory = "D:";

    if (dlg.ShowDialog () == DialogResult.Cancel) return;
    filename = dlg.FileName;
    this.fileName.Text = filename;
    FileStream file;
    try {
      file = new FileStream (filename, FileMode.Create);
    }
    catch (FileNotFoundException) {
      MessageBox.Show ("File " + filename + "does not exist",
            "Error", MessageBoxButtons.OK, MessageBoxIcon.Error);
      return;
    }
    BinaryFormatter writer = new BinaryFormatter ();
    writer.Serialize (file, purchase);
    file.Close ();
  }
 }
}
```

In general, we do not need to look at the Form1.Designer.cs automatically generated design code. In the earlier versions of C# and Visual Studio, both of these were contained in a single .cs file. Now, the automatically generated design coding is in the separate file, making the operational code far easier to read and write.

Commentary on the Difference Between Binary and Serialized Data Files

For one record, the binary file contains 30 bytes while the serialized file contains 231 bytes. Here is what the serialized data looks like in a Hex Editor, Figure 7.2

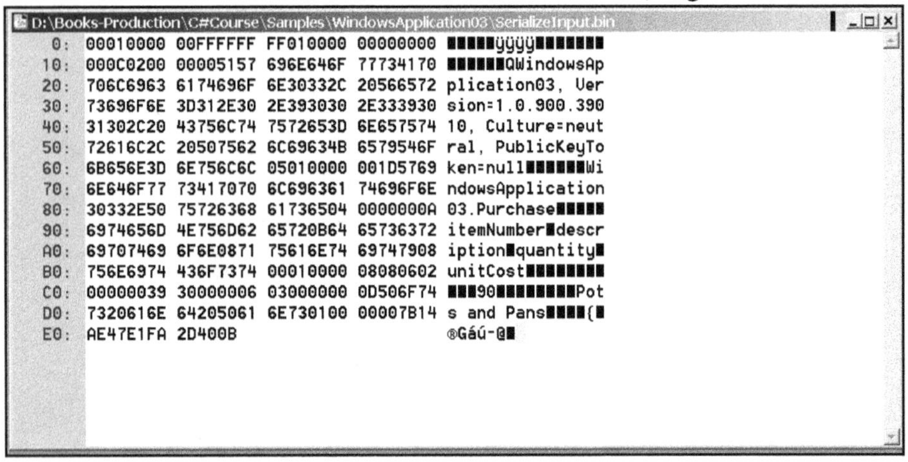

Figure 7.2 Serialized Data in a Hex Editor

This size is used for all records. That is, if you serialized 10 records, each would be 231 in size. Further, notice that part of the information stored is the actual application name. So this prevents other applications from reading this file. Thus, for practical purposes, a regular binary file is best for data sharing situations while serialization is best left for storing application specific information.

Data Structures or Collection Classes or Container Classes

Array Class

The **System.Array** class is a specialized class that provides the basic functionality of all arrays and the Collection classes. While only the .Net components are allowed to derive directly from the **Array** class (this class is reserved to provide the basic C# array processing capabilities), the **Collection** classes are designed for our use. The **Array** class does allow us to use its methods on normal arrays.

```
using System;
class App {
 public static void Main () {
  int[] array = {2, 5, 6, 1, 9, 42, 16};
  Array.Sort (array);
  foreach (int element in array) {
   Console.WriteLine ("{0}", element);
  }
 }
}
```

However, this does not work with classes or structures because the compiler does not know how to sort these items, which field, for example, should be used. This is handled by having our class implement the **IComparable** interface. Let's make an array of the above **Purchase** instances be a sortable array. To do this, we inherit from **IComparable**. We must then implement the **CompareTo** function.

```
[Serializable]
public class Purchase : IComparable {
 int IComparable.CompareTo (object o) {
  Purchase p = (Purchase) o;
  if (this.itemNumber < p.itemNumber) return -1;
  return this.itemNumber > p.itemNumber;
 }
 protected int itemNumber;
 public int ItemNumber {
  get {
   return itemNumber;
  }
  set {
   itemNumber = value;
  }
 }
...
```

Now **Main** can do the following.
```
Purchase[] array = new Purchase[5];
... input 5 instances from a file
Array.Sort (array);
```
and now the array is sorted into increasing item number order.

Further, if the array is sorted, **Array.BinarySearch** can be called.
```
Purchase find = new Purchase ();
... input find data
int index = Array.BinarySearch (array, find);
if (index != -1) {
 // here we have found find at index in the array
```

Note that each class can have only one **IComparable** method.

So how can we have multiple sorting orders? By defining several nested **IComparer** classes within our **Purchase** class. These derived classes have no data items and only one function, **Compare** which is passed two object references. There are two ways to implement this.

Way 1. Add two sort classes derived **IComparer** from to the **Purchase** class

To sort on the **description** strings, typecast to **Purchase** objects and call the **String.Compare** function. To sort on the item number, invoke the existing **IComparable** method.
```
public class SortByDescriptionClass : IComparer {
 public int Compare (object o1, object o2) {
  Purchase p1 = (Purchase) o1;
  Purchase p2 = (Purchase) o2;
  return String.Compare (p1.description, p2.description);
 }
}
public class SortByItemNumberClass : IComparer {
 public int Compare (object o1, object o2) {
  Purchase p1 = (Purchase) o1;
  Purchase p2 = (Purchase) o2;
  return ((IComparable) p1).CompareTo (p2);
 }
}
```
The ugly part lies in the caller who must create instances of these classes to pass to the sorting function.
```
Purchase[] array = new Purchase[5];
... input 5 instances from a file
Array.Sort (array, (IComparer) new
                    Purchase.SortByDescriptionClass());
```

```
Array.Sort (array, (IComparer) new
                          Purchase.SortByItemNumberClass());
```

Way 2. Make **IComparer** a Property

This approach makes it a lot easier on the user. We keep all of the above coding, but now add in two new get properties.

```
public static IComparer SortByDescription {
  get {
    return ((IComparer) new SortByDescriptionClass ());
  }
}
public static IComparer SortByItemNumber {
  get {
    return ((IComparer) new SortByItemNumberClass ());
  }
}
```

Now the user can do the following convenient sorts.

```
Purchase[] array = new Purchase[5];
... input 5 instances from a file
Array.Sort (array, Purchase.SortByDescription);
Array.Sort (array, Purchase.SortByItemNumber);
```

An added benefit, with these comparison functions working, you could go ahead and implement the relational operators for the Purchase class by having them invoke these comparing functions.

The major drawback of using the built in array system is that we always have a fixed upper limit on the array size, whatever value we specify when we create it.

The Collections

The **Collection** classes present a growable set of containers, that is, they resize themselves larger and larger as new items are added to it, subject to the maximum amount of available memory. In production environments, this is usually a very desirable way to go.

The workhorse basic collection is the **ArrayList** class which represents a list stored as a growable array, or an array whose size is dynamically increased as needed.

All of the functions you would expect to find in a list container are here. Items can be added to the list using **Add** or **Insert** and can be removed by using **Remove** or **RemoveAt**. **Sort** and **BinarySearch** apply to the list as well. The **Item** property allows you to access an object at a

153

specific subscript, either to get it or change it.

Of course, for sorting, the same exact coding we just examined for regular arrays is used! Given the above **Purchase** class definition with the fancy Way 2 properties, Main can do the following.

```
ArrayList array = new ArrayList ();
 // the following is part of the input from a file loop
 Purchase p = new Purchase();
 // fill it up
 array.Add (p);
}
array.Sort (); // calls the default method by item number
array.Sort (Purchase.SortByDescription);
array.Sort (Purchase.SortByItemNumber);
foreach (Purchase p in array) {
 Console.WriteLine (p.Description);
}
```

The **Queue** and **Stack** classes also work as expected. **Enqueue** and **Dequeue** are the two key queue methods, while **Push** and **Pop** are the stack main methods.

With these kinds of classes, as well as with the list, how is iteration handled? In a general queue data structure, an **iterator**, often called current pointer, is used to keep track of the current node that is visited. A **Next** and **Previous** function moves current pointer forward and backwards, if the list is double linked.

The container classes support this through the use of the **IEnumerator** interface. Note that through this interface, you can only read the objects being stored and cannot be used to modify the actual collection for that would defeat the purpose of Push-Pop and Enqueue-Dequeue.

When an instance of the enumerator is first created, it is positioned before the first element in the collection. Thus, the first action must be to call the **MoveNext** function. Then, one can call the **Current** function to retrieve the object there. **MoveNext** returns false when there are no more elements in the container. Thus, the processing loop involves calling **MoveNext** and **Current** together. At any time, **Reset** can be called to start over at the beginning. However, if the container's contents are modified, the enumerator is invalid and cannot be reset.

Thus, using the **ArrayList** called array above, we can do the following.

```
using System.Collections;
 IEnumerator myEnumerator = array.GetEnumerator();
 while (myEnumerator.MoveNext()) {
  Purchase p = (Purchase) myEnumerator.Current;
  // use p
 }
```

A Practical Example—ConsoleApplication10

Okay, let's see these things in action. Acme has a binary file of their daily purchase orders and wishes to see a Daily Sales Report. Here is the simple output report.

```
                     Acme Daily Sales Report

    Item       Description        Quantity         Unit          Total
   Number                         Purchased        Cost

   100001      Description 1        2.00          $21.00         $42.00
   100002      Description 2        3.00          $22.00         $66.00
   100003      Description 3        1.00          $23.00         $23.00
   100004      Description 4        2.00          $24.00         $48.00
   100005      Description 5        3.00          $25.00         $75.00
   100006      Description 6        1.00          $26.00         $26.00
   100007      Description 7        2.00          $27.00         $54.00
   100008      Description 8        3.00          $28.00         $84.00
   100009      Description 9        1.00          $29.00         $29.00
   100010      Description 10       2.00          $20.00         $40.00
...
   100049      Description 49       2.00          $29.00         $58.00
                                                                -------
                                                              $2,404.00

Average Order Amount:      $49.06
```

Of course, there is no real need to store the items in a growable array or list. But let's do so to show how it is done.

I used exactly the same **Purchase** class as in the previous example; it is not shown below. I highlighted in bold the new or interesting lines. The only thing that are new are the exceptions that should be caught: **EndOfStreamException** and **IOException**.

Where is the data file to be opened, SalesBinaryFile.dat? If you just use this filename, it will look in the folder where the exe file is located, that is, \bin\debug beneath the project folder. By using "..\\..\\" before the filename, I am telling it to look in the parent folder of the parent folder, which is the project folder where the file is located.

```
Pgm07bConsole.cs
using System;
using System.Collections;
using System.IO;
...
class Class1   {
```

```
    static void Main(string[] args)    {
ArrayList array = new ArrayList ();
Purchase purchase;
FileStream file;
try {
 file = new FileStream ("..\\..\\SalesBinaryFile.dat",
                         FileMode.Open );
}
catch (FileNotFoundException e) {
 Console.WriteLine("File SalesBinaryFile.dat does not exist " +
                 e);
 return;
}
BinaryReader stream = new BinaryReader (file);
try {
 while (true) {
  purchase = new Purchase ();
  purchase.ItemNumber = stream.ReadInt32 ();
  purchase.Description = stream.ReadString ();
  purchase.Quantity = stream.ReadInt32 ();
  purchase.UnitCost = stream.ReadDouble ();
  array.Add (purchase);
 }
}
catch (EndOfStreamException) {
 stream.Close ();
 file.Close ();
}
catch (IOException e) {
 Console.WriteLine ("Error on input: " + e.ToString());
 stream.Close ();
 file.Close ();
 return;
}

double total = 0;
double average;
Console.WriteLine (
            "                         Acme Daily Sales Report\n");
Console.WriteLine (
" Item     Description        Quantity       Unit        Total");
Console.WriteLine (
" Number                      Purchased      Cost\n");
IEnumerator myEnumerator = array.GetEnumerator();
while (myEnumerator.MoveNext()) {
```

```
      Purchase p = (Purchase) myEnumerator.Current;
      double tot = p.Quantity * p.UnitCost;
      total += tot;
      Console.WriteLine (
            " {0}    {1,-16:S}    {2,3:N}        {3,6:C}       {4,8:C}",
          p.ItemNumber, p.Description, p.Quantity, p.UnitCost, tot);
  }

  Console.WriteLine (
  "                                                    -------");
  Console.WriteLine (
   "                                                  {0,10:C}\n",
   total);
  Console.WriteLine ("Average Order Amount: {0,8:C}",
                  total / array.Count);
 }
}
```

Problems

Problem 7-1—Employee Classes With File Processing Revisited

In Problem 4-1, you developed a series of Employee classes. The problem with the main tester program was that we had to create each instance of the Employee class by calling the ctor and passing it the initial values. We are going to rectify that in this assignment.

1. Create an **ArrayList** to store employees.

2. I have provided a binary file of data for your program to load. The first character of the file is a letter indicating which type of employee this one is: H, S, or P. The base class items come first followed by class specific items. Here is the data types and the output sequence of the data in the binary file. Your program should be able to read in this file. Depending upon how you have defined your data members, you may need to input into some temporary variables and then assign to class members. This is how the data were defined and how they were written to the binary file.

```
private char    type;
private int     ssno;
private string  fname;
private string  lname;
private double  yrpay;
private double  hrlyrate;
private double  hours;
private double  baserate;
private double  bonrate;
private int     quota;
private int     made;
...
os.Write (type);
os.Write (ssno);
os.Write (fname);
os.Write (lname);
if (type == 'S') {
 os.Write (yrpay);
}
else if (type == 'H') {
 os.Write (hrlyrate);
 os.Write (hours);
}
else {
 os.Write (baserate);
 os.Write (bonrate);
 os.Write (quota);
 os.Write (made);
```

```
}
```

3. Use file processing to input all of the employees into the array. Note that you should first input the type letter, then allocate a new appropriate employee based on that letter and then input the data. It is wise to make a base class Input function to input its data and then have the derived class's Input function call the base class first and then finish reading in the fields. Note change this to reading the data from the file.

4. With the array loaded, sort the array on the social security number and display the report. Then, sort the array on the last name and display the report.

Chapter 8—Advanced GUI Features

There are many other features we can easily add to a Windows C# application. We must be able to have menus and dialogs along with many other controls. One workhorse control is the list view which shows multiple lines of data, such as all the records in a data base. The list control is one of the more difficult controls to program, but C# has made it fairly easy compared to C++.

Let's see where we are headed with all these features. Figure 8.1 shows Pgm08aWindows in action. I created a small binary file of the **Purchase** information with which we have been dealing. Initially, the list view is empty. Across the top is the main menu. Under "Files," when "Open" is chosen, the common **OpenFileDialog** is displayed enabling the user to pick the database file to open. When the file is opened, the binary purchase records are inputted into an **ArrayList** and then transferred into the list view control as shown in Figure 8.1.

☐ Purchase Database Program						_ □ ✕
File Modifications Help						

Item Number	Description	Quantity	Cost	Total Cost		▲
☐ 100001	Description 1	2	$21.00	$42.00		
☐ 100002	Description 2	3	$22.00	$66.00		
☐ 100003	Description 3	1	$23.00	$23.00		
☐ 100004	Description 4	2	$24.00	$48.00		
☐ 100005	Description 5	3	$25.00	$75.00		
☐ 100006	Description 6	1	$26.00	$26.00		
☐ 100007	Description 7	2	$27.00	$54.00		
☐ 100008	Description 8	3	$28.00	$84.00		
☐ 100009	Description 9	1	$29.00	$29.00		
☐ 100010	Description 10	2	$20.00	$40.00		
☐ 100011	Description 11	3	$21.00	$63.00		
☐ 100012	Description 12	1	$22.00	$22.00		
☐ 100013	Description 13	2	$23.00	$46.00		
☐ 100014	Description 14	3	$24.00	$72.00		
☐ 100015	Description 15	1	$25.00	$25.00		
☐ 100016	Description 16	2	$26.00	$52.00		
☐ 100017	Description 17	3	$27.00	$81.00		
☐ 100018	Description 18	1	$28.00	$28.00		
☐ 100019	Description 19	2	$29.00	$58.00		
☐ 100020	Description 20	3	$20.00	$60.00		
☐ 100021	Description 21	1	$21.00	$21.00		▼

Figure 8.1 List View After File Open

Notice that the first four columns of the list view come from a Purchase record, but the last column is a calculated result. Further, notice that a checkbox appears to the left of each row. The check boxes make a very simple way for the user to select one or more rows for modifications. Yes, we could implement the standard multiselect operations, but that is a harder feature to add as we begin with this complex control.

This list view is in "Details" or report mode. A list view can also be in "Large Icon," "Small Icon," and "List" modes, depending upon your needs. With a database record display, details mode makes the most sense.

Under the Modifications Menu, the user can add new purchases to the database, update check marked purchases, and delete check marked purchases. If the user makes any changes, then if they attempt to terminate the application without saving those changes, a MessageBox appears querying them about unsaved data loss.

If you think about how one could implement the add and update process, it is clear that we need to display an Add Purchase Dialog box and an Update Purchase Dialog box to the user. Thus, we can see how to create our own dialogs.

Thus, there is quite a lot of new features in this application. Plus, I added another, separate .cs files for the classes. Figure 8.2 shows the Project Class View window.

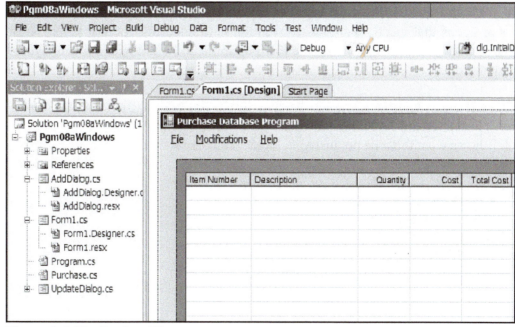

Figure 8.2 The Project View

Menus

Menus are easy to add to a form. Simply drag the MenuStrip icon from the Windows Forms of the Toolbox onto the application form and drop at the top left corner of the form. When you click on it up at the top, boxes appear saying "Type Here." Whatever you type in, becomes the text of that menu item.

Some terminology. A menu item is a single entity that represents some action to be performed, such as Open a file or Add a New Purchase. Menu items are normally grouped into a larger Popup menu which is displayed on the main menu bar, which goes across the top of the form window.

When deciding what popup menus to have, try to maintain the look and feel of other Windows applications. That way, your users will have a much easier time learning how to use your application. If there is to be a File popup menu, it appears first on the far left of the menu bar. Help is always the last popup menu. Others lie in between.

Of course, there can be popup menus within popup menus. It can become as complex as the application requires.

Each menu should have a hot key which is a letter pressed in conjunction with the Alt key that fires or opens that menu. Windows convention is to underline the hot letter. So on the File popup menu, if the user pressed Alt-F, the File popup menu would open up displaying the menu items in that group.

To tell the system what the hot letter is to be, precede that letter in the text with an & character. Thus, to create the File popup menu text, I actually typed in the "Type here" box, &File. Figure 8.3 shows what this File popup menu looks like when it is activated either by a mouse click on that menu or by Alt-F.

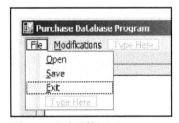

Figure 8.3 File Menu

Figure 8.4 shows the Modifications popup.

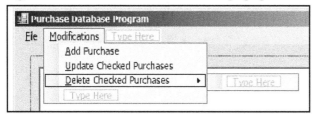

Figure 8.4 Modifications Menu

The first action is to setup the menus the way you want them to appear. Figure 8.5 shows the "Type here" messages when you are editing the main menu in design view.

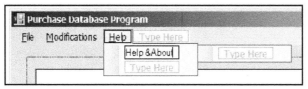

Figure 8.5 Help Menu

The second action is to tie to each menu item a function to be called when that menu item is chosen by the user. Note the functions are tied to menu items, not popup menus. As you would expect, you right click on each menu item and choose Properties.

Each menu item can also have a shortcut key, which the user can press instead of using the mouse. If you use these, available on the Properties page, be sure to use the normal ones that users would expect, such as Ctrl-O for Open and Ctrl-S for Save. Figure 8.6 shows that I have chosen Ctrl-B for the Help About item. This is entered in the **ShortcutKeys** property. Also add the text in the **ShortcutKeyDisplayString**, so that it is shown beside the menu item. Add a **ToolTipText** message to be shown when the mouse is over this menu item.

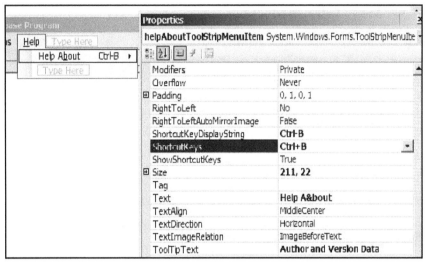

Figure 8.6 Set Shortcut Keys, Display String, and Tool Tip Text

Next, we tie the selection of a menu item with the function to call. If you double click a menu item, a function is automatically created for you. However, its name is usually awfully long and cumbersome and not too indicative of its meaning. Usually, programmers call these functions OnXXX, such as OnFileOpen, for example. To use your own function name, choose Properties on that menu item and then click on the lightening bolt to get to the messages this item can fire. In the Click text box, enter your desired name for the function, Figure 8.7.

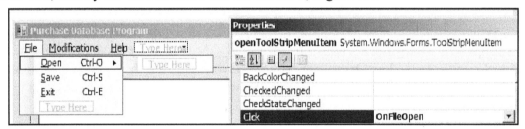

Figure 8.7 Entering the Function to Call When Open Is Chosen

There are some additional properties that a menu item can have. One is the ability to display check mark beside the menu item under some circumstance or not under others. Experiment with these additional effects.

Adding Additional cs Files

Next, I chose File-Add New Item and chose Class and entered Purchase.cs. Then I copied our existing Purchase class exactly as it was previously. There are no changes in it. It encapsulates the Item Number, Description, Quantity, and Unit Cost. When we go to add a new dialog class, it is automatically going to be in a separate cs file.

The List View Control and File Open and Save

Okay. Let's tackle the hardest part of the new implementation effects, the list view control in Details mode. I put a simple panel on the form first and dropped the list view control on top of the pane for a better visual appearance. One drags a list view control from the tool box onto the form and resizes as desires.

Look back to Figure 8.1 once more and notice some details about the control in use. It has five columns and at the top of each column is a button like heading, called a **ColumnHeader** control. One of the very first actions is to set some critical properties, and the number of columns and their headers is paramount.

Right click on the form and choose properties. I chose to use the group them into categories. Figure 8.8 shows the key initial settings that I made. The **View** is set to **Details**; the **FullRowSelect** is set to **true** to enable the user to click anywhere on the row to select and highlight all five columns. I also set **CheckBoxes** to **true** to enable the check boxes to appear to the left. In other application, you may have some icon images that are to appear on the left. By making **GridLines** true, when the control is drawn, row and column lines are drawn making it easier to view in my opinion.

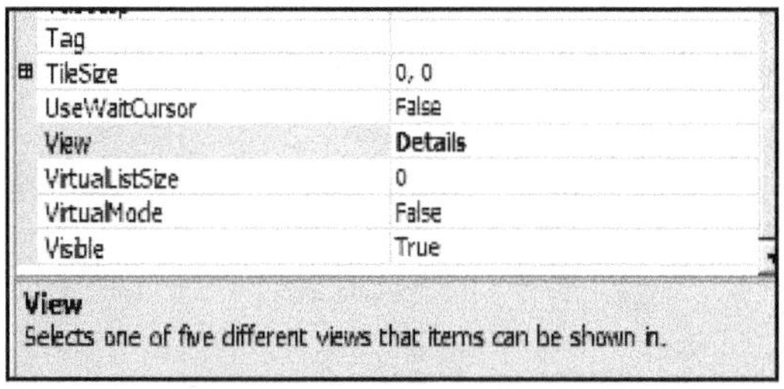

	Tag	
⊞	TileSize	0, 0
	UseWaitCursor	False
	View	**Details**
	VirtualListSize	0
	VirtualMode	False
	Visible	True
View		
Selects one of five different views that items can be shown in.		

Figure 8.8 View Set to Details

Next, we must add in the column heading controls which also defines the number of columns this control will have. Click on the ... box beside **Columns** Listview property. This brings up a dialog in which the **ColumnHeader** controls are added and their properties set. This is shown in Figure 8.9 below.

When it first appears, the controls are all empty. Choose Add and enter the information. In Figure 8.9, I have added five controls. Notice the three key Miscellaneous properties. These are important. One provides the alignment of data, usually left or right. Another provides the actual text of the column heading. The **Width** is the actual width of this column when the control first appears. Make sure that you have them set wide enough initially. Yes, the user can drag the dividers between the headers to resize the columns while the application is running. However, it is far better for the columns to begin at a reasonable width.

One would add in all the headers that are needed at this point in time.

Examine the other properties that could be set. However, I needed no others, especially the Sort property. I need to be able to tie an item in the control back to the Purchase item in the array, so I don't want them sorted.

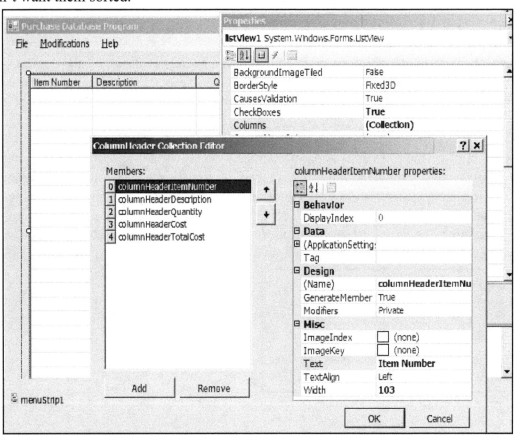

Figure 8.9 Adding the Column Headers

The only event I added was responding to the double click. I thought it would be nice if a double click automatically Updated any selected records.

C# Programming

OnOpen

Next, we must supply the coding to fill the list view with the **Purchase** items contained in the array. When the user chooses the File-Open menu item, we do the following in response. The key lines to add these items into the list view control are in bold face. Also note that we must also clear or empty all **Purchase** items from the array list before we begin adding in the new ones from this file.

```
private void OnOpen(object sender, System.EventArgs e) {
 OpenFileDialog dlg = new OpenFileDialog();
 dlg.CheckFileExists = true;
 dlg.CheckPathExists = true;
 dlg.Filter = "Binary Files (*.dat)|*.dat";
 dlg.InitialDirectory = "..\\..\\";
 if (dlg.ShowDialog() == DialogResult.Cancel) return;
 string filename = dlg.FileName;

 Purchase purchase;
 FileStream file;
 try
 {
  file = new FileStream(filename, FileMode.Open);
 }
 catch (FileNotFoundException ex)
 {
  Console.WriteLine("File " + filename +
                    " does not exist " + ex);
  return;
 }
 BinaryReader stream = new BinaryReader(file);
```

With the file opened, empty the existing data from the array and then input the file of records. Allocate a new Purchase object and try to input it. If it is successful, add it to the array. If it is not successful, catch the errors and handle them.

```
 array.Clear();
 try
 {
  while (true)
  {
   purchase = new Purchase();
   purchase.ItemNumber = stream.ReadInt32();
   purchase.Description = stream.ReadString();
   purchase.Quantity = stream.ReadInt32();
   purchase.UnitCost = stream.ReadDouble();
   array.Add(purchase);
  }
 }
```

```
catch (EndOfStreamException)
{
  stream.Close();
  file.Close();
}
catch (IOException ex)
{
  Console.WriteLine("Error on input: " + ex.ToString());
  stream.Close();
  file.Close();
  return;
}
```

Now set the modified flag to false, indicating the data has not yet been changed. Remove all items in the list view. Next, iterate through the array and add each one to the list view.

```
modified = false;
this.listViewPurchases.Items.Clear();
IEnumerator myEnumerator = array.GetEnumerator();
while (myEnumerator.MoveNext())
{
  Purchase p = (Purchase)myEnumerator.Current;
  double tot = p.Quantity * p.UnitCost;
  ListViewItem item =
                new ListViewItem(p.ItemNumber.ToString(), 0);
  item.SubItems.Add(p.Description);
  item.SubItems.Add(p.Quantity.ToString());
  item.SubItems.Add(String.Format("{0,8:C}", p.UnitCost));
  item.SubItems.Add(String.Format("{0,8:C}", tot));
  this.listViewPurchases.Items.Add(item);
}
}
```

The first action is to call the **Items.Clear** function. The **Items** represents a collection of all the items stored in the list view. The **Clear** function removes all the items currently in the control.

The class **ListViewItem** encapsulates an item to be stored in the list view control. When there are more than one column of data in a list view, the second and subsequent columns are known as **SubItems**, normally. That is, the offset 0 or column 0 is usually the first field of a row. Here, it is given the text string of the **ItemNumber**. The remaining **SubItems** are added in the order they appear by using **SubItems.Add** and passing it the text string to be displayed. Notice that I chose to also nicely format these currency fields. The last **SubItem** is actually a calculated result field and is not even in the **Purchase** record.

Finally, the **Items.Add** function is called passing the complete **ListViewItem** instance.

When this loop is finished, all of the purchase data appears in the list view and the control handles all necessary scrolling and column resizing.

OnFileSave

To save the data to a binary file, first bring up the common file save dialog and get the name of the file to use. Next, create the file. If all is okay, then get an enumerator into the array and use it to get at each record in the array and save its data.

```csharp
private void OnFileSave(object sender, EventArgs e)
 {
  if (array.Count == 0) return;
  SaveFileDialog dlg = new SaveFileDialog();
  dlg.CheckPathExists = true;
  dlg.Filter = "Binary Files (*.dat)|*.dat";
  dlg.InitialDirectory = "..\\..\\";
  if (dlg.ShowDialog() == DialogResult.Cancel) return;
  string filename = dlg.FileName;
  FileStream file;
  try
  {
   file = new FileStream(filename, FileMode.Create);
  }
  catch (FileNotFoundException)
  {
   MessageBox.Show("File " + filename + "does not exist",
        "Error", MessageBoxButtons.OK, MessageBoxIcon.Error);
   return;
  }
  BinaryWriter stream = new BinaryWriter(file);
  IEnumerator myEnumerator = array.GetEnumerator();
  while (myEnumerator.MoveNext())
  {
   Purchase p = (Purchase)myEnumerator.Current;
   stream.Write(p.ItemNumber);
   stream.Write(p.Description);
   stream.Write(p.Quantity);
   stream.Write(p.UnitCost);
  }
  stream.Close();
  file.Close();
  modified = false;
```

```
}
```

OnUpdate Process

The **OnUpdate** method which is called either by the menu Modifications-Update Checkmarked Items or by a double click within the list view control itself. Herein lies the hardest portion of the coding.

The first action is to obtain a list collection of all checkmarked items. The method **CheckedItems** returns this list of **ListViewItems** for us. Now it is a simple matter to iterate through each item in this list and update it. The **Checked** property of the **ListViewItem** is true if it is checked. If one is checked, we can update it. However, first we must have access to the **Purchase** information to which this item is referring. The **Text** property returns the text the item contains. It is always the main item text, not the subitem's text. In this case, it is the **ItemNumber** that is being returned. I convert it back into an integer and call a look up function, **FindPurchase** which finds this purchase item in the array.

```
private Purchase FindPurchase(int itemnum)
{
  IEnumerator myEnumerator = array.GetEnumerator();
  while (myEnumerator.MoveNext())
  {
   Purchase p = (Purchase)myEnumerator.Current;
   if (p.ItemNumber == itemnum) return p;
  }
  return null;
}

private void OnUpdate(object sender, System.EventArgs e) {
 ListView.CheckedListViewItemCollection list =
                    this.listViewPurchases.CheckedItems;
 foreach (ListViewItem lv in list) {
  if (lv.Checked == true) {
   int index = lv.Index;
   int itemnum = Int32.Parse (lv.Text);
   Purchase p = FindPurchase (itemnum);
   if (p != null) {
    UpdateDialog dlg = new UpdateDialog ();
    dlg.ItemNumber = p.ItemNumber.ToString();
    dlg.Description = p.Description;
    dlg.Quantity = p.Quantity.ToString();
    dlg.UnitCost = p.UnitCost.ToString();
    if (dlg.ShowDialog (this) == DialogResult.Yes) {
```

170

```
        p.ItemNumber = Int32.Parse (dlg.ItemNumber);
        p.Description = dlg.Description;
        p.Quantity = Int32.Parse (dlg.Quantity);
        p.UnitCost = Double.Parse (dlg.UnitCost);
        double tot = p.Quantity * p.UnitCost;
        lv.Text = dlg.ItemNumber;
        ListViewItem item =
                   new ListViewItem (p.ItemNumber.ToString(), 0);
        item.SubItems.Add(p.Description);
        item.SubItems.Add(p.Quantity.ToString());
        item.SubItems.Add(String.Format ("{0,8:C}", p.UnitCost));
        item.SubItems.Add(String.Format ("{0,8:C}", tot));
        this.listViewPurchases.Items.RemoveAt (index);
        this.listViewPurchases.Items.Insert (index, item);
        modified = true;
      }
    }
  }
 }
}
```

Ignore for a moment the coding to create and run the UpdateDialog. Just assume that we have the revised Purchase information available to us. We must store the revised information into the array an get the list view's corresponding row of data replaced with the new information.

Unfortunately, we cannot just replace the strings and substrings. Instead, we must remove that old row and insert a new **ListViewItem** collection representing the new data in its place. This is done by creating a new instance of **ListViewItem** and adding in the four subitems as shown above.

The two key methods are **RemoveAt** and **InsertAt**. First, we remove at this index and then insert at this index the new instance.

Making Dialog Classes

The next step is to create the two dialog classes, one for updating and one for adding. Actually, you could make just one dialog and use it for both, but I wanted to show a couple dialog classes.

To add a new dialog class to your project, choose File-Add New Item and choose Windows Form, since a dialog is actually a window. If you fail to enter a good name for the dialog, you can right click on the form and rename it to something suitable, such as UpdateDialog. At this point, it is just another Windows form, and does not behave as a modal dialog.

We must change the **FormBorderStyle** to **FixedDialog** in order for this form to behave as a dialog should. This is shown in Figure 8.10 below. Also change the **Text** property to what you want to appear in the dialog's caption.

There are many other properties you could experiment with, including the automatic supplying of Ok and Cancel buttons. However, I am going to add in my own pair of buttons to show you how to hook into the dialog interface.

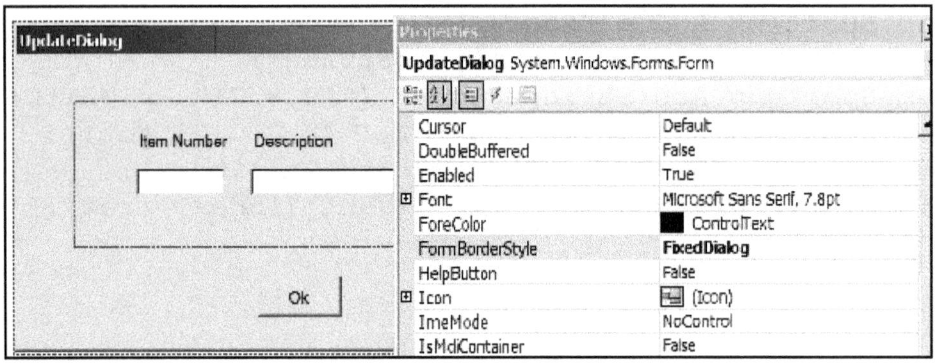

Figure 8.10 Changing the Form to Fixed Dialog

Next, one would add in all of the dialog controls that are needed. Here I used a copy-paste trick. We have already had a control to allow the user to enter this Purchase information in WindowsApplication03. So I opened up another instance of Visual Studio and opened that project. Then I selected the entire group of controls and did Edit-Copy. Then, back in our current project, I did Edit-Paste. Presto, instant dialog controls. I then also copied over the properties to set them.

Finally, I added a pair of buttons, Ok and Cancel. Next, I choose Properties on each button and added a method to be called when the button is clicked: **OnUpdateOk** and **OnUpdateCancel**.

Now I need these two buttons to perform just like the Ok and Cancel buttons of an ordinary dialog box. This is easily done by just setting the form property **DialogResult** to either **Yes** or **No.**

```
private void OnUpdateOk(object sender, System.EventArgs e) {
   DialogResult = DialogResult.Yes;
}

private void OnUpdateCancel(object sender, System.EventArgs e) {
   DialogResult = DialogResult.No;
}
```

Here is the complete **UpdateDialog** coding. Notice I provide properties to retrieve and set the actual text boxes of the dialog.

```
using System;
using System.Collections.Generic;
using System.ComponentModel;
```

```
using System.Data;
using System.Drawing;
using System.Linq;
using System.Text;
using System.Windows.Forms;

namespace Pgm08aWindows
{
 public partial class UpdateDialog : Form
 {
  public UpdateDialog()
  {
   InitializeComponent();
  }
  public string ItemNumber
  {
   get
   {
    return this.itemNumber.Text;
   }
   set
   {
    this.itemNumber.Text = value;
   }
  }
  public string Description
  {
   get
   {
    return this.description.Text;
   }
   set
   {
    this.description.Text = value;
   }
  }
  public string Quantity
  {
   get
   {
    return this.quantity.Text;
   }
   set
   {
    this.quantity.Text = value;
   }
```

```
  }
 public string UnitCost
 {
  get
  {
   return this.unitCost.Text;
  }
  set
  {
   this.unitCost.Text = value;
  }
 }

 private void OnUpdateOk(object sender, System.EventArgs e)
 {
  DialogResult = DialogResult.Yes;
 }

 private void OnUpdateCancel(object sender, System.EventArgs e)
 {
  DialogResult = DialogResult.No;
 }
 }
}
```

The **AddDialog** is totally parallel. See the program on disk.

Now how do we create and run these new dialog classes? We construct an instance, set its properties which fill its controls with the initial values, and call **ShowDialog**, just like the common file dialogs.

```
     UpdateDialog dlg = new UpdateDialog ();
     dlg.ItemNumber = p.ItemNumber.ToString();
     dlg.Description = p.Description;
     dlg.Quantity = p.Quantity.ToString();
     dlg.UnitCost = p.UnitCost.ToString();
     if (dlg.ShowDialog (this) == DialogResult.Yes) {
      p.ItemNumber = Int32.Parse (dlg.ItemNumber);
      p.Description = dlg.Description;
      p.Quantity = Int32.Parse (dlg.Quantity);
      p.UnitCost = Double.Parse (dlg.UnitCost);
      double tot = p.Quantity * p.UnitCost;
```

Notice that the key design feature is that the dialog class provided member properties to get and set the various controls. So we allocate an instance, call the set property functions, and can then run the dialog. When it completes, we use the get property functions to retrieve the data from the

174

dialog controls.

Here is how the **AddDialog** is called. I highlighted the list view coding.

```
private void OnAdd(object sender, System.EventArgs e) {
 AddDialog dlg = new AddDialog ();
 if (dlg.ShowDialog (this) == DialogResult.Yes) {
  Purchase p = new Purchase ();
  p.ItemNumber = Int32.Parse (dlg.ItemNumber);
  p.Description = dlg.Description;
  p.Quantity = Int32.Parse (dlg.Quantity);
  p.UnitCost = Double.Parse (dlg.UnitCost);
  double tot = p.Quantity * p.UnitCost;
  array.Add (p);
  ListViewItem item =
                new ListViewItem (p.ItemNumber.ToString(), 0);
  item.SubItems.Add(p.Description);
  item.SubItems.Add(p.Quantity.ToString());
  item.SubItems.Add(String.Format ("{0,8:C}", p.UnitCost));
  item.SubItems.Add(String.Format ("{0,8:C}", tot));
  this.listViewPurchases.Items.Add (item);
  modified = true;
 }
}
```

Handling the Delete Operation

Deletions are easier to handle. Again, acquire a collection of the **CheckedItems** and iterate through it. Retrieve the Index property of each item and convert its Text into the ItemNumber integer. FindPurchase returns the matching item in the array list. But before just deleting them, we should prompt the user and ask if it is okay to go ahead and delete these. A message box is idea.

```
private void OnDelete(object sender, System.EventArgs e) {
 ListView.CheckedListViewItemCollection list =
                          this.listViewPurchases.CheckedItems;
 foreach (ListViewItem lv in list) {
  if (lv.Checked == true) {
   int index = lv.Index;
   int itemnum = Int32.Parse (lv.Text);
   Purchase p = FindPurchase (itemnum);
   if (p != null) {
    string show = p.ItemNumber.ToString() + " " +
              p.Description + " " + p.Quantity.ToString() +
              " " + String.Format ("{0,8:C}", p.UnitCost);
    if (MessageBox.Show (show,
```

```
            "Do you really want to delete this purchase?",
            MessageBoxButtons.YesNo,
            MessageBoxIcon.Information) == DialogResult.Yes) {
      this.listViewPurchases.Items.RemoveAt (index);
      array.RemoveAt (index);
      modified = true;
        }
      }
    }
  }
}
```

If the user clicks Ok, then since we have its index and since the list is in the same order as the array, we can call the **RemoveAt** methods of both classes to remove this purchase item.

Tracking Modified Status

Continually, whenever any change is made, our bool modified must be set to true. This way, when the user is about to quit, we can prompt them about unsaved data. We add the **OnClosing** function this way. Notice if the user wants to save it, I set **Cancel** to true, which avoids closing the application. The user can then choose the Save menu item.

```
private void OnClosing(object sender, FormClosingEventArgs e)
  {
   if (modified)
   {
    if (MessageBox.Show(
       "Do you want to quit and not save the changes?",
       "Changes have not been saved",
       MessageBoxButtons.YesNo, MessageBoxIcon.Information)
       != DialogResult.Yes)
    {
     e.Cancel = true;
    }
   }
  }
```

Finally, we need to make our menu item "Exit" actually exit the application. This is done by calling **Application.Exit**. This will in turn call **OnClosing**.

```
private void OnExit(object sender, EventArgs e) {
  Application.Exit ();
}
```

Other Controls

Two other controls you should also master are a simple list box and a combo box (which represents a text box and a list box merged) because these are very common controls. Each of these has an array of strings that are being stored and displayed.

The tree view is also sometimes used. The Explorer window is actually a tree control on the left in which you pick a drive and folder with a list view on the right that displays the contents of the selected folder on the left.

And there are many other controls available from the tool box. If you are interested in any of these, use the Help system. Begin by finding the class description. Then take the link to "List Member Functions" to see the available functions. Usually, on one of these help pages are examples of how to create and use these controls.

You really do need to get good at looking things up if you are going to become successful in writing C# applications.

Problems

Problem 8-1—Employee Classes GUI

In previous problems, you developed a series of Employee classes and read them in from a binary file of employee data. In this assignment we are going to write a fancy Windows application to display the data and perform a weekly payroll calculation.

The File menu should contain at least a Load Employees File and a Save Employees File menu items. The Edit menu should contain Add, Update and Delete menu items. The Actions menu should include Display Weekly Payroll. The Help should contain Help About.

Construct a list view that contains columns for each possible value but not the final total pay field. Have one column indicate which kind of employee this one is, such as Piece Rate. Obviously when an employee is displayed, not all of the columns will contain data for this employee.

Implement the two file menu items.

Implement an Add employee dialog and, if Ok is chosen, add the new employee to the list view. Implement the Update and Delete menu items in any manner you desire. Somehow, the user must be able to change employee data and to remove an employee. Careful about switching between an hourly worker and a salaried worker and a piece rate worker.

When the application terminates, if the data has been changed and the file not saved, prompt the user about the situation and handle it accordingly.

When the Display Weekly Payroll item is chosen, run a dialog that displays the Weekly Payroll report in a manner of your choosing.

Chapter 9—Graphics

It's time to examine the many graphical drawing capabilities of a Windows form. Further, we can now write reasonable graphical games which often need the graphical facilities of Windows. The game example is called Balls, in which the player controls the movement of one moving ball. The objective it to hit as many of the other balls as possible in the allotted time span of the game. Figure 9.1 shows a game in progress.

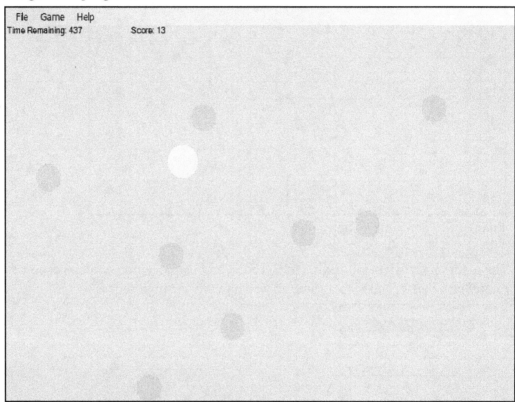

Figure 9.1 The Balls Game in Progress

When the game is done, the top ten scores are saved in a file. If the player's score is high enough to rank in the top ten scores, a dialog appears asking for the player's name, Figure 9.2.

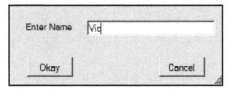

Figure 9.2 Enter Name Dlg

Then the High Scores dialog is shown. This dialog can also be shown from the main menu item Game-View High Scores. It is shown in Figure 9.3.

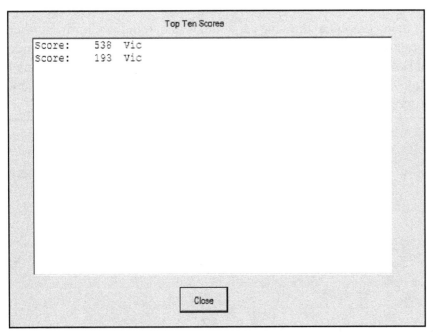

Figure 9.3 The Game's High Scores

The main menu offers File-Exit, Help-About, and Game popup, which is shown in Figure 9.4. One can Start, Pause, and Stop a game as well as view the high scores.

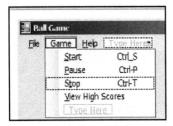

Figure 9.4 Game Menu

This sample uses a timer to track the time remaining for the player, updating it on the screen as well as the player's current score as the game progresses. The player controls the ball with the four arrow keys, adding an impulse of velocity to his or her yellow ball specified by the direction of the arrow key. Note random numbers are used for each ball's initial position and velocity.

When a ball collides with another, it is an elastic collision. Based upon the angle of collision, some or even all of a ball's momentum can be transferred to the other ball, resulting in a ball halting all motion, much like a game of pool. All balls have the same weight and no momentum is lost in any collision.

In order to make the collisions realistic, I had to employ a bit of physics of motion. While the actual physics and math behind these collisions is key to the realism of the game, such is not important to our discussion of C#. If you are interested in learning more about the physics, please read my Game Programming Theory ebook.

The Ball Game Form

The starting point is the actual main form itself. It has the main menu strip at the top. The entire surface of the form becomes the playing field. In order to display anything upon the client area of the form, we must have an instance of the Graphics class, which encapsulates the GDI drawing surface.

The usual way to obtain an instance is responding to the Paint message that is sent to the form when Windows determines that the form or part of it needs to be re-shown. In the Properties of the form, click on the lightening bolt to get to the messages sent to the form. We want to override the Paint message. I called the function OnPaint as shown in Figure 9.5.

Figure 9.5 Setting the OnPaint Function

The only other message or event to which I need to respond is the pressing of an arrow key. When a key is pressed, three messages or events are sent. The first is sent when the key is pressed down, The second occurs when the key is released. The third is then sent indicating the key and its potential repeat count. The three events are shown in Figure 9.6, where I added an event for the KeyDown event.

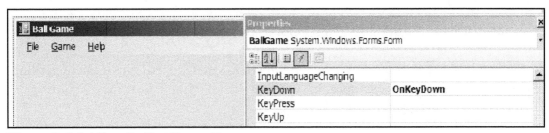

Figure 9.6 Adding OnKeyDown Event

181

In this program, I only need to know if an arrow key has been pressed. Thus, I respond only to this one message for faster game control. This is about all to the Design View, very simple.

In the form's operational coding, there are three key new actions to study: painting, the keyboard interface, and the timer. Let's begin with the timer actions and generating random numbers.

To use a timer, one must allocate a **static** instance of the **Timer**. Timers must be static instances.

```
static System.Windows.Forms.Timer myTimer =
                           new System.Windows.Forms.Timer();
```

Next, you must allocate a new event handler which will be called every time the time interval has passed.

```
    myTimer.Tick += new EventHandler(TimerEventProcessor);
```

When you want to start the timer, you must set the desired interval in milliseconds (1/1000 second). Then, call the **Start** method and the timer is active.

```
    myTimer.Interval = 10;
    // Sets the timer interval to .01 seconds.
    myTimer.Start();
```

When the interval elapses, the system calls your event function. Here, you can respond to the time interval having passed. At some point, you can stop the timer by calling the **Stop** method. Notice that the event handler is a member function, not a static function. Thus, you have the this parameter or instance data available for your use.

```
    private void TimerEventProcessor(Object myObject,
                                       EventArgs myEventArgs)
    {
...
      myTimer.Stop();
    }
```

To create random numbers, you need an instance of the Random class.

```
private Random random;
```

When you allocate one, the default constructor seeds the number generator with the current time on the computer, ensuring a different set of numbers with each launching of the program.

```
    random = new Random(); // time dependent seed value used
```

To obtain the next random number, call the **Next** method, passing it the upper limit of the desired range of numbers, for example 50.

```
    int vx = random.Next(50);
```

The Ball class encapsulates a ball, both the opponents and the player's ball. C# provides some handy classes to help encapsulate drawing data: **Point** and **Rectangle**. The **Point** members are integers, **X** and **Y**. The **Rectangle** members are integers, **Left**, **Top**, **Right**, and **Bottom**.

Further, we must know the actual dimensions of the client area of our form. Why? As a ball moves around, we must "bounce" off of the sides of the client area. Otherwise, the ball would simply disappear from the screen. The form's **ClientRectangle** contains the current size of the form and is updated whenever the form is resized. Unfortunately, this size includes the menu bar. To keep things simple, I just added 25 pixels to the Top dimension to avoid having a ball partially disappear beneath the menu bar at the top of the form.

Timer specifics for this game are a bit more involved than just setting a timer. I need to start, pause, and stop a game. These are menu commands. I used a bool to track whether or not a game is in progress, gameRunning. The interval is set to 10 milliseconds, but that would create a total count of 5000 for the game. Hence, I lowered the count for the game to 500 and decremented it every tenth time that the timer went off. If Pause Game is selected, I set a bool pausing to true and stop the timer. When the user chooses to continue the game, I set pausing to false and restart the timer again.

Here is the start of the BallGameForm file with the key items highlighted in boldface.

```
using System;
using System.Collections.Generic;
using System.ComponentModel;
using System.Data;
using System.Drawing;
using System.Linq;
using System.Text;
using System.Windows.Forms;
using System.Collections;

namespace Pgm09aWindows
{
  public partial class BallGame : Form
  {
    static System.Windows.Forms.Timer myTimer =
                              new System.Windows.Forms.Timer();
    static int hundredths;
    static bool pausing = false;
    static int endCount = 500;
    static double deltaTime = .1;
```

The **deltaTime** is passed to the Ball class to indicate the amount of time that has elapsed so that a ball can determine its new position, based on its current velocity. There are eight opponent balls stored in the array **balls** and one player ball stored in **ball**.

```
const int MAXBALLS = 8;
```

```
private Ball[] balls;
private Ball ball;
private Rectangle client;
private bool gameRunning;
private Random random;

 public BallGame()
 {
  InitializeComponent();
  myTimer.Tick += new EventHandler(TimerEventProcessor);

  gameRunning = false;
  random = new Random(); // time dependent seed value used
 }

 private void OnHelpAbout(object sender, EventArgs e)
 {
  MessageBox.Show("Written by Vic Broquard Feb 2009",
              "Ball Game Program Version 1.0",
       MessageBoxButtons.OK, MessageBoxIcon.Information);
 }

 private void OnExit(object sender, EventArgs e)
 {
  Application.Exit();
 }
```

The MakeBalls function allocates a new set of Ball instances, eight opponents and one player. Random numbers are used for the object's location and velocity. However, a random number is also used to determine the initial direction of the x and y velocity component.

C# provides a **Color** class to encapsulate a color. It has a large number of predefined colors available and one can make your own color as well by setting the red, green, and blue intensities. Here, I chose to use **Yellow** for the player's ball and **SkyBlue** for the opponent's balls.

```
 private void MakeBalls()
 {
  balls = new Ball[MAXBALLS];
  for (int i = 0; i < MAXBALLS; i++)
  {
   int px = random.Next(client.Right);
   int py = random.Next(client.Bottom);
   int vx = random.Next(50);
   int vy = random.Next(50);
   int plusMinusX = random.Next(1);
   int plusMinusY = random.Next(1);
```

```
    if (plusMinusX == 0) vx = -vx;
    if (plusMinusY == 0) vy = -vy;
    balls[i] = new Ball(20, new Point(px, py), Color.SkyBlue,
                        new Point(vx, vy));
  }
}

private void MakePlayerBall()
{
  int px = random.Next(client.Right);
  int py = random.Next(client.Bottom);
  int vx = random.Next(50);
  int vy = random.Next(50);
  int plusMinusX = random.Next(1);
  int plusMinusY = random.Next(1);
  if (plusMinusX == 0) vx = -vx;
  if (plusMinusY == 0) vy = -vy;
  ball = new Ball(25, new Point(px, py), Color.Yellow,
                  new Point(vx, vy));
}

private void OnStart(object sender, EventArgs e)
{
  client = new Rectangle(this.ClientRectangle.Left,
                         this.ClientRectangle.Top,
                         this.ClientRectangle.Width,
                         this.ClientRectangle.Height);
  MakeBalls();
  MakePlayerBall();
  pausing = false;
  hundredths = 1;
  endCount = 500;
  myTimer.Interval = 10;
  // Sets the timer interval to .01 seconds.
  myTimer.Start();
  gameRunning = true;
}
```

In **OnStart**, I reacquire the client area of the form, since between games, the user may have altered the window's size. A new set of balls are created with the garbage collector deleting any previous set. The counts are reset and the interval timer started and the game is launched.

When the interval elapses, I increment **hundredths**. To get the objects redisplayed on the screen, I must send the **Paint** event. This is done by telling Windows that the entire client area of the form needs to be repainted. The **Invalidate** function does this, triggering a paint event at this point.

When **hundredths** has gotten to ten, I decrement the time remaining in **endCount**. If **endCount** is at or below zero, the game is over.

```csharp
// This is the method to run when the timer is raised.
private void TimerEventProcessor(Object myObject,
                                 EventArgs myEventArgs)
{
 hundredths++;
 this.Invalidate();
 if (hundredths > 10)
 {
  endCount--;
  hundredths = 1;
 }
 if (endCount <= 0)
 {
  myTimer.Stop();
  gameRunning = false;
  this.OnStop(this, null);
 }
}

private void OnPause(object sender, EventArgs e)
{
 pausing = !pausing;
 if (pausing)
 {
  myTimer.Stop();
  gameRunning = false;
 }
 else
 {
  myTimer.Start();
  gameRunning = true;
 }
}

private void OnStop(object sender, EventArgs e)
{
 myTimer.Stop();
 gameRunning = false;
 ScoresForm dlg = new ScoresForm();
 if (dlg.CheckThisScore(ball.score))
 {
  dlg.ShowDialog();
 }
}
```

When **OnStop** is called, the timer is stopped and the game is no longer running. Now it is time to check the current score to see if it is in the top ten. I allocate an instance of the **ScoresForm** dialog and call a member function **CheckThisScore**. If this current score belongs in the high ten scores, only then do I actually run the dialog and get the player's name and add it to the top ten. We will examine the top ten coding later on.

In **OnPaint**, the **PaintEventArgs** provides us with a reference to the canvas upon which we can draw. The **e.Graphics** returns the desired reference. We must have a **Graphics** reference if we are to do any drawing on the form.

The function to display a string on the screen is DrawString, which requires the string to display, the font to use, a brush with the color to use, and the screen coordinates at which to start the displaying of the string. Thus, I first created a new brush using the SolidBrush function, which is passed the color to be used, here Black. The time remaining is always shown.

However, if the player's ball object is not null, then I also display the current player's score as well. Finally, if the game is running, I first reposition all of the balls. That is, the new positions are calculated, collisions handled, and the player's score updated. To draw a circle, the FillElipse function is used. I use that ball's color for the fill color brush and the drawing rectangle stored in the ball object. If the rectangle is a square, a circle is drawn, that is, a circle is a degenerate ellipse or an ellipse whose two focii are the same point.

```csharp
private void OnPaint(object sender, PaintEventArgs e)
{
 Graphics graphics = e.Graphics;
 SolidBrush textBrush = new SolidBrush(Color.Black);
 graphics.DrawString("Time Remaining: " + endCount, this.Font,
                     textBrush, 0, 25);
 if (ball != null)
 {
  graphics.DrawString("Score: " + ball.score, this.Font,
                      textBrush, 200, 25);
 }
 if (gameRunning)
 {
  RepositionBalls();
  graphics.FillEllipse(new SolidBrush(ball.color), ball.draw);
  for (int i = 0; i < MAXBALLS; i++)
  {
   graphics.FillEllipse(new SolidBrush(balls[i].color),
                        balls[i].draw);
  }
 }
}
```

There are a large number of other drawing functions available. We will look at some of these shortly. Next comes the keyboard interface, here it is extremely simple: respond only to the four arrow keys. The **KeyEventArgs** contain key data about the key being pressed, along with the possible use of the ctrl, alt, and shift keys. The property **KeyValue** contains the key code of the key pressed. Here is where I check for the specific values of the four arrow keys. I simply add or subtract an arbitrary amount, 10, from the ball's velocity X or Y property.

```
private void OnKeyDown(object sender, KeyEventArgs e)
{
 if (gameRunning)
 {
  if (e.KeyValue == 40) // down arrow
  {
   ball.velocity.Y += 10;
  }
  else if (e.KeyValue == 38) // up arrow
  {
   ball.velocity.Y -= 10;
  }
  else if (e.KeyValue == 37) // left arrow
  {
   ball.velocity.X -= 10;
  }
  else if (e.KeyValue == 39) // right arrow
  {
   ball.velocity.X += 10;
  }
 }
}
```

Here is the remainder of the form coding. We will return to the **RepositionBalls** function after we discuss the **Ball** class.

```
private void RepositionBalls()
{
 if (gameRunning)
 {
  ball.Move(deltaTime);
  ball.CheckForScreenCollisions(this.client);
  int i;
  for (i = 0; i < MAXBALLS; i++)
  {
   balls[i].Move(deltaTime);
   balls[i].CheckForScreenCollisions(this.client);
   if (ball.CheckForBallCollision(balls[i]))
   {
    ball.ApplyCollisionImpulse(balls[i]);
```

```
    ball.score++;
    }
  }
  ball.MakeRectangle();
  for (i = 0; i < MAXBALLS; i++)
  {
    for (int j = 0; j < MAXBALLS; j++)
    {
      if (i != j)
      {
        if (balls[i].CheckForBallCollision(balls[j]))
        {
          balls[i].ApplyCollisionImpulse(balls[j]);
        }
      }
    }
    balls[i].MakeRectangle();
  }
  }
}

private void OnViewHighScores(object sender, EventArgs e)
{
  ScoresForm dlg = new ScoresForm();
  dlg.ShowDialog();
}
}
}
```

The Ball Class

The Ball class started out simple, storing the radius of the ball, its color, the location of its center, and its current velocity in the x and y directions. To simplify its drawing, I store the drawing rectangle coordinates in a Rectangle instance. Each period of time, the velocity times the time interval gives how much the ball has moved in the x and y directions.

xnew = xold + velocityX * time

ynew = yold + velocityY * time

where the velocity components could be negative, indicating going up or left.

However, this did not yield sufficient realism to the game. In fact, collisions are key to the game. Thus, a bit of physics and math must be added to the ball. At once, new problems develop since velocity and other items needed for collision analysis are actually vectors, that is a magnitude and a direction. In comes vector mathematics at once. Again, you are not responsible for any of this physics or math, though I will give such a short discussion. The vector math must be done using doubles, not integers. Hence, I created a simple Vector class that handles just the very few operations that I need here for this problem. It is not by any means a complete **Vector** class. See the Game Theory Programming for a complete **Vector** class if you are interested in this aspect. The data members of the **Vector** class are three doubles, **x**, **y**, and **z**, which hold the respective positive or negative values that define the vector.

The Ball class stores one Vector instance for convenience, the collisionNormal. If you draw a line from the center of one ball to the center of the colliding ball, the collision normal is a vector that is perpendicular to that line, where the two balls touch. The double velocityClosing is the speed at which the two balls hit. If two balls traveling at the same speed hit each other square on, the closing velocity is twice that of a single ball. Further, they will fly off in exactly the opposite directions that they were traveling and at the same speed. Play some pool and see all of the collision possibilities in action.

Ball.cs
```
using System;
using System.Collections.Generic;
using System.Linq;
using System.Text;
using System.Windows.Forms;
using System.Drawing;

namespace Pgm09aWindows
{
 class Ball
 {
  public int radius;
  public Point loc;
  public Color color;
  public Point velocity;
  public Rectangle draw;
  public Vector collisionNormal;
  public double velocityClosing;
  public int score;
```

The **score** member is only used in the player's ball. The **Move** function adds velocity times time to the current location to obtain the new location in the x-y plane. **MakeRectangle** counstructs the drawing rectangle for **OnPaint**.
```
  public Ball(int r, Point l, Color c, Point v)
  {
   radius = r;
   loc = l;
   color = c;
```

```
 velocity = v;
 MakeRectangle();
 score = 0;
}

public void Move(double dt)
{
 loc.X += (int)(velocity.X * dt + .5);
 loc.Y += (int)(velocity.Y * dt + .5);
}

public void MakeRectangle()
{
 draw = new Rectangle(loc.X - radius, loc.Y - radius,
                      radius * 2, radius * 2);
}
```

After the ball is moved to its new location, a check must be made to see if it has reached the edges of the client area. If so, it is put back onto the screen such that all of the ball is visible and the corresponding velocity that caused it to hit that side is negated, indicating a pure bounce off of the side. The 25 pixel amount added to the top accounts for the height of the menu strip, which is unfortunately included in the client area.

```
public void CheckForScreenCollisions(Rectangle screen)
{
 if (loc.X - radius <= screen.Left)
 {
  loc.X = screen.Left + radius;
  velocity.X = -velocity.X;
 }
 else if (loc.X + radius >= screen.Right)
 {
  loc.X = screen.Right - radius;
  velocity.X = -velocity.X;
 }
 if (loc.Y - radius <= screen.Top + 25)
 {
  loc.Y = screen.Top + radius + 25;
  velocity.Y = -velocity.Y;
 }
 else if (loc.Y + radius >= screen.Bottom)
 {
  loc.Y = screen.Bottom - radius;
  velocity.Y = -velocity.Y;
 }
}
```

To check for a collision with another ball, calculate how far apart the two centers are, the square root of the sum of the differences of their x and y distances. If this distance is less than the sum of the two radii, the balls have collided.

```
public bool CheckForBallCollision(Ball b)
{
  double dx = b.loc.X - loc.X;
  double dy = b.loc.Y - loc.Y;
  double distance = Math.Sqrt (dx*dx + dy*dy);
  return distance < b.radius + radius;
}
```

To find the collision point vector, subtract the current center locations. If they are almost zero, the two balls are on top of each other. Use either one's location, but add in the radius to the surface. Usually, this is not the case. Calculate the slope of the difference, m. Use the slope intercept form of the equation of a line to obtain the new vector to return.

```
public Vector GetCollisionPoint (Ball e) {
  double x = loc.X - e.loc.X;
  double y = loc.Y - e.loc.Y;
  if (Math.Abs (x) < .0000001) {
   return new Vector (loc.X, loc.Y + radius, 0);
  }
  else {
   double m = y / x;
   double x3 = loc.X + Math.Sqrt (radius *radius / (m * m + 1));
   double y3 = loc.Y + m * (x3 - loc.X);
   return new Vector (x3, y3, 0);
  }
}

public Vector LocToVector () {
  return new Vector (loc.X, loc.Y, 0);
}

public Vector VelocityToVector () {
  return new Vector (velocity.X, velocity.Y, 0);
}
```

The above two functions merely convert the location and velocity to a vector, converting integers into doubles. To apply the collision exchange of momentum or impulse, calculate the relative velocity vector and the location of collision vector, normalized to a unity vector. Taking the dot product of the relative velocity and the normalized position of collison vector gives us the scalar closing velocity. If less than zero, a collision has occurred and now calcuate the exchange of velocities between the two balls. Here all collisions are fully elastic, no energy is lost during the collisions, so the coefficient of restitution is unity. The mass of the balls are the same and here chosen to be one unit. The +.5 being added to the final values handles rounding from a double into an integer.

```csharp
public void ApplyCollisionImpulse (Ball e) {
Vector relativeVelocity =
        new Vector (VelocityToVector() - e.VelocityToVector());
Vector norm = new Vector (LocToVector() - e.LocToVector());
norm.Normalize ();
collisionNormal = e.collisionNormal = norm;
velocityClosing = e.velocityClosing = relativeVelocity * norm;
if (velocityClosing < 0)
{
 // is a collision
 double J = -(2 /* + CoefficientOfRestitution*/) *
            velocityClosing / 2; //(1. / mass + 1. / e.mass);
 Vector v = VelocityToVector () + J * collisionNormal;
 // ignoring the division by / mass; assume equal ball masses
 Vector ev = e.VelocityToVector () -J * collisionNormal;
 // ignoring the division by / e.mass;
 velocity.X = (int)(v.x + .5);
 velocity.Y = (int)(v.y + .5);
 e.velocity.X = (int)(ev.x + .5);
 e.velocity.Y = (int)(ev.y + .5);
 }
 }
 }
}
```

Next, let's look at the BallGameForm's **RepositionBalls** function from above. The delta time interval is passed to the ball's Move function so that the ball is moved to its new position based on that small interval of time. Next, collisions with the edges of the client area are checked for and handled. Then, all of the balls are similarly moved and screen edge collisions handled. Now I check to see if the player's ball hits any of the opponent's balls and if so, apply the exchange of impulse or momentum and increment the player's score. Finally, each individual opponent ball is checked for collisions with other opponents and handled. The **MakeRectangle** call finalizes the resultant new position of each ball.

```csharp
private void RepositionBalls()
{
 if (gameRunning)
 {
  ball.Move(deltaTime);
  ball.CheckForScreenCollisions(this.client);
  int i;
  for (i = 0; i < MAXBALLS; i++)
  {
   balls[i].Move(deltaTime);
```

193

```
    balls[i].CheckForScreenCollisions(this.client);
    if (ball.CheckForBallCollision(balls[i]))
    {
     ball.ApplyCollisionImpulse(balls[i]);
     ball.score++;
    }
   }
   ball.MakeRectangle();
   for (i = 0; i < MAXBALLS; i++)
   {
    for (int j = 0; j < MAXBALLS; j++)
    {
     if (i != j)
     {
      if (balls[i].CheckForBallCollision(balls[j]))
      {
       balls[i].ApplyCollisionImpulse(balls[j]);
      }
     }
    }
    balls[i].MakeRectangle();
   }
  }
 }
```

The **Vector** class is shown here for completeness. It is not important to our discussion of the GDI. If your math is up to it, look it over.

```
using System;
using System.Collections.Generic;
using System.Linq;
using System.Text;

namespace Pgm09aWindows
{
 class Vector
 {
  public double x;
  public double y;
  public double z;

  public Vector()
  {
   x = y = z = 0;
  }

  public Vector(double xx, double yy, double zz)
```

```csharp
{
 x = xx;
 y = yy;
 z = zz;
}

public Vector(Vector v)
{
 x = v.x;
 y = v.y;
 z = v.z;
}

public double Magnitude () {
 return Math.Sqrt (x * x + y * y + z * z);
}

public void Normalize () {
 double mag = Magnitude ();
 if(mag <= .000001) mag = .000001;
 x /= mag;
 y /= mag;
 z /= mag;
 if (Math.Abs(x) < .000001) x = 0;
 if (Math.Abs(y) < .000001) y = 0;
 if (Math.Abs(z) < .000001) z = 0;
}

static public Vector operator- (Vector a, Vector v) {
 return new Vector(a.x - v.x, a.y - v.y, a.z - v.z);
}

// Vector dot product
static public double operator* (Vector a, Vector v) {
 return a.x * v.x + a.y * v.y + a.z * v.z;
}

// scaler *
static public Vector operator* (Vector a, double s)
{
 return new Vector(a.x * s, a.y * s, a.z * s);
}
static public Vector operator *(double s, Vector a)
{
 return new Vector(a.x * s, a.y * s, a.z * s);
}
```

```
static public Vector operator+ (Vector a, Vector v)  {
  return new Vector(a.x + v.x, a.y + v.y, a.z + v.z);
 }
}
}
```

The Ten High Scores Dialogs and Data

The starting point is to construct a class **Score** to hold the score and player's name. Each instance is going to be serialized to a binary file.

```
using System;
using System.Collections.Generic;
using System.Linq;
using System.Text;

namespace Pgm09aWindows
{
 [Serializable]
 class Score
 {
  private int score;
  public int PlayerScore
  {
   get
   {
    return score;
   }
   set
   {
    score = value;
   }
  }

  private string name;
  public string Name
  {
   get
   {
    return name;
   }
   set
   {
    name = value;
   }
```

```
    }
  }
}
```

Next, we need a container class to store the data and deal with lookup and insertion type functions, **ScoresList**. I used an **ArrayList** to hold up to ten top **Score** instances. The constructor allocates the list and initializes the filename to be used. Then, it calls **LoadScores** to input the top ten instances, if present.

```
using System;
using System.Collections;
using System.Linq;
using System.Text;
using System.Windows.Forms;
using System.IO;
using System.Runtime.Serialization;
using System.Runtime.Serialization.Formatters.Binary;

namespace Pgm09aWindows
{
 class ScoresList
 {
  public ArrayList list;
  public string filename;

  public ScoresList()
  {
   filename = "..\\..\\Scores.bin";
   list = new ArrayList();
   LoadScores();
  }
  private void LoadScores()
  {
   FileStream file;
   try
   {
    file = new FileStream(filename, FileMode.Open,
                          FileAccess.Read);
   }
   catch (FileNotFoundException)
   {
    return;
   }
   BinaryFormatter reader = new BinaryFormatter();
   try
   {
    while (true)
```

```
      {
        Score score = (Score)reader.Deserialize(file);
        list.Add(score);
      }
    }
    catch (SerializationException)
    {
      // eof
      file.Close();
    }
  }
```

Later on, when a game is finished, ShouldScoreBeInList is called with that new score. The function returns true or false. If it is freater than one of the top ten, it should be in the list. Even if it is not there, if there are less than ten top scores, it should be added.

```
  public bool ShouldScoreBeInList(int newScore) {
    int count = list.Count;
    IEnumerator myEnumerator =list.GetEnumerator();
    while (myEnumerator.MoveNext())
    {
      Score s = (Score)myEnumerator.Current;
      if (newScore > s.PlayerScore)
        return true;
    }
    return count < 10;
  }
```

Just because it is allowed to be in the top ten does not mean that the player wishes to add it. After the main form checks with the player to see if they wish to add their name and final score to the top ten list, **AddScore** is called. This function had the complicating factor that not only does this one have to be inserted into the list in the proper position, highest score is first, but also, if there are more than ten, the lowest one must be removed. I will handle the removal of an eleventh bottom most score when the file is saved.

```
  public void AddScore(Score newScore)
  {
    int i = 0;
    IEnumerator myEnumerator = list.GetEnumerator();
    while (myEnumerator.MoveNext())
    {
      Score s = (Score)myEnumerator.Current;
      if (newScore.PlayerScore > s.PlayerScore)
      {
        list.Insert (i, newScore);
        return;
      }
```

```
    i++;
   }
   list.Add (newScore);
  }

 public void SaveList()
 {
  FileStream file;
  try
  {
   file = new FileStream(filename, FileMode.Create);
  }
  catch (FileNotFoundException)
  {
   MessageBox.Show("File " + filename + "does not exist",
                   "Error", MessageBoxButtons.OK,
                   MessageBoxIcon.Error);
   return;
  }
  BinaryFormatter writer = new BinaryFormatter();
  IEnumerator myEnumerator =list.GetEnumerator();
  int i = 0;
  while (myEnumerator.MoveNext())
  {
   Score s = (Score)myEnumerator.Current;
   writer.Serialize(file, s);
   i++;
   if (i == 10) // keep only top ten scores
    break;
  }
  file.Close();
  }
 }
}
```

The check of i == 10 and break keeps only a maximum of ten scores in the file.

The ScoresForm dialog controls the whole top ten scores operation. It allocates an instance of the ScoresList. Recall that the ScoresList constructor has already opened the file and inputted the data, so that it is ready to be shown in the listbox of this dialog.

When adding a whole new set of items into a listbox, first you must empty out all of its previous lines. Within the listbox instance, the collection Items holds the strings to be shown in the listbox. Its Add member is used to actually insert a string into the listbox. Key lines are highlighted in boldface below.

```
using System;
```

```csharp
using System.Collections;
using System.ComponentModel;
using System.Data;
using System.Drawing;
using System.Linq;
using System.Text;
using System.Windows.Forms;
using System.IO;
using System.Runtime.Serialization;
using System.Runtime.Serialization.Formatters.Binary;

namespace Pgm09aWindows
{
 public partial class ScoresForm : Form
 {

  private ScoresList list;

  public ScoresForm()
  {
   InitializeComponent();
   list = new ScoresList();
   LoadListBox();
  }

  public bool CheckThisScore(int newScore)
  {
   if (list.ShouldScoreBeInList(newScore))
   {
    if (MessageBox.Show (
       "Do you want to add your score to the High Score List?",
       "Query", MessageBoxButtons.YesNo, MessageBoxIcon.Question)
        == DialogResult.Yes) {
     EnterNameDlg dlg = new EnterNameDlg();
     if (dlg.ShowDialog(this) == DialogResult.Yes)
     {
      string s = dlg.PlayerName;
      Score score = new Score();
      score.PlayerScore = newScore;
      score.Name = s;
      list.AddScore(score);
      LoadListBox();
      return true;
     }
    }
   }
  }
```

```csharp
   return false;
 }

 private void LoadListBox()
 {
  listBoxScores.Items.Clear();
  IEnumerator myEnumerator = list.list.GetEnumerator();
  while (myEnumerator.MoveNext())
  {
   Score s = (Score)myEnumerator.Current;
   string m = String.Format(
               "Score: {0,6:D}  ", s.PlayerScore) + s.Name;
   listBoxScores.Items.Add(m);
  }
 }

 private void OnCloseDialog(object sender, EventArgs e)
 {
  list.SaveList();
  DialogResult = DialogResult.No;
 }
 }
}
```

When the dialog is closed, the file is saved. If you wish to be more efficient, you could maintain a bool isModified, initializing it to false. If a new score is added, then it could be set to true. When closing, if it is true, only then save the list to the binary file. The EnterName dialog is not shown. See the source code for this very simple dialog.

Double Buffering to Reduce Flicker

When doing a lot of fast time drawing on the form, flicker results. The solution to the massive flicker is to use an off screen buffer. The idea is to do all of the drawing in this off screen buffer and then when done, display that whole screen.

C# has made the use of an off screen buffer an automatic action. One Form Property that I set in Pgm09aWindows was **DoubleBuffered** set to true. Once this is set, the C# framework handles all of the details. We draw as normal in **OnPaint**, however, this drawing is actually occurring in the off screen buffer. When we end the **OnPaint** function, C# now makes this off screen buffer the on screen buffer and the final results are shown. The next time we arrive in **OnPaint**, once again, all painting is done in the off screen buffer.

The results of this is a drastic reduction in flicker. In my opinion, this is a fantastic bit of automatic coding done for us. In C++, we are used to dealing with the myriad details of construction and maintenance of such a buffer. In C#, it is totally automatic!

Bring up this sample and right click on the main form and change the **DoubleBuffered** property to false and re-run the program. Notice how badly it flickers. Then change this property back to true and re-run it. Compare just how valuable this bit of automation actually is for game programming in particular!

More GDI Details

When all or a portion of the form's client area is "dirty," Windows fires the **Paint** event, constructing a paint **Graphics** object ready for your use in re-displaying that area. From any point in your program, you can call either

```
Invalidate();
```

or

```
Invalidate (myRectangle);
```

to invalidate the whole area or some rectangular portion of the client area.

You can also obtain a **Graphics** object from some other portion of the form than the **Paint** event. The function call is

```
Graphics g = this.CreateGraphics();
```

Brush objects and **SolidBrush** objects are used to fill the interior of spaces created by such functions as **FillEllipse**, as well as to paint larger surfaces. **Pen** objects and **SystemPen** objects are used to draw lines and curves. Closely associated with these is the **Color** object, which provide a large number of static read-only colors.

In addition to **Point**, **Rectangle**, and **Size** classes, which have integers as their data members, there are also **PointF**, **RectangleF**, and **SizeF** which hold floating point numbers.

The **Font** object allows one to specify a specific font to use in the drawing of text. **BufferedGraphics** allows you to use double buffering to reduce flicker by drawing on an off screen buffer and then making it the active buffer. **Image** objects allow you to show various image files on the screen.

Some of the available drawing functions include **DrawArc**, **DrawCurve**, **DrawLine**, **DrawLines**, **DrawRectangle**, **DrawRectangles**, and **DrawString**. Also, **FillPolygon** is sometimes useful for filling an irregular shape.

With forms, there are numerous controls that can be placed upon them as well. At this point, you should begin to thoroughly examine the various possibilities shown in the C# documentation Help system.

Image Processing

Next, let's examine the displaying of images and their processing. Figures 9.7 and 9.8 show the program in operation. A bmp or jpg file is loaded. If the Zoom menus are used, the image is zoomed by powers of two centered on the image. If the mouse buttons are used, the image is zoomed on the mouse location within the image.

Figure 9.7 Image Viewing Program

Figure 9.8 Image Zoomed 2X

Notice also, I added a tool bar, called a tool strip in C#. The menu and tool bar buttons always zoom from the center of the image. Also, a mouse left click zooms the image in by increasing powers of two, while a right click zooms the image out by successive lower powers of two. Both use the point of the mouse click as the zoom point.

The **Image** class handles the inputting of the image file, a bmp or jpg, via the **FromFile** function. Once loaded, the **Height** and **Width** properties give us the dimensions of the loaded image. The **Graphics** function **DrawImage** displays the image into the provided screen rectangular area, stretching it to fit those dimensions.

```
g.DrawImage(image, screenRect);
```
Here, I have made the screen's rectangle be the dimensions of the actual image.

However, an overloaded **DrawImage** will allow you to specify what rectangular area of the source image is to be displayed in what rectangular area of the screen. This allows you to expand or contract portions of the image. In other languages, this is called stretch blitting.

```
g.DrawImage(image, dest, sourceRect, GraphicsUnit.Pixel);
```
The dest parameter is a bit unusual. It is an array of three **Point** objects, which specify the display area's upper left corner on the screen, the upper right corner, and the lower left corner. From these three points, the function determines the lower right corner automatically.

When displaying the image, I added three colored rectangles around the image, forming a nice border. Except for the zooming calculations, most of the coding is straightforward.

```
using System;
using System.Collections.Generic;
using System.ComponentModel;
using System.Data;
using System.Drawing;
using System.Linq;
using System.Text;
using System.Windows.Forms;

namespace Pgm09bWindows
{
 public partial class FormImageViewer : Form
 {
  string    filename;      // name of the image file to be shown
  Image     image;         // the image from the file
  Rectangle outerBorder;   // outer border rectangle around image
  Rectangle middleBorder;  // middle border rectangle
  Rectangle innerBorder;   // inner border rectange
  Rectangle screenRect;    // the screen area of image
  Point     imageCenter;   // actual x,y coords of image's center
  int       ix;            // current x,y spot from which to zoom
  int       iy;
```

```
int         ihzoom;      // height of the zoom portion of image
int         iwzoom;      // width of the zoom portoni of image
int         zoomFactor;  // how much to zoom in or out by
Rectangle   sourceRect;  // original complete image rectangle
Point       ulCorner1;   // the zoomed ul corner to be shown
Point       urCorner1;   // the zoomed ur corner to be shown
Point       llCorner1;   // the zoomed ll corner to be shown
Point[]     dest;        // the screen points where zoomed image
                         // is to be shown

public FormImageViewer()
{
 InitializeComponent();
 zoomFactor = 1;
}

private void OnFileOpen(object sender, EventArgs e)
{
 OpenFileDialog dlg = new OpenFileDialog();
 dlg.CheckFileExists = true;
 dlg.CheckPathExists = true;
 dlg.Filter ="bmp files (*.bmp)|*.bmp|jpg files (*.jpg)|*.jpg";
 dlg.InitialDirectory = "..\\..\\images";
 if (dlg.ShowDialog() == DialogResult.Cancel) return;
 filename = dlg.FileName;
 LoadImage();
 this.Invalidate();
}
```

The OnFileOpen function displays the common File Open dialog, looking for bmp and jpg files. If one is chosen, the filename is stored for future use. The LoadImage function is then called to input the image and set up all of the various values. The **Invalidate** call displays the image on the screen via **OnPaint**.

I arbitrarily chose so show the image at an upper left corner at 10, 100 and set up two const ints to keep track of this point. This point is then used to establish the many other drawing locations.

```
const int ImULX = 10;    // image upper left X
const int ImULY = 100;   // image upper left Y

private void LoadImage () {
 image = Image.FromFile(filename);
 if (image == null) return;
 screenRect = new Rectangle(ImULX, ImULY, image.Width,
                            image.Height);
 innerBorder = new Rectangle(ImULX, ImULY, image.Width,
```

```
                                    image.Height);
innerBorder.Inflate(new Size(2, 2));
middleBorder = new Rectangle(ImULX, ImULY, image.Width,
                            image.Height);
middleBorder.Inflate(new Size(4, 4));
outerBorder = new Rectangle(ImULX, ImULY, image.Width,
                            image.Height);
outerBorder.Inflate(new Size(6, 6));
```

Notice how I use the **Inflate** function to enlarge the **Rectangle** objects. In the above **Inflate**, from the **Size** width value, 6 is added to both the **Left** and **Right** members, while 6 is also added to the **Top** and **Bottom** members. Actually, the 6 is subtracted from the **Left**, while it is added to the **Right** integers.

Next, the actual center point of the image is found and saved in the imageCenter **Point**. For zooming, we need the point within the image which will be centered in the screen rectangular area. Integers ix and iy hold this center point for zooming. When the menu or tool bar buttons are pressed causing zooming, always the center of the actual image will remain centered within the screen rectangle. However, when the mouse clicks are used, the center point for zooming will become the point within the image that corresponds to where the mouse is currently pointing at the time of the click.

The integers ihzoom and iwzoom hold the current width and height of the zoom, initially none. I then construct the array of three Point objects which define the destination rectangle on screen when zooming in or out. These values are held constant for a particular image.

```
imageCenter = new Point(image.Width / 2, image.Height / 2);
ix = imageCenter.X;
iy = imageCenter.Y;
ihzoom = image.Height;
iwzoom = image.Width;
ulCorner1 = new Point(ImULX, ImULY);
urCorner1 = new Point(ImULX + image.Width, ImULY);
llCorner1 = new Point(ImULX, ImULY + image.Height);
dest = new Point[3];
dest[0] = ulCorner1;
dest[1] = urCorner1;
dest[2] = llCorner1;
zoomFactor = 1;
}
```

OnPaint is relatively simple. After obtaining a Graphics canvas on which to display, if an image has not yet been loaded, the function returns. This is the minimal painting of the background. However, if the image has been loaded, then a title is displayed above the image which gives the current magnification in use. Initially, it is one or none. Notice in this DrawString call, I use the default brush and font. This is followed by drawing the three border rectangles around the image itself.

```
private void OnPaint(object sender, PaintEventArgs e)
{
 Graphics g = e.Graphics;
 if (image != null)
 {
  g.DrawString("Magnification: " + zoomFactor,
               SystemFonts.DefaultFont,
               SystemBrushes.WindowText, new Point(100, 75));
  g.DrawRectangle(new Pen(Color.Green), outerBorder);
  g.DrawRectangle(new Pen(Color.Red), middleBorder);
  g.DrawRectangle(new Pen(Color.Black), innerBorder);
  if (zoomFactor != 1)
  {
   g.DrawImage(image, dest, sourceRect, GraphicsUnit.Pixel);
  }
  else
  {
   g.DrawImage(image, screenRect);
  }
 }
}
```

Finally, if the zoomFactor is one, a simple **DrawImage** is done, placing the whole image within the screen rectangular area. However, if we are zooming, then the indicated source rectangular portion of the image is scaled pixel by pixel into the screen display area.

When **OnZoomIn** is called, the **zoomFactor** is doubled. The new height and width is found by dividing the image width and height by the current zoom factor. For example, if the width is 100 and the zoom factor is 2, then the width of the image to be shown will be 50, giving a magnification of 2. Based on the new width and height to be shown, the source rectangle is re-created by moving from the center point **ix** left by the width to show divided by two. Likewise, the top becomes the center point **iy** less the new height over two. The **Invalidate** causes a repainting to occur, showing the zoomed-in image.

```
private void OnZoomIn(object sender, EventArgs e)
{
 if (image == null) return;
 zoomFactor *= 2;
 ihzoom = image.Height/zoomFactor;
 iwzoom = image.Width/zoomFactor;
 sourceRect = new Rectangle(ix - iwzoom / 2, iy - ihzoom / 2,
                            iwzoom, ihzoom);
 if (sourceRect.Height <= 1 || sourceRect.Width <= 1)
 {
  zoomFactor /= 2;
```

```
    Invalidate();
  }
  Invalidate();
}

private void OnZoomOut(object sender, EventArgs e)
{
  if (image == null) return;
  zoomFactor /= 2;
  if (zoomFactor <= 1)
  {
    zoomFactor = 1;
    ix = imageCenter.X;
    iy = imageCenter.Y;
    Invalidate();
  }
  ihzoom = image.Height / zoomFactor;
  iwzoom = image.Width / zoomFactor;
  sourceRect = new Rectangle(ix - iwzoom / 2, iy - ihzoom / 2,
                             iwzoom, ihzoom);
  Invalidate();
}
```

Handling the Mouse

When any of the mouse events occur, the **MouseEventArgs** hold the many details, such as the location of the mouse and the button which was clicked, if any, and the status of the control and alt keys as well. The member **Button** contains which button was pressed, if any. The members **X** and **Y** contain the mouse position.

In this case, a left button click means to zoom in, while a right button click means zoom out. Depending upon which button is pressed, **OnZoomIn** or **OnZoomOut** is called. The real problem is determining the location within the image that will now become the new center point for the zoom action. This is complicated by the fact that we could already be zoomed in a factor of say 4 when the mouse click occurs at some location over the area image. Worse, the mouse click could be outside the image on the screen!

The first action is to make sure the click is over our image on the screen. The member **screenRect** hold the area on the screen where the image is located. I construct a **Rectangle** based upon the mouse click location. The **Rectangle** function **IntersectsWith** returns true if the mouse rectangle intersects with the screen rectangle. This means the mouse location is within the image area. If it is not, I just return, doing nothing.

```
    private void OnMouseClick(object sender, MouseEventArgs e)
    {
```

```
if (image == null) return;
 Rectangle mouse = new Rectangle(e.X, e.Y, e.X, e.Y);
 if (!screenRect.IntersectsWith(mouse)) return;
```

The tricky part is to determine the new image center x-y location. First, I take the old center location, **ix** and **iy**, and back them off to the upper left corner coordinates.

```
// find the new center point of the image
int ixo = ix - iwzoom / 2; // the old UL corner shown
int iyo = iy - ihzoom / 2;
```

Next, I take the mouse position, corrected for the slight screen coordinate offset, here 10,100, and scale them by the current zoom factor. That is, if the mouse is at a corrected x coordinate of say 100 and the zoom factor is 1, then each mouse pixel value is worth 1. However, if the zoom factor is 2, then each mouse pixel is worth half a pixel. Adding these adjusted factors to the upper left corner, gives me the new location for zooming.

```
int ixd = (e.X - ImULX) / zoomFactor; //offset from UL coorner
int iyd = (e.Y - ImULY) / zoomFactor;// scaled by zoom factor
ix = ixo + ixd; // the new center point from which to zoom
iy = iyo + iyd;
if (e.Button == MouseButtons.Left) // zoom in at this spot
{
 OnZoomIn(null, null);
}
else if (e.Button == MouseButtons.Right)// zoom out this spot
{
 OnZoomOut(null, null);
}
}
```

The Tool Strip

The toolstrip control allows you to display a series of tool bar buttons. When pressed, they signal an event. Toolbar buttons should always be triggering the same event as a corresponding menu item.

The first action is to create the actual button images. Each button is a separate bmp image, 16x16 or so pixels in size. I borrowed some images from a toolbar from a C++ application, toolbar.bmp. I created three files, Open.bmp, zoomin.bmp, and zoomout.bmp. These are in the same folder as the project files.

Click on the Add Toolstrip Button and then chose Properties. The framework installs a default image. We must replace this default image with our new bmp image via the Properties dialog. Find the Image property and click the ... button to bring up the Select Resource dialog as shown in

Figure 9.9 below. Choose Import Resource and select the new bmp image. Once chosen, it is then displayed in the center of the Choose Import Resource dialog and also beside the Image in the properties window.

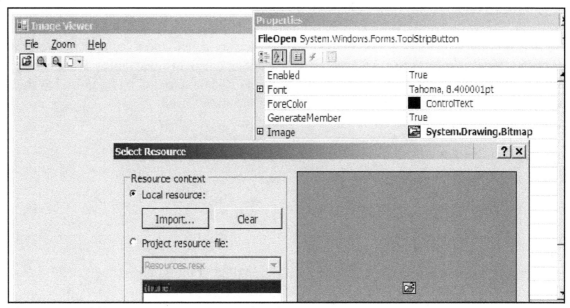

Figure 9.9 Adding an Image to the Tool Strip

Next, I changed the Name property, the Text property, and the Tooltip property to File Open in this case. Then, click on the lightening bolt to get to the associated events. Click on the Click property and enter the existing OnFileOpen function. Thus, the user can click on this button or chose the menu item Load Image File to open up a new bmp or jpg file to be shown.

Problems

Program 9-1 A Solo Yahtzee Game

Write a Solo Player Yahtzee game. Five six-sided dice are rolled and a yahtzee is five of a kind. However, after each rolling turn, a player puts the result on one of thirteen tallies. If a second yahtzee is rolled, the player may use the values as usual in a tally, but also add one hundred to their final points per each extra yahtzee rolled. Only thirteen turns are allowed.

    The categories are as follows.
1's (count and add only the 1's)
2's (add all of the 2's together)
3's
4's
5's
6's
if the total of this group is 63 or more, add an additional 35 point bonus to the score

3 of a kind (total all 5 dice)
4 of a kind (total all five dice)
full house 25 points (3 of a kind + 2 of a kind)
small straight 30 points (a series of 4 increasing values, such as 1, 2, 3, 4)
large straight 40 points (a series of 5 increasing values)
yahtzee 50 points (five of a kind)
chance (add the total of all five dice no matter what they are)

    The player roll begins by rolling all five dice. If they do not want to stop and score the dice, they can roll any number of the dice two more times. That is, three dice rolls is the maximum. When they have finished rolling, they choose where to place the results. A previously placed result cannot be overwritten, this roll must be scored in an empty category. If they cannot use the roll in any way and chance is already used, then it is a scratch and is not counted. We will give them a break and not make them indicate which one of the thirteen categories they wish to scratch.

    When the player has completed his thirteen rolls, display the final total score.

    You will need to devise a mechanism to indicate which of the five dice are to be re-rolled for the second and third time. Similarly, you have to create a mechanism for the player to indicate which category he or she wishes this roll to be counted. Once the player indicates where this roll should be placed, the program performs the correct summation and stores the number in that category. All categories and their current scores for the player must be visible on the screen during the game.

As a suggestion, have the thirteen categories on the left side of the screen with a letter in front of each. When the player wants to stop and place this roll in a scoring category, he or she enters the letter that corresponds to the category. An 'S' can be used for scratch. Again as a suggestion only, use text boxes to make column of scores next to these categories to hold the player's scores. Alternatively, you could have the player click on the category in which this roll is to be scored.

A possible way to indicate which dice are to be re-rolled, you could have a number beneath each die result, 1 through 5. If the player wishes to re-roll, he or she can enter an 'R' for re-roll and then enter the number that corresponds to the dice to be re-rolled. Alternatively, you could have the player click on the dice to be kept, drawing a highlight box around them and then provide a Roll button, which would roll all non-highlighted dice.

Chapter 10—Database Operations

A database is an integrated collection of data organized for some purpose. It is organized and stored by the database's DBMS—DataBase Management System. DBMS provides us with a uniform method of data access independent of how the data are physically stored in the database itself. The relational databases utilize SQL Structured Query Language to perform operations on the database. An SQL statement can ask the database to find a person whose social security number is 123456, for example. These are called database queries. (SQL is pronounced either by its letters or "sequel".)

A programming language communicates SQL statements to a database through Microsoft ActiveX Data Objects (ADO) and ADO.NET.

While many of you know SQL already as well as database organization, some may not. So first we'll cover the very basics of database organization, then the SQL statements, and finally the ADO.NET interface. My discussion is rather brief and limited. The text offers a more detailed discussion of these principles.

Relational Database Concepts

Consider a database to store customer invoices for a company. The printed invoice would contain the invoice number, the customer data and the order data. Customer data may include the customer's name, address, city, state and zip code. The order information might include an item number, description, the quantity ordered, the unit cost, and the subtotal cost of that item. There would likely be an invoice total at the bottom. Certainly, other fields could be on the invoice as well, such as a date of purchase and so on.

How do we store all of these data in a database? We do not just create a field for every item on the invoice and stuff all of it into one pile.

A database consists of one or more Tables. Think of a table as being similar to a file. Each row of the table corresponds to a single record of data. The columns of a row are the individual fields of data that make up this record. A row can be thought of as a structure of data.

Databases are normalized. This means that duplicative data are not stored. For example, each item has a lengthy character string description field. In the invoice table, we would not store that description. Why? Suppose that we had 100 invoices in the table and each one purchased the same item. We would be duplicating that description string endlessly over and over. Instead, we make an Items table which stores the item's number, description and unit cost fields. Then in the Invoices

214

table we need only store a pointer of some kind to the corresponding Items table record. Viola, duplicated data is eliminated. However, if you look at Figure 10.1, one table is not yet fully normalized. This illustrates one of the all to common errors in database design. Can you spot it?

This pointer is called a "key" and in this case is the ItemNumber field, which must be a unique number. That is, no two different products have the same item number value.

The same holds true for the customer data. We have a Customer table that stores the customer information. For its key, we can use the customer id number that the company assigns. Each separate purchaser is assigned their own unique id number. Figure 10.1 shows the Purchase.mdb tables not yet **normalized**

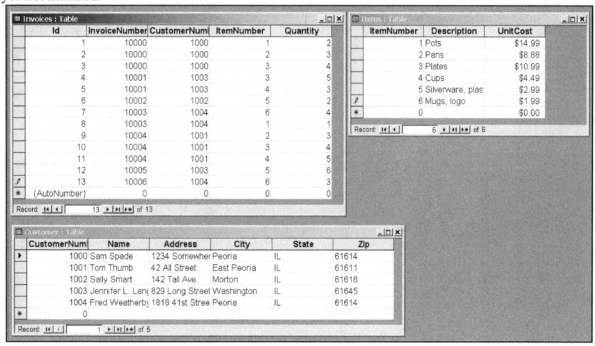

Figure 10.1 The Purchase.mdb Set of Tables Not Yet Fully Normalized

For example, using the invoice number 10000, to find the customer data for this order, we must match the customer number of 1000 in the Customers table. To find the items ordered, we match each ItemNumber in the invoice with the Items table to obtain the description and the cost of that item. This matching process is called a "query."

The names on the list view Column Header controls are the actual field names in the table. The primary key of the Invoices table is an arbitrary number assigned by the system. However, in the Customers and Items tables, the primary keys are CustomerNumber and ItemNumber fields.

Okay. So what is not properly normalized here? In the Invoices table, there are duplicate entries for each invoice number, one for each item being purchased on that invoice. A better design is to provide a fourth table, ItemsPurchased, that contains the invoice number, item number and quantity. The better version of the Purchases database is shown in Figure 10.2.

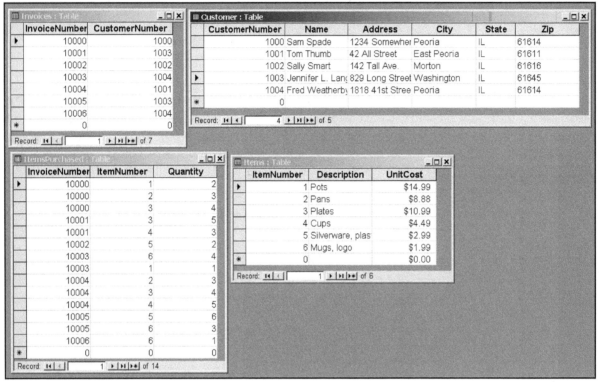

Figure 10.2 The Purchase.mdb Properly Designed for Easy Usage

When done this way, the entrance point is usually the Invoices table. Pick the desired invoice number, and then access the corresponding customer information and/or the actual items purchased.

What kind of actions might we wish to perform on these tables? Certainly finding a match is needed; this is SELECT statement. We might want to INSERT some new information. We might want to UPDATE or possibly even DELETE something that is incorrect. We must construct statements in some query language to accomplish these. In fact, the uppercased items above are the SQL verbs we code for those actions.

Beginning SQL Statements

To query a database, one often uses a SELECT statement to retrieve a set of records. The basic format is

```
SELECT * FROM tablename
```

The * means that you want all of the fields in the record to be in your result collection. The table name must be provided.

We could say

```
SELECT * FROM Customer
```

and the query results collection would contain all five records from that table, each with all of their fields.

Sometimes, we only want certain key fields in the result. We specify the field names separated by commas in place of the *. To include only the Description and UnitCost fields from the Items table we could code

```
SELECT Description, UnitCost FROM Items
```

This would provide us with a results collection that included these two fields for all six records in that table.

Sometimes, we want to narrow the result down to one specific record or subset of records. To do so, we must supply the matching criteria with a WHERE clause. To retrieve the Description and UnitCost of only the plates, we need to match the ItemNumber with that of plates, a 3. The WHERE clause uses the operators: >, <, >=, <=, =, and <>. Thus, we could code it this way.

```
SELECT Description, UnitCost FROM Items WHERE ItemNumber = 3
```

Sometimes when we obtain a sub-collection of records, we would like them sorted or ordered by a specific column. Suppose that we wanted a result consisting of all of the Description and UnitCost fields of the Items table sorted into ascending order on Description. We use the ORDER BY clause with ASC or DESC for ascending or descending.

```
SELECT Description, UnitCost FROM Items ORDER BY Description ASC
```

If you wish a secondary ordering, separate the field names in the ORDER BY clause by commas.

The INNER JOIN clause allows us to join two or more tables into one results collection. Its syntax is

```
INNER JOIN table2 ON table1.fieldname = table2.fieldname
```

Suppose that we wish to print out a bill for a specific invoice item. We would need to join each Invoices table record with its corresponding Items data which match the invoice's ItemNumber field.

```
SELECT InvoiceNumber, ItemNumber, Quantity, Description,
```

```
        UnitCost
FROM Invoices
INNER JOIN Items ON Invoices.ItemNumber = Items.ItemNumber
```
This yields a result collection of all the records from the Invoices table (ie. no WHERE clause) each of which contains these fields InvoiceNumber, ItemNumber, Quantity, Description, UnitCost.

To add a new record to the database, we use the INSERT statement whose simplest syntax is
```
INSERT INTO table (field1, field2, ..., fieldn)
        VALUES (val1, val2,...valn)
```
If the value is a character string constant, surround it with ' ' single quote marks.

Some fields are "auto increment" which means that the DBMS system will automatically supply that value. The Id number of the Invoices table is an auto increment field.
```
INSERT INTO Items (ItemNumber, Description, UnitCost)
        VALUES (7, 'Party Napkins', 1.99)
```
Adds a new record to the Items table with these values.

To update an existing record, use the UPDATE statement whose basic syntax is
```
UPDATE table SET field1 = val1, field2 = val2 WHERE find criteria
```
You control the field(s) that are to be altered in a specific record by coding the desired SET assignments. Fields not mentioned in the SET are unchanged. However, it is vital that the WHERE clause specify which record is to be altered by using a proper matching test.

For example, to change the Description of item number 6 in the Items table, we can code
```
UPDATE Items SET Description = 'Mugs, Company Logo'
WHERE ItemNumber = 6
```

Finally, to delete a record, we use the DELETE statement whose syntax is
```
DELETE FROM table WHERE criteria
```
To remove the Mugs item from the Items table, we code
```
DELETE FROM Items WHERE ItemNumber = 6
```

The ADO.NET Object Model

The ADO.NET object model is the next generation of ActiveX Data Objects (ADO) and provides the programming interface for database access. System.Data is the root namespace for all these classes. System.Data.OleDb contain classes designed to work with any data source. System.Data.SqlClient contains classes optimized to work with Ms SQL Server databases. Working with databases requires the use of several classes.

There are a wide variety of database providers and Visual Studio provides support directly for some of the more common ones, such as Ms SQL Servers. We will be using Access databases because Access is more readily available to students. There is not a Jet Db Engine provider per se, but Microsoft provides support for Access databases through its OleDb system.

When working with databases, you can view the actions conceptually in two ways: connected and disconnected. When working in the connected manner, you connect directly to the database and then interact with it directly until such time as you then disconnect. Often while you are working with the database, others can be locked out. When you use the disconnected approach, you make the connection and then function as a client-side copy of the actual database. The copy is stored in a DataSet with which you then perform your operations. In the disconnected model, the making and breaking of the connections is done automatically for you when actually needed. This often used approach helps quickly free up database connections for other users and increases scalability of your system.

First, one must make the connection to the database. At the low level, for an Access database, this can be an instance of the **OleDbConnection** class. This class provides the information such as the database filename, login and password and so on. Normally, only one connection to the database is needed.

Next, an application requires one **OleDbDataAdapter** instance per query or table access. This class encapsulates the series of SQL query commands that you want to execute. Although the wizard will create a model SQL statement for us, that SQL command often must be modified when we actually are ready to run the query. Calling its **Fill** function causes the query command currently installed to be run. The results of the query, namely another table or set of records, is placed in the third class.

The **DataSet** class holds the results of the just run query. This collection of rows and columns (rows are the records found and columns contain the fields) can be empty (no matching records were found) or can have one or more rows of data each with the same number of columns (one or more as per the query).

Now one powerful feature of the Windows controls is that the control can be "bound" to the results in the **DataSet** instance. When this is done, whenever the **DataSet** is updated, the control automatically displays the new information. Other than providing the initial binding to the fields or columns in the **DataSet**, we need do nothing further. It is all automatic! In this sample, I will show how this is done with a combobox and with text controls.

Another powerful feature is the **DataGrid** which shows the contents of a **DataSet** automatically. This object is also bound to a **DataSet** that often contains a number of rows and columns. It automatically displays the entire contents of the **DataSet**. The control is really a **ListView** in details mode with **ColumnHeader** controls that implement sorting on the columns. It is an amazing amount of functionality with virtually no coding of ours required. I will show how this is done as well.

Finally, other times, one may need to iterate through the actual rows within the **DataSet** so that some additional processing can be done, such as finding a total not created by the query. Processing of the data in a **DataSet** is done by using an instance of the **DataView** class. I will also show how this is done.

Let's begin by making a simple table viewer to see how these objects are constructed. Incredible as it may seem, we can get a view of a table within a database without coding a line of code!

Making a Table Viewer

Make a new project (here Pgm10bWindows) and widen the form. Drag a **DataGridView** object from the tool box onto the form. A DataGridView Tasks dialog appears. If you loose this dialog, clicking on the tiny arrow at the top of the object brings it back up. This is shown in Figure 10. Choose Add Project Data Source from the Choose Data Source drop down box.

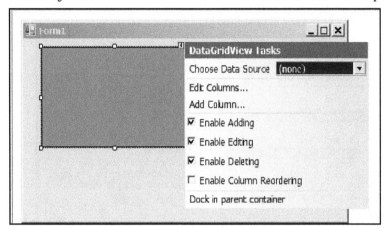

Figure 10.3

This brings up the Data Source Wizard, shown in Figure 10.4. Choose Data base and click Next.

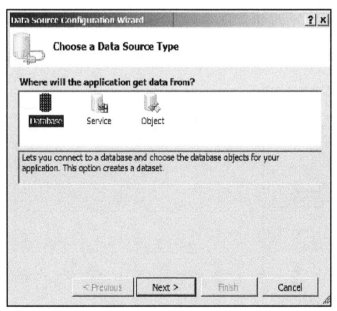

Figure 10.4 Data Source Wizard

This brings up Choose Your Data Connection Dialog. Click New Connection, as shown in Figure 10.5. Select Access Database File and click Continue.

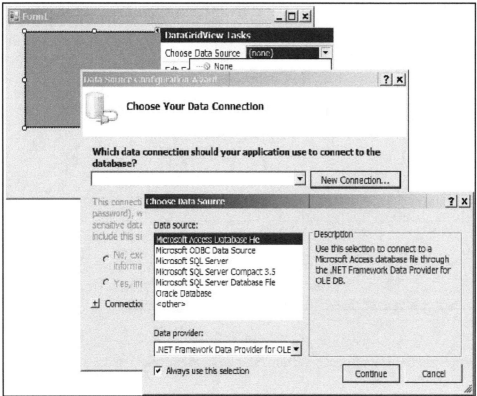

Figure 10.5 Choosing Database Connection Dialog

Next, in the Add Connection dialog, select Browse and find the Purchase.mdb file, Figure 10.6.

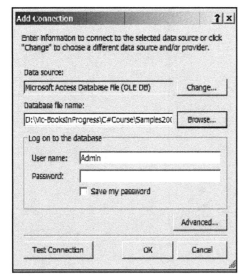

Figure 10.6 Add Purchase.mdb

Notice that the dialog inserted the full drive and path specification to the file. If you keep this full file spec, then you cannot move this project or program from this location because you are locked in to this specific path to the file. Later on, I will show you how to change this path.

When you click okay and get back, a message box appears as shown in Figure 10.7, stating that a local data file that is not in the project. Click Yes so that it copies the Purchase.mdb file into the bin folder each time it runs.

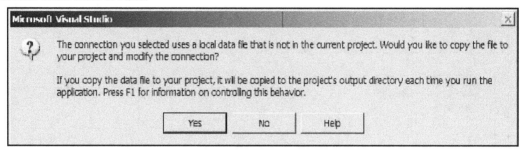

Figure 10.7 The Warning Message Box

Next, it asks if you want to save the connection string in the application configuration file. Yes is the default. Let's allow this and click Next, as shown in Figure 10.8.

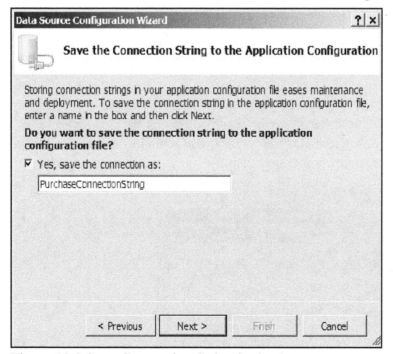

Figure 10.8 Save Connection String in the App Configuration File

Next, we are presented with the Choose Your Database Objects. Expand the Tables icon or checkmark the Tables. You can choose a specific table or tables or even columns within a table. In this case, let's take all the tables as shown in Figure 10.9.

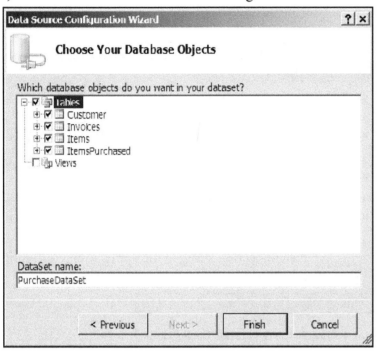

Figure 10.9 Choose Your Database Objects

Now we are back close to the starting point where we select the Customer Table as shown in Figure 10.10. If you should loose this dialog, select the **DataGridView** and click on the tiny arrow at the top and you can get back to this point once again.

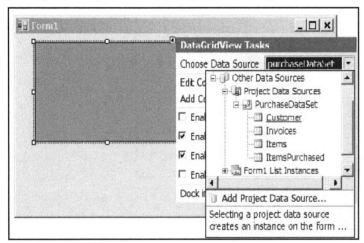

Figure 10.10 Select the Customer Table

When it is done, it will load the column headers for all of the fields in the Customer Table into the **DataGridView**. I had to enlarge the form and grid to be able to see all the fields. This is shown in Figure 10.11.

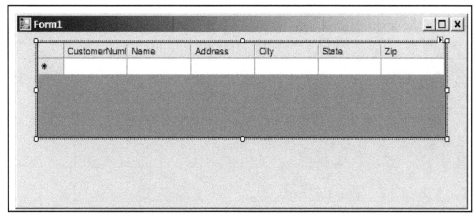

Figure 10.11 The DataGridView Ready to Go

Now build the program and run it. Automatically, the program loads the Customer Table for us, Figure 10.12. We've done no real coding as yet!

	CustomerNuml	Name	Address	City	State	Zip	
▶	1000	Sam Spade	1234 Some...	Peoria	IL	61814	▲
	1001	Tom Thumb	42 All Street	East Peoria	IL	61611	
	1002	Sally Smart	142 Tall Ave.	Morton	IL	61616	
	1003	Jennifer L. L...	829 Long St...	Washington	IL	61645	▼

Figure 10.12 Pgm10b Executing

Now notice the four new objects added to a grey strip at the bottom of our design view, shown in Figure 10.13.

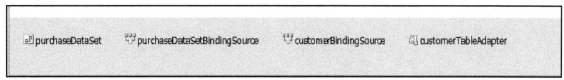

Figure 10.13 The Database Objects Added to Our Program

Specifically, we have a **BindingSource** for the database itself, purchase, and a purchase **DataSet** object for the database. We also have a **BindingSource** for the customer table for the **DataGridView** and a **TableAdapter** for the customer table, which holds the SQL commands to be followed.

Next, I added three more DataGridView objects, selecting the other tables within the purchase DataSet Binding. Now a pair of BindingSource and TableAdapter objects have been added for each of these three. See Figure 10.14.

When you run the application, the contents of all four tables are shown. Still, I have not written one line of coding. Figure 10.15 shows the program running.

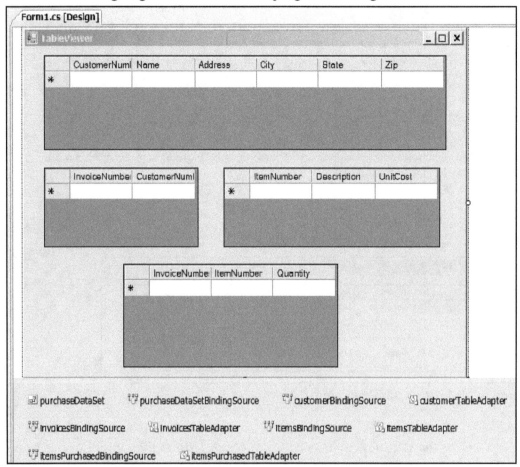

Figure 10.14 The Complete Pgm10bWindows Design View

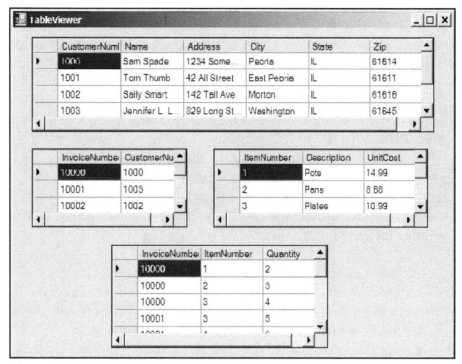

Figure 10.15 The Table Viewer Executing

Notice that in the tool box window area, a new tab has been added, the Server Explorer. You can also drag items from here and drop them on the form as well.

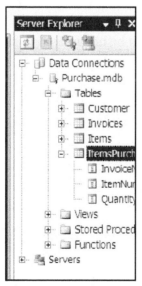

Figure 10.16 Server

Database Classes and Details

In the System.Data namespace, some key types are defined. Let's examine some of these key underlying classes, because such will greatly help your understanding of the specific objects that we will be using.

DataSet —represents an in-memory cache of the data from any number of tables, stored as **DataTable** objects

DataTable —represents a complete table (rows and columns)

DataRow —represents a single row within a **DataTable**

DataColumn—represents a single column within a **DataTable**

DataView —represents a customized view of a **DataTable** which can be used for sorting, editing, or searching, for example

IDataAdapter —defines the core processes for a data adapter object

IDbDataAdapter—extends the basic data adapter object to push and pull data from the data store itself, handling Insert, Delete, Update, and Select commands

IDbCommand —defines a command to be followed—the SQL commands

IDbConnection —handles making the database connections, open and close

IDbTransaction —handles the execution of a set of commands

A database transaction consists of one or more inserts, deletes, and updates that must either all work or all fail as a collective whole. This ensures that the changes are safe and valid. For example, you make a charge on a charge card for say $100.00. This involves two separate actions: take the money from your charge card account and add the funds to the company who is selling you the item. Both actions must be done successfully. The merchant will be unhappy if your funds does not get transferred to his account, though you might enjoy having the funds not taken from your account. Thus, a transaction has two key functions: **Commit** and **RollBack**.

The model that we are using in the disconnected approach is this.

```
Client Application
   DataSet Object ------- Data Adapter -------> Database
                  <------ Data Adapter ------- Database
```

The **DataSet** object holds the memory image of the data from the database. The data adapter handles the two-way flow of information via commands. It keeps the connection open for the least amount of time to handle the flow of data. Once the client has a copy of the data, it is free to take all the time it wishes to insert, update, and delete data in its local copy, the **DataSet**. When it is ready to perform the actual modification of the real database, it then passes the **DataSet** to the data adapter who then physically updates the real database.

228

Many key operations can be done on the **DataSet** and we need to spend some time examining it and its features. Here are some key functions of the **DataSet**. Remember that a **DataSet** can contain one or more **DataTables**.

Clear—Clears all data from the **DataSet**, all rows in all **DataTables**

AcceptChanges—Commits all the changes made since it was loaded or the last **AcceptChanges** was called

RejectChanges—Rolls back all the changes made since it was created or the last **AcceptChanges** was called

In the purchaseDataSet of Pgm10bWindows, there are four **DataTables**, named Customer, Invoices, Items, and ItemsPurchased.

The **DataTable**, which holds the data and is contained within the **DataSet**, has **DataColumn** objects which are tied to the database schema. That is, they represent the column names, type of data it holds and so on.

DataSet   —gets the **DataSet** that holds this table

TableName —gets or sets this table's name

PrimaryKey—gets or sets an array of columns that act as the primary keys for the data

Columns   —a **DataColumnCollection** holding the individual **DataColumn** objects

Rows   —a **DataRowCollection** holding the actual **DataRow** objects which contain the data values

These last two members we often need. A **DataColumnCollection** is a container to hold the array of **DataColumn** objects, while a **DataRowCollection** holds the actual **DataRow** objects which contain the data values.

The **DataColumn** holds key information about this column.

AutoIncrement—property used to automatically increment this column's data when new records are added

Caption   —the string caption to be displayed for this column

ColumnName —gets or sets the name of this column of data

DataType   —defines how the data is stored, integer, float, string, Boolean, etc.

DefaultValue —any default value if no data is entered in this column when inserting a new record

The **DataRow** contains the data and methods. The first one, the **ItemArray**, is often needed in programming.

ItemArray   —gets or sets all of the values for this row using an array of objects

AcceptChanges—accepts all changes made since the row was loaded or the last **AcceptChanges**

RejectChanges —rejects all changes since the row was loaded or the last **AcceptChanges**

BeginEdit   —starts an edit operation on this row

229

EndEdit   —ends the edit operation
CancelEdit   —cancels the current edit in progress
Delete   —marks this row to be removed when **AcceptChanges** is called
IsNull   —returns true if the specified column contains a null value

Handling Inserts, Deletes, and Updates

Handling of deletes is easy. Assume that customerTable.Rows is an instance of **DataRowCollection** of the customer table.

```
int rowToDelete = 0; // the row we've decided to delete
customerTable.Rows[rowToRemove].Delete ();
customerTable.Rows.AcceptChanges ();
```

It is only marked as deleted until **AcceptChanges** is called. If **RejectChanges** is called, it is unmarked as deleted.

Inserting a row is also easy.

```
DataRow newRow = customerTable.NewRow ();
newRow["Name"] = newNameString;
...
customerTable.Rows.Add (newRow);
```

Updating a row is more involved. First, you have to find the row or rows to be updated. Let's take one row at a time first. From customerTable.Rows, you have found the row to be updated as rowIndex = 42, where this is a local integer that contains the row number to be updated.

```
DataRow updateRow = customerTable.Rows[rowIndex];
updateRow.BeginEdit ();
if (MakeChanges (updateRow)) { // function makes changes
                              // returns true if made okay
 updateRow.EndEdit ();
}
else {
 updateRow.CancelEdit ();
}
```

The other possibility is to search for the needed row(s) to be updated. For example, suppose that we need to update the customer data for customer number 1000. We need to find this row of data in the DataSet. There are several ways to do this. One is to use the Filter Criteria option of the DataTable.

```
int num; // currently holds 1000
string filter = string.Format("CustomerNumber= '{0}'", num);
DataRow[] results = customerTable.Select (filter);
```

```
for (int j = 0; j<results.Length; j++) {
  results[j]["Name"] = newname;
  ...
}
```

The second possibility is use the primary key to find the row in question. In the case of a table having a primary key, the Table has added a **FindBy...** function. In the case of the Customer table, I defined the CustomerNumber to be the primary key. Hence we can do the following to find this row.

```
this.customerDataSet.Customer.FindByCustomerNumber (
                                customerNumberPicked);
```

Now we can retrieve the **DataRow** and proceed to do the update using BeginEdit-EndEdit as above.

Yet another way can be used to find rows. In the case of the ItemsPurchased table, there is no primary key. Further, we really need to join the Items table and the ItemsPurchased table so that we have all of the fields together to be shown to the user. A way to do this is to create our needed SQL SELECT command and store it in the **DataAdapter** and then call Fill to load a query with the results.

```
this.itemsPurchasedTableAdapter.Adapter.SelectCommand.CommandText
= "SELECT ItemsPurchased.InvoiceNumber, ItemsPurchased.ItemNumber,
  ItemsPurchased.Quantity, Items.Description, Items.UnitCost,
  ItemsPurchased.Quantity * Items.UnitCost AS Total FROM ItemsPurchased
  INNER JOIN Items ON ItemsPurchased.ItemNumber = Items.ItemNumber
  WHERE ItemsPurchased.InvoiceNumber = " + invoiceNumberPicked.ToString();
this.itemsPurchasedTableAdapter.Fill(itemsPurchasedDataSet.ItemsPurchased);
DataView items = new DataView(itemsPurchasedDataSet.ItemsPurchased);
invoiceTotal = 0;
foreach (DataRowView r in items)
 {
  invoiceTotal += Double.Parse(r["Total"].ToString());
 }
```

A **DataView** is an alternative representation of your table, allowing you to extract a subset from a table or in the above case, a joined table. A **DataGridView** can be bound to a **DataView** as well.

Let's put some of these to work and make a better way to view the purchase data.

Making an Invoice Picker Program

To illustrate step by step how database operations are done, let's create an Invoice Viewer application that allows the user to pick which invoice number they wish to view and the viewer then displays that invoice in detail. Figure 10.17 shows what Pgm10cWindows looks like when run.

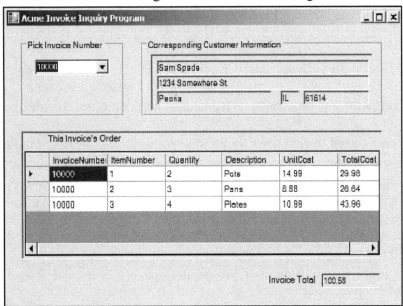

Figure 10.17 Pgm10cWindows Inquiry Program

When the user chooses another invoice number from the Pick Invoice Number combobox, the customer information text boxes are updated along with the Invoice Order details (the **DataGridView**) and the Invoice Total.

With the more recent versions of Visual Studio, Microsoft has opted to alter the database wizard and tool bar widgets with the idea of making simple database applications easier to write. That is, the new **BindingSource** and **DataGridView** objects attempt to make the process simpler to do, with much of the drudgery coding being automatically generated. Yet, with this streamlined process, more involved situations are harder to implement. Such is the case with the **DataGridView**, which replaces the older **DataGrid**. Although Visual Studio still supports the **DataGrid**, they no longer provide a graphical way to drag and drop such a control onto your form.

Specifically, this change impacts the Invoice Order control shown in Figure 10.17 above. With the older **DataGrid**, dynamically one could perform a database join operation, joining the Items and the ItemsPurchased tables to obtain all of the fields needed to be shown in the **DataGrid**. This is shown in Pgm10aWindows. With the **DataGridView**, I was not able to do this on the fly with a SQL JOIN command. Instead, I needed to provide an Access Query to perform the join and then bind the **DataGridView** to the Access Query resultant table.

Most all of the coding in this sample was automatically generated by the wizard. Thus, the best way to see how to do database programming is to actually see if you can reproduce this sample using the wizard. Thus, let's go through the steps needed one at a time. Interestingly enough, this is also how one should develop an application, in steps or stages, not trying to code everything at once and then debug the lot.

Step 1 Getting the Combobox and the Text Boxes Working

Start up a new Windows Application. Copy my Purchase.mdb Access file from Pgm10cWindows into that folder just created for the project. Then add a group box saying to Pick the Invoice Number and add a combobox inside the group box. Now we need to add the database and support for the combobox.

Drag the BindingSource from the tool box onto your form and follow the steps shown in Figures 10.4 through 10.9 to install the Purchase.mdb Access database. I chose to have all of the tables selected.

Click on the Properties of the combobox and set the Data Source property. It will create a new binding. Tie it to the Invoices table. Then set the Display Member property to InvoiceNumber. Next, when the user makes a new selection in this combobox, we need to respond to that change and update all of the other tables. Hence, click on the Events lightening bolt of the properties and set SelectedIndexChanged property to the function OnInvoiceChanged.

Obviously, we will need to retrieve this new invoice number and use it to reload the other tables. Since we also need to load all of the controls when the application begins, let's add a function LoadControls which will be passed the selected zero-based index of the chosen item in the combobox. When the application starts, that value will be 0, indicating the first invoice number in the control. Later, when the user picks a different invoice to view, in OnInvoiceChanged, we can get the index of the selection and pass it to the LoadControls.

We will need to save the actual invoice number and the corresponding customer number as well. Why? We will need to search the invoice table to find this invoice and retrieve the customer number. Given the customer number, we must find that one in the Customers table and then use that record to fill the text boxes with the customer information.

Here is what we have so far.
```
private int invoiceNumberPicked;
private int customerNumberPicked;
PurchaseDataSet.CustomerRow customerRow;
. . .
```

```
private void Form1_Load(object sender, EventArgs e)
{

 this.customerTableAdapter.Fill(this.purchaseDataSet.Customer);
 this.invoicesTableAdapter.Fill(this.purchaseDataSet.Invoices);
 int row = 0;
 LoadControls(row);
}

private void LoadControls(int row)
{
 DataView dv = new DataView(purchaseDataSet.Invoices);
 customerNumberPicked = Int32.Parse(dv[row]["CustomerNumber"].ToString());
 invoiceNumberPicked = Int32.Parse(dv[row]["InvoiceNumber"].ToString());
 customerRow = this.purchaseDataSet.Customer.FindByCustomerNumber(
                                        customerNumberPicked);
 textBoxName.Text = customerRow.Name;
 textBoxZip.Text = customerRow.Zip;
 textBoxAddress.Text = customerRow.Address;
 textBoxState.Text = customerRow.State;
 textBoxCity.Text = customerRow.City;
```

The wizard added the two adapter **Fill** function calls. I added the LoadControls function. In order to retrieve the selected invoice number, I wrap a **DataView** around the Invoices table. As long as we have not sorted the invoice numbers in the combobox, the combobox zero-based index of the selected one should correspond to the index of the row we need in the Invoices **DataSet**. The DataView is then subscripted as an array to get to the desired row. To get the column within that row, use the table's column name. Here, I got the invoice number and customer number selected by the user.

To look up the customer, I make use of the fact that the Customer table has a numerical key field, the CustomerNumber. The **DataSet** then adds a special function for just this purpose, **FindByCustomerNumber**. This is very convenient indeed, as long as we have a key field in the table. The function returns the row picked. Its data type is **PurchaseDataSet.CustomerRow**.

To respond to the comboxbox selection changed, I coded the following.

```
private void OnInvoiceChanged(object sender, EventArgs e)
{
 DataRowView s = (DataRowView)comboBoxChooseInvoice.SelectedItem;
 int row = comboBoxChooseInvoice.SelectedIndex;
 if (row == -1) return;
 LoadControls(row);
}
```

There are two ways that you can obtain the invoice and customer number selected. One way is to wrap a **DataRowView** around the combobox's **SelectedItem**, which is coming from the invoices **DataSet**. Both numbers are then available from this object. Alternatively, one can use the **SelectedIndex**, a zero-based index.

Step 2 Getting the Items Purchased DataGridView Working

Next, I added a panel and a label for the items purchased. Then, I dropped a **DataGridView** on to the panel and resized it. Finally, I added a label and text box to hold the total cost of the order. In the Access QueryReport, the query adds a calculated field, the total cost of the item, quantity * unit cost. Again, open the properties of the **DataGridView** and click the DataSource property. Add in a new binding to the QueryReports table.

I added a new variable to hold the total cost of the order. The database wizard added an adapter Fill function call in the Form1_Load function.

```
  private double invoiceTotal;
...
  private void Form1_Load(object sender, EventArgs e)
  {
 this.queryReportTableAdapter.Fill(this.purchaseDataSet2.QueryReport);
...
   int row = 0;
   LoadControls(row);
  }

  private void LoadControls(int row)
  {
   DataView dv = new DataView(purchaseDataSet.Invoices);
  customerNumberPicked = Int32.Parse(dv[row]["CustomerNumber"].ToString());
  invoiceNumberPicked = Int32.Parse(dv[row]["InvoiceNumber"].ToString());
  customerRow = this.purchaseDataSet.Customer.FindByCustomerNumber
                                               (customerNumberPicked);
   textBoxName.Text = customerRow.Name;
   textBoxZip.Text = customerRow.Zip;
   textBoxAddress.Text = customerRow.Address;
   textBoxState.Text = customerRow.State;
   textBoxCity.Text = customerRow.City;
  this.queryReportTableAdapter.Adapter.SelectCommand.CommandText =
     "SELECT ItemsPurchased.InvoiceNumber, ItemsPurchased.ItemNumber,
     ItemsPurchased.Quantity, Items.Description, Items.UnitCost,
     ItemsPurchased.Quantity * Items.UnitCost AS TotalCost
      FROM ItemsPurchased
      INNER JOIN Items ON ItemsPurchased.ItemNumber = Items.ItemNumber
      WHERE ItemsPurchased.InvoiceNumber = " +invoiceNumberPicked.ToString();
  this.queryReportTableAdapter.Fill(purchaseDataSet2.QueryReport);
```

```
DataView items = new DataView(purchaseDataSet2.QueryReport);
invoiceTotal = 0;
foreach (DataRowView r in items)
{
 invoiceTotal += Double.Parse(r["TotalCost"].ToString());
}
textBoxInvoiceTotal.Text = invoiceTotal.ToString();
}
```

Notice the bold faced coding in the LoadControls function. First, I need to run the QueryReport query. To do so, I must tell the query which invoice number to use. If I don't, then I get a result data set which contains all of the items purchased by everyone. Notice that I do an INNER JOIN on the two tables, Items and ItemsPurchased. The WHERE clause allows me to only find those records which match the currently selected invoice number. This SQL command is stored in the adapter's **CommandText** member. Then, the query is run by calling the adapter's Fill function. Automatically, the **DataGridView** is then filled with those records now in the QueryReport **DataSet**.

However, I need to accumulate the total cost of this order. Again, I wrap a **DataView** around the **DataSet** and can then utilize a **foreach DataRowView** in the **DataView** to access each row. Again, to access the specific column in the row, use the character string name of that column as a subscript.

Thus, with minimal coding, we have a complete invoice inquiry program. Now we need to examine how to insert, update, and delete records.

Problems

None

Chapter 11—Database Updates

There are many ways to handle database updates, some easier than others to code. If we use a **DataGridView** to display the **DataSet** on our form, the process is fairly simple to code. If we use the Purchase Database as our base, updates in general can be tricky to implement. For example, changing a customer's id number impacts not only the Customer table but also related tables, in this case the Invoices table, which contains the customer number who made the purchase. Changing an item number for an existing item in the Items table impacts potentially all records in the Items Purchased table, as one or more invoices might contain this item.

Instead of getting bogged down in such details, let's only examine how to Add, Update, and Delete records from the Customer table, ignoring any related table impacts. This way, we can focus only upon the methods and procedures needed to implement these three key database actions. Figure 11.1 shows Pgm11aWindows in operation. Notice the **DataGridView** is displaying one extra blank row in the view. This will become significant when deleting.

	Customer	Name	Address	City	State	Zip
▶	1000	Sam Spade	1234 Somewhere St	Peoria	Il	61614
	1001	Tom Thumb	42 All Street	East Peoria	IL	61611
	1002	Sally Smart	142 Tall Ave	Morton	IL	61616
	1003	Jennifer L. Lan...	829 Long Street	Washington	IL	61645
	1004	Fred Weatherby	1818 41st Street	Peoria	IL	61614
*						

Figure 11.1 Pgm11a with a DataGridView of the Customer Table

Now one could program the grid to allow you to click in a cell and begin editing it, much like the Windows Explorer. One could program the grid to allow you to add a new record by typing in the * blank line. These take a bit more coding and message handling than the simpler case.

Our interface consists of button presses for the desired actions. If Add is pressed, a new record will be added. If a line is selected, Update will allow the user to change it, while Delete will delete the record. Notice that both the add and update process will require an identical dialog in which the six data values can be entered or changed. Thus, there will be a common CustomerAddUpdateDlg form as well as the main form class.

237

Notice a few of the properties that I set in the **DataGridView** instance. The **DataSource** is bound to the customerBindingSource's Customer Table. The **SelectionMode** is set to **FullRowSelect**. Figure 11.2 shows the main form in Design View with the database binding sources, data connections, and classes.

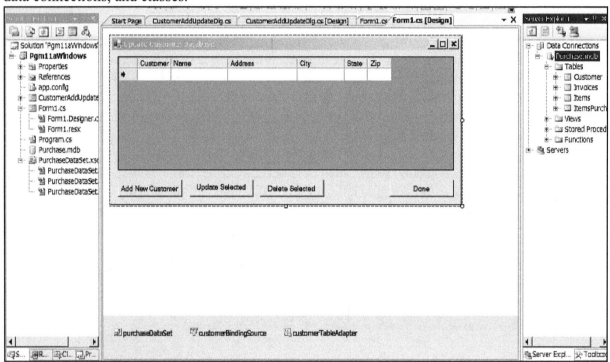

Figure 11.2 The Main Form in Design View

Figure 11.3 shows the CustomerAddUpdateDlg form.

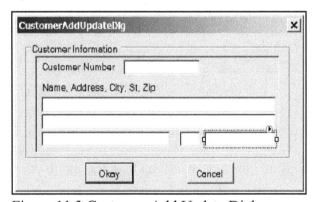

Figure 11.3 Customer Add Update Dialog

Coding the Add Update Dialog

The only difference between an add dialog and an update dialog is that the text boxes will contain nothing in the add case, while they contain the current data in the update case. It makes sense to make only one physical dialog class to handle both situations. The real question is how to transfer data to and from the dialog and its controls.

There are a number of ways this can be accomplished. One method is to provide get/set properties. For example one might have the following.

```
public string Name {
  get {
   return textBoxName.Text;
  }
  set {
   textBoxName.Text = value;
  }
}
```

This method is fine when there are only a couple of members. However, in this case we have seven members. This method places more of a coding burden on the caller of the dialog instance.

An alternate way is to provide a data transfer buffer which contains the seven members. Since we are dealing with a **DataGridView**, we could pass a **DataRowView** which contains all of the seven members of the row to be updated. The constructor is passed a reference to this **DataRowView** and uses it to load the seven text boxes. However, if we then save this reference in a protected data member of the dialog class, when the user clicks OK, we can then retrieve the current updated contents of the seven text boxes, storing them back into the passed **DataRowView** instance of the caller. This then lessens the workload on the caller of the dialog.

Here is the AddUpdateDlg.cs coding.

```
using System;
using System.Collections.Generic;
using System.ComponentModel;
using System.Data;
using System.Drawing;
using System.Linq;
using System.Text;
using System.Windows.Forms;

namespace Pgm11aWindows
{
 public partial class CustomerAddUpdateDlg : Form
 {
  DataRowView r;
```

```csharp
public CustomerAddUpdateDlg(DataRowView row)
{
 r = row;
 InitializeComponent();
 textBoxName.Text = r["Name"].ToString();
 textBoxCustomerNumber.Text = r["CustomerNumber"].ToString();
 textBoxAddress.Text = r["Address"].ToString();
 textBoxCity.Text = r["City"].ToString();
 textBoxState.Text = r["State"].ToString();
 textBoxZip.Text = r["Zip"].ToString();
}

private void OnOkay(object sender, EventArgs e)
{
 r["Name"] = textBoxName.Text;
 r["CustomerNumber"] = textBoxCustomerNumber.Text;
 r["Address"] = textBoxAddress.Text;
 r["City"] = textBoxCity.Text;
 r["State"] = textBoxState.Text;
 r["Zip"] = textBoxZip.Text;
 DialogResult = DialogResult.Yes;
}

private void OnCancel(object sender, EventArgs e)
{
 DialogResult = DialogResult.No;
}
}
}
```

Coding the Main Form for Pgm11aWindows

The main program begins by initially connecting to the database and loading the Customer table into our **DataGridView**. Then, the database connection is dropped, allowing other applications to access the database, while we work on our updates, thereby minimizing the overhead cost to the database itself.

```csharp
using System;
using System.Collections.Generic;
using System.ComponentModel;
using System.Data;
using System.Drawing;
using System.Linq;
using System.Text;
using System.Windows.Forms;
```

```
namespace Pgm11aWindows
{
 public partial class Form1 : Form
 {
  public Form1()
  {
   InitializeComponent();
  }

  private void Form1_Load(object sender, EventArgs e)
  {
   this.customerTableAdapter.Fill(this.purchaseDataSet.Customer);
  }
```

Let's examine how the add new record is handled. Here, we must fabricate an empty record to pass, that is an empty, new, **DataRowView**. Using the Customer table **DataSet**, I allocated a new instance of the **DataView** and then called the **AddNew** function, which returns a completely new **DataRowView**, which has all seven of the members in it, ready for us to supply the new values. This new instance, r, is then passed to the dialog constructor, who stores this reference to be later filled with the text boxes when OK is pressed within the dialog.

```
   private void OnAdd(object sender, EventArgs e)
   {
    DataView item = new DataView(purchaseDataSet.Customer);
    DataRowView r = item.AddNew();
    CustomerAddUpdateDlg dlg = new CustomerAddUpdateDlg(r);
    if (dlg.ShowDialog() == DialogResult.Yes)
    {
```

If OK is pressed, then we need to actually insert this new row in the database Customer table itself. First, I called the **Add** function of the **DataSet** to add this row. Of course, there is always the possibility that this action can fail. The **HasErrors** property is true if there were errors. In such an event, I display a **MessageBox**. One could also use the **DataRow** array s to further pinpoint the errors.

```
     purchaseDataSet.Customer.Rows.Add(r.Row);
     if (purchaseDataSet.Customer.HasErrors)
     {
      DataRow[] s = purchaseDataSet.Customer.GetErrors();
      MessageBox.Show("Customer Number = " +
              r["CustomerNumber"].ToString(),
              "Error Adding the record",
       MessageBoxButtons.OK, MessageBoxIcon.Information);
     }
```

Second, if the row was successfully added to the **DataSet**, then one must actually make the database connection and physically update the database itself. Call the **Update** function of the adapter to physically connect to the database, update the table, and break the connection, thereby minimizing our actual connection to the database once more.

```
    else
    {
      customerTableAdapter.Update(purchaseDataSet.Customer);
    }
  }
}
```

The update process requires us to find the desired row and pass it to the AddUpdateDlg constructor. The record to be updated must be selected in the **DataGridView**. It's member **Count** contains the number of rows that are currently selected. If one row is not selected, the function returns, doing nothing. The **SelectedRows** property returns a collection of all of the selected rows, here only one could be selected, index 0. One could allow a series of selected rows to be updated one after the other. In such a case, wrap the rest of the coding in a while or for loop. Since the **DataGridView** rows could potentially be sorted into a different order than the actual records in the **DataSet**, the Index property provides the tie-back to the index of this record in the **DataSet**. Then, a new **DataView** is constructed and the correct row's data is retrieved into a **DataRowView**, r.

```
private void OnUpdate(object sender, EventArgs e)
{
  if (grid.SelectedRows.Count != 1) return;
  DataGridViewSelectedRowCollection rows = grid.SelectedRows;
  int i = rows[0].Index;
  DataView item = new DataView(purchaseDataSet.Customer);
  DataRowView r = item[i];
  CustomerAddUpdateDlg dlg = new CustomerAddUpdateDlg(r);
  if (dlg.ShowDialog() == DialogResult.Yes)
  {
```

There is one serious design flaw in the above coding, which is handled properly in the OnDelete function. Notice when running the program, the **DataGridView** shows an empty row at the bottom of the view. Here, one could implement an in-column add new record. That is its purpose. What if the user selects that row? Ah, there is no record or data at this location and the program crashes! How to handle this possibility is shown in the OnDelete function below. Try it and watch the program crash.

If OK is pressed, again, we need to do two actions. First, we must update the **DataSet** with the new revised data and then physically connect to the database and perfrom the update there. Again, I access the **DataSet's** row to be updated and then call the **BeginEdit** function. The individual columns of the row are modified from the returned data from the dialog. Then, **EndEdit** is called.

```
DataRow dr = purchaseDataSet.Customer.Rows[i];
dr.BeginEdit();
dr["Name"] = r["Name"];
dr["CustomerNumber"] = r["CustomerNumber"];
dr["Address"] = r["Address"];
dr["City"] = r["City"];
dr["State"] = r["State"];
dr["Zip"] = r["Zip"];
dr.EndEdit();
```

Of course, there is once again the potential for errors to occur. One ought to check for errors using the **HasErrors** property, which is true if errors arose during the edit. Again, I produced a simple message, but one could also use the array of **DataColumns** to add further information on the reason(s) for the errors.

```
if (dr.HasErrors == true)
{
 DataColumn[] s = dr.GetColumnsInError();
 MessageBox.Show("Customer Number = " +
          r["CustomerNumber"].ToString(),
          "Error Updating the record",
  MessageBoxButtons.OK, MessageBoxIcon.Information);
}
```

If there were no errors in updating the **DataSet**, use it to physically update the database by once more calling the **Update** function of the data adapter.

```
 else
 {
  customerTableAdapter.Update(purchaseDataSet.Customer);
 }
 }
}
```

Handling requests to delete records again requires that one record in the view be selected. If none are, the function returns. If one is selected, I again use the **SelectedRows** property to return a collection of all those rows. However, there can only be one element in this collection, index 0. Ah, but what if the user selects the dummy bottom row, which is present to implement an in-place add new record? In the OnUpdate, the program crashes if this one is selected. To prevent this accidental selection, we must make sure that the retrieved index of the **DataSet** is within range of zero to the number of records minus one.

```
 private void OnDelete(object sender, EventArgs e)
 {
  if (grid.SelectedRows.Count != 1) return;
  DataGridViewSelectedRowCollection rows = grid.SelectedRows;
  int i = rows[0].Index;
```

```
if (i < grid.Rows.Count-1 && i >=0){
```

The above line prevents selection of the dummy bottom row. Only if the index is within range, do we proceed to obtain the actual row from the DataSet.

```
DataRow dr = purchaseDataSet.Customer.Rows[i];
```

One does not now immediately delete the record. It is wise to ask the user for confirmation. This prevents accidental deletion of records.

```
if (MessageBox.Show("Customer Number and Name = " +
    dr["CustomerNumber"].ToString() +
    "  " + dr["Name"].ToString(),
    "Confirm deletion of this record",
    MessageBoxButtons.YesNo,
    MessageBoxIcon.Information) == DialogResult.Yes)
{
```

If the user really does want this record deleted, then the same two-step process is used. First, it is deleted from the Customer DataSet using the **Delete** function. Again, it is wise to check for errors before proceeding to make the physical database connection and requesting the physical deletion. The database physical deletion occurs when we call the Update function of the database adapter.

```
    dr.Delete();
    if (dr.HasErrors == true)
    {
     DataColumn[] s = dr.GetColumnsInError();
     MessageBox.Show("Customer Number = " +
            dr["CustomerNumber"].ToString(),
            "Error Deletint the record",
            MessageBoxButtons.OK, MessageBoxIcon.Information);
    }
    else
    {
     customerTableAdapter.Update(purchaseDataSet.Customer);
    }
   }
  }
 }
}

private void OnDone(object sender, EventArgs e)
{
 Application.Exit();
}
 }
}
```

These are the basics of handling add, update, and delete. However, there are other ways of accomplishing the same thing. Specifically, users like to be able to simply click in a column of a row and go into Edit mode, altering the data. They like to click in the empty dummy row and start typing in data into the columns to add a new record. Often, they like to select a record and press the delete key. All of these are possible and more. It depends upon the degree of functionality that you wish to provide your users. Obviously, in-place adding and editing requires responding to many additional messages sent by the **DataGridView** control.

Problems

Program 11-1— Building an Employee Database

In previous problems, you developed a series of Employee classes and read them in from a binary file of employee data. In this assignment, we are going to build an Employee database and provide a user application to allow them to add, update, and delete employees.

First, look over the actual data members of the Employee classes. Then, build a database that contains all of these members. One member will contain a character that tells you whether this is a salaried, hourly, or piece-rate employee. This field in turn tells you which remaining columns are appropriate for the employee. The physical database can be any of your choice, but Access is recommended. If you have access to SQL, you may use it as well.

When adding a record, be sure to put zeros into all of the unused columns. For example, with a salaried employee, most all of the remaining fields are not used, such as hourly rate. These should be set to zero.

Once the underlying physical database is created, you must then load the database with the binary data used in the previous problems. Again, I do not care how you do this. One way would be to write a quick application that reads in each binary record and then adds it to the database. Alternatively, you could finish the implementation of this assignment and then use its Add function to manually enter all of the previous problem's records.

The main application loads a **DataGridView** of the Employees Table. Provide a way for the user to add, update, and delete records. You may use the easy way that I did it in this sample, providing three action buttons. Implement all three functions to allow the user to add new employees, update existing employees, and delete employees.

Caution. When updating an employee, their pay type can change, from salaried to hourly or piece-rate, etc. Thus, you need to make sure that the various fields that are no longer valid for that type of employee are zeroed out as well.

Thoroughly test your program.

Chapter 12—ASP.NET and Web Actions

Now armed with the basics, we can at last address the creation of Web-based applications. Such applications create the content for the Web browsers to display. The content can include HTML, client side scripting (such as validation of data in a form), images, and so on. The technology is called ASP.NET.

One common use is to create Web Forms to collect information. Typically these Web Forms have text boxes and list boxes as well as labels, radio buttons and similar controls to gather up the user's request and then send them to the server for processing.

Web applications are very different from the desktop applications that we have been writing. Web programs always involve at least two networked machines, except in development where one machine can serve both sides. One machine will become the client, browser-based, and the other machine will become the Web server machine, processing and handling requests from the client machine or browser. How do the two machines "talk" to each other? Communication is done via the communications protocol known as HTTP, Hypertext Transfer Protocol.

HTTP is a protocol that specifies a set of methods and headers to allow client and servers both to interact with each other and share information in a uniform way.

A client machine launches a web browser, such as Firefox or Internet Explorer. An HTTP request is made to access a resource, usually a web site on a remote machine. In the case of my ebook site, you request it's initial action by typing in: http://Broquard-ebooks.com. You are entering a domain name and the browser uses the DNS services (Domain Name Services) to look up the actual four-part numerical 32-bit address of the server hosting the ebook site. This is the IP address. It sends the request out to the internet via port 80, usually.

The web server, monitoring port 80, then sees the incoming request and it handles the request. The server's job is to construct a web page, by dealing with check box results, listbox selections, text box choices and so on, in order to provide the correct information to be sent back to the client's browser. The server then sends back to the client the web page in HTML format, Hypertext Markup Language.

The client browser receives this message in HTML and proceeds to follow its commands to display the web page. It can also be sent back some data verification and checking functions that the browser can use to validate subsequent user choices on the page's controls. For example, on the ebook order page, the Calculate Total button instructs the browser to call a function within the server's sent web page to compute the total cost of the order, thereby not making the server have to do this calculation itself, lessening the workload of the server.

One of the most troubling aspects of web programming is that HTTP is a stateless protocol. As soon as the server sends off the responds to the client browser, the server forgets completely what it has sent! We are so used to having our data members being safely stored on the stack. That is, Function A holds a number of data members whose values are nicely established. Now Function A calls Function B. When Function B returns back to Function A, Function A has no memory of any of its previously stored data members!

Thus, a web programmer must take very specific steps to "remember" information as it goes from web page to web page. Such information might be the credit card number, the login id, the person's address, and so on. Cookies are one way to "remember" information, but storing the data in a database is, in my opinion, a far better way to do it. In fact, my ebook site does not use cookies at all, all data is stored in a database instead.

A **web application** is really a collection of files, .htm, .asp, .aspx, image files, XML files, and so on. These are stored on the server machine in one or more directories. A **web server application** is in charge of hosting your web applications, providing a number of services, such as security, email services, even FTP, file transfer protocol.

The early web applications used CGI (Common Gateway Interface) which consumed large amounts of server resources and required separate application instances, which made sites based on them difficult to scale to large volumes. Later, ASP (Active Server Pages) became the norm. With these, scripts were sent to both the client and server to assist in the processing of user entered data. However, the parser was now faced with alternating between rendering ordinary HTML and then interpreting and executing your script code, a much less efficient process than simply executing compiled code.

The ASP.NET model is a major evolution forward. It is a fully compiled application that is run by the server utilizing the full capabilities of the .NET framework, which consists of a large toolkit of development tools. ASP.NET blurs the line between program development and web development. It is fully object oriented in nature, including an event driven architecture, and is dedicated to high performance. It is fully integrated with the .NET framework, you have access to all of the classes we've seen so far and then some. It is fully compiled, not interpreted, yielding fast execution.

ASP.NET provides support for two different types of web page controls. First, it supports the older **HTML Controls**. These are the controls, such as text boxes, which can be by normal HTML tags, using any kind of editor, including Notepad. These provide a fast migration path for older ASP pages. The down side of using these older controls is the heavy burden of programming placed upon the programmer. ASP.NET now provides support for the newer **Web Controls**. These are OOP replacements for the older HTML Controls, providing vastly more and easier programming support.

Web Controls are always prefixed with asp: followed by the class name. `<asp:TextBox id="name" Text="Hello World" runat="server" />`

The benefit of using these newer controls is enormous. Now we can interact with them as we would other types of OOP controls: `Name.Text = "New Value";` I will be using these new controls predominately.

Deployment of an ASP.NET web site to a production server is a breeze. One simply copied all of the file and folders of the development site. A web.config file handles all of the registration duties. In short, you do not need to tinker with the Windows registry or even the IIS server.

Setting Up Visual Studio .NET 2008 For Web Projects

Visual Studio supports the old way of making web projects and the new way. The old way is to make a solution project with the .sln and related files. However, the new way is called a Projectless Web Site. With the new way, it assumes that every file in the web folder and subfolders are part of the web site and doesn't need to compile anything. The new way is vastly superior in many ways, the least of which is deployment. When you are ready to deploy your new site, you just copy the whole thing onto the service provider and you are all set. This is a great convenience and will be the way that I am going in this text.

However, to make best use of this new method, one should save all of your Visual Studio settings. Go to Tools—Import Export Settings. Export all of your current settings to a file. Name it Non-Web or something that you can remember. The use the same menu selection and choose Reset All Settings and pick Web Development Settings. Presto, you will have all of the most optimum settings for creating projectless web applications.

When you go to create a new Web Project or to open an existing one, on the File menu, choose, File New Web Site or Open Web Site, not projects.

Setting Up Web Servers

This text is geared toward students, not web service providers. Hence, for students and others who are in the process of developing a web site, we need ways to create and test web sites. Fortunately, there are several options available. None of these are intended to act as a final, production host.

Method 1—Two Or More Computers with One Being the Server

Microsoft's server is called IIS, Internet Information Services and it supports ASP (active server pages) as well as ASP.NET. With many computers, IIS is already installed. However, with some operating systems, it is not automatically selected when the operating system is installed. Thus, you may need to install IIS on your computer to be able to make and run web applications. To install, go to the Control Panel and select Add/Remove Windows Components, then select IIS.

Note, with Visual Studio .NET 2008, you should have IIS installed before you install Visual Studio. If you install IIS afterwards, it may not run properly. To fix it, you will need to run the DOS command line utility: `aspnet_regiis.exe /i`

A single IIS installation is able to host many different web sites. It accomplishes this by using virtual directories, one for each site. Each virtual directory is tied to a specific physical folder.

This method is particularly suited for those who have two or more computers for development. For example, I have one of my networked desktops with IIS setup on it. I can then create and/or install my web applications on this machine and then use the other machines to test and browse the site. Alternatively, I can create the web site on one of the other machines and then copy it to this server for final testing before I copy the site off to the real web service provider's site. The details using of this method are the same as Method 2.

Method 2—Single Computer Using IIS

Typically, when IIS is installed, it creates a folder usually on C drive called Inetpub. Beneath this directory are the various web sites. Under Windows XP, Control Panel—Administrative Tools is the IIS program, Internet Information Services, shown in Figure 12.1

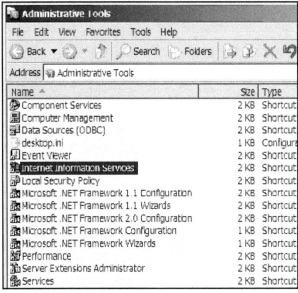

Figure 12.1 Starting IIS

Launch IIS. You will see an icon for the Web Sites, FTP Sites, and email (SMPT). Click on the Default Web Site icon, right click and bring up the context sensitive menu. Select New | Virtual Directory. We need to organize our web sites for this course. Let's make a new folder to contain them called C#Programming. Our new various sample and testing web sites can then be created in folders beneath this one. The wizard will take you step by step through the process. Later on, you can use properties on this virtual directory to alter such things as permissions, if you don't get them setup initially as they need to be. See Figure 12.2 below.

The Alias ought to be the same name as the folder, C#Programming in this case. Next, enter the actual folder name by pressing the Browse button. Keep the alias and the folder the same name to avoid confusion later on. You will need to navigate to C:\Inetpub\wwwroot and then press Make New Folder to actually create this new folder which will eventually contain the various web site project folders that you make, one for each sample web site. Next, check the security access rights that a client browsing these sites must have. By default, Read and Run Scripts are checked. If database actions storing new data are going to be needed or if your web site will be writing new files to the folder, then check Write as well. Remember, you can always later on come back and change the permissions.

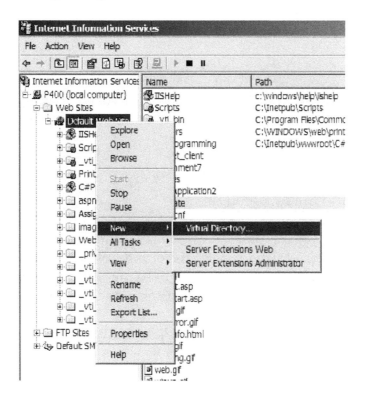

When done, again right click on the Default Web Site icon and make sure that it is Started. If so, Started will be grayed out and Stop will be active, shown in Figure 12.2 above. Use Method 3 below to begin browsing to this new web site.

Method 3—Using Visual Studio's Web Server to Setup a Local Host to Any Web Folder on Your Computer

You can create new Web Sites in any folder on your computer and then use Visual Studio's Web Server to establish a local host to that site so you can then browse with any browser. To do this, open a Visual Studio DOS prompt. **Tools—Visual Studio 2005 Command Prompt**. This launches a DOS window.

Run the **weddev.webserver.exe** program. Specify some port number and the path to the folder containing the website. I copied the first sample Pgm12aWeb site from the Sample programs folder which comes with the ebook and placed it into the IIS folder. However, I could just as easily entered the full path to where this folder is located where the ebook was installed.

```
C:\Program  Files\Microsoft  Visual  Studio  9.0\vc\bin>webdev.webserver.exe
/port:12346 /path:"C:\Inetpub\wwwroot\c#programming\Pgm12aWeb"
```

In your browser, enter http://localhost:12346/ and the web page is shown. This assumes that the initial page to be shown is default.aspx.

This method is convenient when you wish to examine sample web pages from this ebook or from other textbooks. Usually the web pages are in sample program folders beneath some arbitrary folder where you have installed them.

Method 4—Letting Visual Studio .NET 2008 Automatically Run Your Web Site When You Choose Debug—Start without Debugging

When you make a new Web Site project, you can simply click on Start without Debugging as you normally would to run any program. Visual Studio handles the details, launching your default browser and showing the page automatically. Obviously, this will be the easiest approach for a student to use while working on their homework and practice assignments.

In summary, you will most likely use Methods 3 and 4 to view my sample web sites and to create and view your own sites.

Making New Web Site Projects Using Visual Studio .NET 2008

Vitally important: when making a new web site, do not choose New Project! Rather, choose New Web Site as shown in Figure 12.3 below.

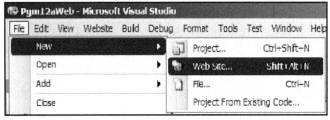

Figure 12.3 Making a New Web Site Project

Choose ASP.NET Web Site. The location should be File. The alternatives are HTTP and FTP. These two allow you to connect directly to a Web Server to upload the project as you go. File will be the default. To the right will be the proposed folder. Alter it as desired. The language should be C# not Visual Basic. When you click Finish, the wizard will create a basic starting page along with the needed files and folders. This is shown below in Figure 12.4

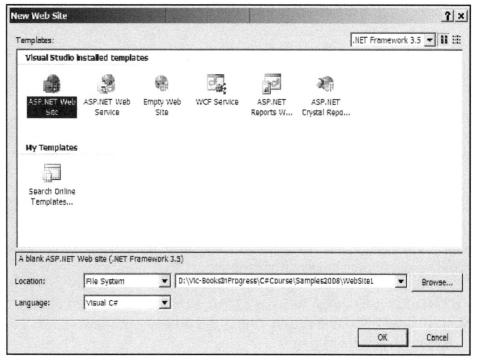

Figure 12.4 Making a New Web Site

Immediately, we are into html coding. This test does not assume that you have any prior exposure to html coding. Let's begin by covering the fundamentals.

Basic HTTP Logic

The simplest Web page consists of plain text files that contain **markups** or **tags** defining how the browser is to show or what it is to do with the item between the tags. These tags are surrounded by < >. Between the angle brackets is the start of tag or the end of tag keywords.

For example, the tag <title> tells the browser to display as a title the text immediately after the tag. The end of the title text is marked by the end title tag, </title>. In general, the end tags all begin with a /. Thus, we could code
<title>ACME Manufacturing Web Page</title>
The browser will then display this text as a title, usually in a large style font prominently on the page.

Commonly, a Web page also has hyperlinks, which are links to other sections of this page or other pages of this site or even totally different sites.

Every HTML document on the Web has a URL, a Uniform Resource Locator, that defines where this document is located. For example, coding this url into a browser
http://www.broquard-ebooks.com

causes the browser to find my site's host server. Since no specific web page is requested, the browser requests a page called default.htm. One could enter this
http://www.broquard-ebooks.com/**default.htm**
This directs the browser to my server and requests the server to send the default.htm document back using the http protocol. There are other file extensions used, such as .asp and .aspx for ASP.NET files of C#.

A part of the action that occurs under the hood is the resolution of the www.broquard-ebooks.com into an actual IP address which happens to be: 64.225.80.185. This translation into the real IP address is done by a DNS, a Domain Name Server, which is a computer that maintains a huge table of all of these addresses. The translation operation is called a DNS Lookup.

Sometimes you may see additional information in the URL such as
http://www.broquard-ebooks.com/**scripts/main.asp**
Here scripts is a folder on the server system. Files that have the asp extension are Active Server Pages. Asp pages contain script that the server executes to build the page that is to be returned to the client browser to display. Asp pages allow the server to meet various requirements such as displaying a page with links to the books you have purchases. Aspx files are C# files.

However, for security reasons, these folders we enter are not the actual folder names but are "virtual folders" which the server translates into the actual folder names on the server. This allows hiding of the real folders from hackers.

When a client requests a Web page, it sends a GET HTML command including the protocol and its version, such as

GET /scripts/main.htm HTTP/1.1

The server gets this command and first returns an acknowledgment.

HTTP/1.1 200 OK

or the famous or infamous

HTTP/1.1 404 Not Found

The server then sends some headers that identify what it is about to send, such as

Content-type: text/html

or perhaps

Content-type: image/jpg

Then after sending a blank line which means end of headers, the server sends the actual page or HTML document itself.

Some Additional Terminology

Most Web-based applications are **multi-tiered**. That is, multi-tier applications divide their functionality into separate groups or tiers, logical groupings of functionality. Each tier can be on the same machine or reside on totally different machines.

Typically, the **client tier** or **top tier** runs the browser; this is typically your computer running its browser. The information often lies in a database located on a **data tier** machine or **bottom tier**. The Web server is often called the **middle tier** and implements the presentation logic or business rules for the system. Such rules try to guarantee that the information is correct before it is given to the database tier.

For example, when one purchases an ebook from a site, first you enter your charge information in the browser page. Then it is sent to the middle Web-server for processing. The server verifies all is okay before it sends the actual charge request to the Charge Card Web Server which actually bills your card. Thus, the processing workload is spread among various systems and computers.

The HTML Document

The html file consists of a set of html tags. Each html file has basically the same overall structure. Let's examine this first. In Visual Studio, without any project open, chose File—New File and then pick HTML Page. Figure 12.5 shows what is generated for us.

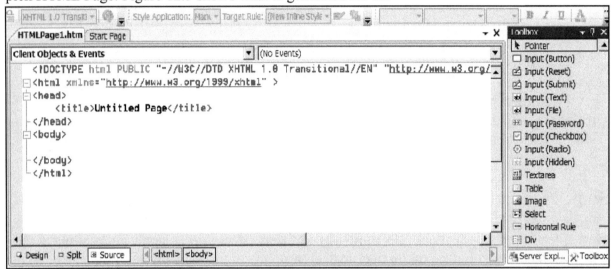

Figure 12.5 A New HTML Page

There are a number of things to note here. The first is the document type tag. This tag tells the IDE to validate this document coding against the XHTML standard. HTML is very loose in its syntax. XHTML is an attempt to improve upon this. Just above this window is a drop down box that allows you to select alternatives.

Notice the entire page is contained bewteen the <html> and </html> tags. Next comes the header section denoted by tags <head> and </head>. Within the header is the <title> </title> tags which defines the caption that the browser will show when it displays this page. Here it would show "Untitled Page."

Most all of our coding goes into the next section denoted by the tags <body> </body>, representing the body of the document to be shown. Here we can display all manner of information. Before we get into those details, let's look more closely at the Visual Studio Editor which is showing our page, Figure 12.5 above.

Across the bottom of the editor window, you will see Design, Split, Source, and a tabbed series, in this case showing html and body tags. Clicking on one of the tags will select all of the coding within those tags. At any time, you can click on Design view which will show you approximately what your page currently looks like, if it were to be shown in a browser. Source view displays the actual html coding. Split divides the window into halves, showing both views simultaneously.

Across on the right side is the tool box which contains items that can be dragged onto our page, including the usual things one expects to see on a web page. Text boxes, check boxes, radio buttons, and tables, for example. Across the top area of tool bars, we have some new ones that have appeared. Some of these allow us to easily select colors, fonts, and font sizes.

In the Design view, right click and get Properties up. Choose Body. Now click on the BgColor property. This allows you to set the background color for the whole body. This brings up the color picker dialog, shown in Figure 12.6. You can enter hex or click on a color.

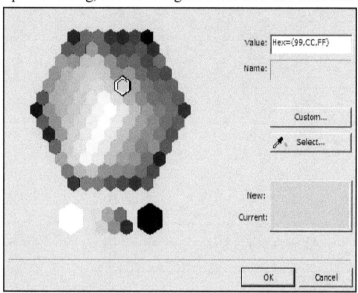

Figure 12.6 Selecting the Background Color Property

To illustrate more of the html tags and their use, let's make a sample web site. **Choose File—New Web Page**. I called it Pgm12aWeb. When it finishes creating our basic shell, notice the html coding. It has two additional elements within the <body>.

```
<form id="form1" runat="server">
<div>

</div>
</form>
```

Many web pages contain a form, which is used to group a lot of controls, such as text boxes, together to be able to send that collection of user choices back to the server. The use of a form greatly aids the gathering of user entered data for processing. Hence, the default web page installs this for us. Each form on a page has an id, but commonly there is only one form per page. The run at server option states that the server will be running server side logic to help fill up this page.

257

The <div> tag identifies a division within the form. It is used to group items together, often to apply a given set of styles to all of the items within the division, unless they specifically override those styles. A form can have many divisions. Again, notice that the Visual Studio adds these two new items to the list of tab items at the bottom of the editor window.

Let's go ahead and set some overall properties. I right clicked and brought up the Properties box and clicked on the <body> tag. I set the BgColor to a light blue. Next, I clicked on the <div> tag and clicked on the style property, pressing the ... button on the left of it. Under the Font category, I chose x-large for the font size and under Block I chose the text center property as shown in Figure 12.7.

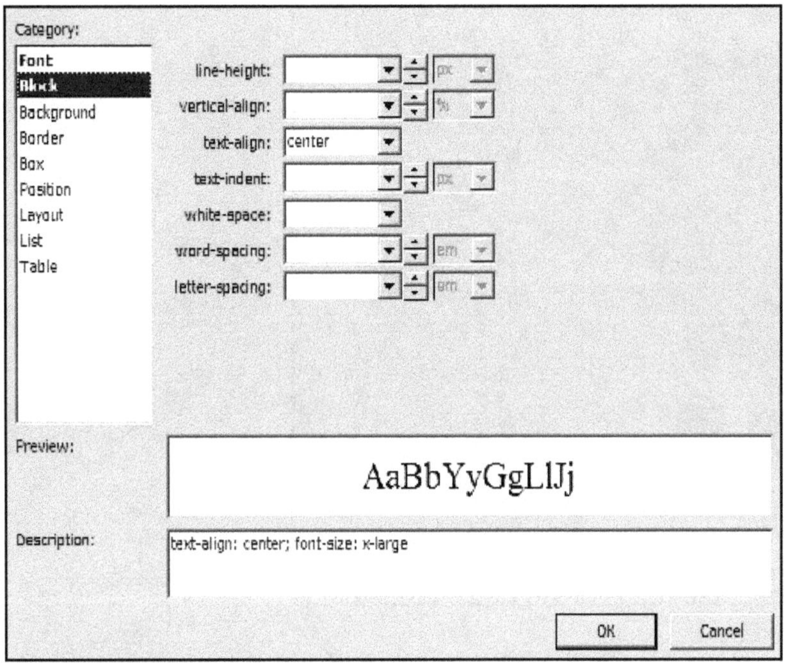

Figure 12.7 Choosing Div Style Properties

Figure 12.8 shows what we now have.

What are the coding rules, so to speak? It is a wise policy to follow the XHTML standard.

Tag and attribute names must be in lower case.
All elements must be closed either with an end tag or one that is self closing, as in
        <p> </p> or <br/>.
Attribute values must be enclosed in double quotes as in runat="server."
The id attribute is used to name the control instead of the name attribute.

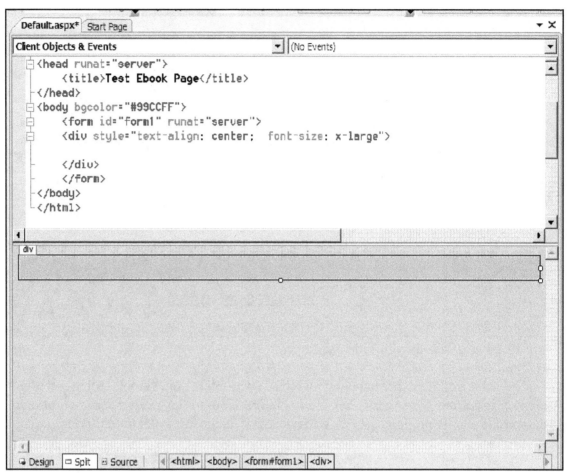

Figure 12.8 Pgm12aWeb with the Basic Styles Set

Now let's add a title. There are several types of headers, but the tag <h1> is the larger. I added

```
<h1> Broquard eBooks Test Page</h1>
```

as the first line inside of the division.

The tag <p> defines the start of a paragraph. As with normal writing, when the browser gets to the next <p> tag, it double spaces. If you want the next line of text not to be double spaced, embed the </br> line break tag, which causes single spacing. Below the header tag in the source view, type a <p> and notice that the editor gives you a choice of all of the possible tags and when you chose "p," it then adds the end tag </p> for you.

I added an image to the project folder called logo1s.jpg. Let's add this image to this first paragraph. On the tool box, find the Image icon and drag it into the source view within this new paragraph. Get its properties up and enter logo1s for the ImageUrl property. Notice the image is not shown in the Design view. Here's what we have coded so far.

```
<div style="text-align: center;  font-size: x-large">
<h1> Broquard eBooks Test Page</h1>
<p>
<asp:Image ID="Image1" runat="server" ImageUrl="logo1s.jpg" />
</p>
```

Now let's see what it looks like so far. Chose Debug—Start without Debugging. Your browser should be launched and the web page shown. Figure 12.9 shows what it looks like in mine.

Figure 12.9 Pgm12aWeb with Title and Image

Now let's add another paragraph which says to Pick Your Ebook. After entering <p> and then enter to get the </P>, enter Pick Your Ebook. Now in the Design view, right click on the paragraph and choose properties. Click on Style. Let's set the font color to red. Your line should now look like this.

```
<p style="color: #FF0000">Pick Your Ebook</p>
```

Now make a new paragraph and then drag the Radio Button List icon and drop it into this new paragraph. We are going to add a set of radio buttons to pick which book is desired. Once it is added, in Design View, click on properties once more. We are going to add the actual radio buttons with their text. In this case, the actual choices are going to be hard coded into the group of radio buttons as opposed to having the server build them dynamically on the fly for us.

Click on the Items property. This brings up the add strings dialog. Add a new one and then enter the desired text in the value property of the added string. Figure 12.10 shows all that I have entered. Also set the BorderColor to black, the BorderStyle to Solid, and the BorderWidth to 2. Finally, let's set the background color to say yellow. Here's what code is generated.

```
<p>
<asp:RadioButtonList ID="RadioButtonList1" runat="server"
   BackColor="Yellow" BorderColor="Black" BorderStyle="Solid"
   BorderWidth="2px">
   <asp:ListItem    Value="Cpp    for    Computer    Science    and
Engineering"></asp:ListItem>
   <asp:ListItem Value="Beginning Data Structures"></asp:ListItem>
```

```
<asp:ListItem Value="Advanced Data Structures"></asp:ListItem>
<asp:ListItem Value="Object Oriented Programming"></asp:ListItem>
<asp:ListItem Value="Windows MFC Programming I"></asp:ListItem>
</asp:RadioButtonList>
</p>
```

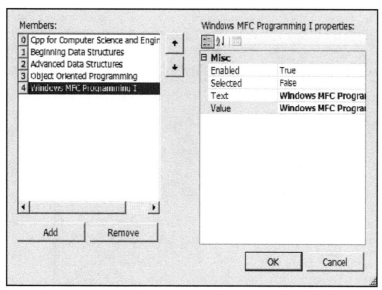

Figure 12.10 Adding the Radio Button String Values

Now we again test it and see what it looks like in our browser. Start without Debugging. What a second! Firefox has our yellow box up against the left edge of the window and all of the radio buttons are centered, instead of being left justified as the default alignment of the control properties says. In IE, the yellow box is indeed centered in the window as desired, but it also has the buttons centered instead of left aligned as they should be!

Welcome to the slight differences between browsers! When developing a web page, be sure to check how the page appears in all of the browsers that you anticipate will be coming to your site. Each displays things slightly differently.

Let's leave this problem go for now and return to its fix later on. Next, add another paragraph. This time, let's drag a list box into this paragraph. Next, right click on its properties and choose Items. Again, add the same five items as we just did for the radio button group. You should have the following added.

```
<p>
<asp:ListBox ID="ListBox1" runat="server">
    <asp:ListItem>Cpp     for     Computer     Science     and
Engineering</asp:ListItem>
<asp:ListItem>Beginning Data Structures</asp:ListItem>
<asp:ListItem>Advanced Data Structures</asp:ListItem>
<asp:ListItem>Object Oriented Programming</asp:ListItem>
<asp:ListItem>Windows MFC Programming I</asp:ListItem>
</asp:ListBox>
```

261

```
</p>
```

Now let's run it in two browsers and see the results. Viola, both browsers display the list box properly centered. Finally, let's add one more paragraph and drag a button into it. Change its text to read "Submit," simulating what the user of this page would do once he or she has made their selection.

```
<p>
 <asp:Button ID="Button1" runat="server" Text="Submit" />
</p>
```

The next two figures, 12.11 and 12.12 show the results in Firefox and then IE6. Compare the results.

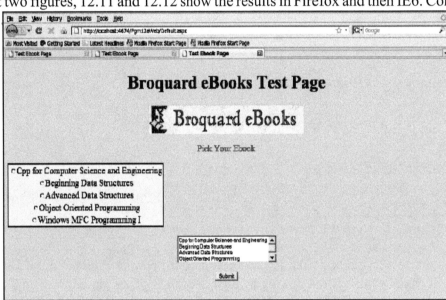

Figure 12.11 Firefox 3.0 Showing Our Web Page

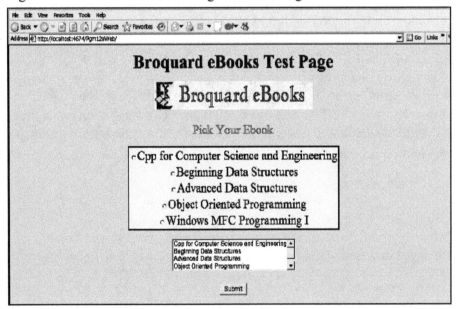

Figure 12.12 IE 6 Showing Our Web Page

Again, I cannot emphasize that you should always test with several browsers. We will need to fix these problems. The font size of "Pick Your Ebook" text is different between the two browsers. The centering of the radio button list is wrong in Firefox, while both browsers are centering the radio buttons and their text incorrectly.

To fix the errors, I resorted to using a deprecated option, align="center" on the radio button list properties. This then aligns the whole radio button list centered. To fix the incorrect alignment of the buttons themselves, from centered to left aligned, I resorted to using a style for table rows. Why? The radio button list is actually rendered as if it were a table of rows with one column, rather like a spreadsheet with only one column active. I used the following in the header section.

```
<style type="text/css"> td{text-align:left}</style>
</head>
```

Figure 12.13 shows the corrected web page in Firefox. Still IE6 uses the wrong font in the radio button text.

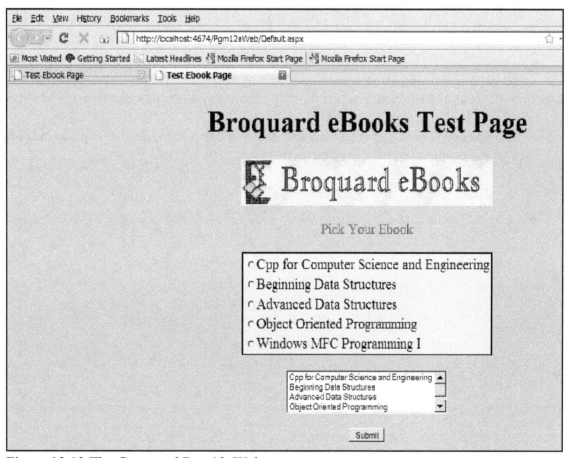

Figure 12.13 The Corrected Pgm12aWeb

Some Design Tips

By now, you've played around with this sample web page. You can drag asp: items onto your source view or design view. You can select it and change its many properties. You can also type in the tags directly into the source view as well, which is the easiest way to add heading and title lines, in my opinion.

Normally, the positioning of the lines and controls is on a flowing basis, one after the other. Sometimes, you want specific locations. In such cases, you can use absolute positioning which is also known as grid layout. Be careful with this, because items at absolute positions will be located at those precise spots and cannot move around when the client browser window changes sizes, sometimes leaving one's item off of the browser's current window area.

Where absolute positioning is often used is with divisions <div> where one wishes to keep a menu plastered against the left edge of the browser window, for example. Think of a div as a floating box, invisible usually, though you can give it borders and colors, etc.

Some controls have a smart tag, which is a tiny arrow on its upper right corner. Clicking this brings up key actions that one can perform with it, such as adding new items in the listbox.

The fancy style builder can be used to create one time only styles for specific items or it can be placed in the header and referenced by many subsequent controls.

Scripting

In the previous web program, we have a static page. Further, nothing happens when the Submit button is pressed. Obviously, there is more that must be coded. Enter scripting, which is coding designed to perform a special task. Scripting is done in JavaScript or VBScript. In this text, I will use JavaScript exclusively because it is much like C++ and C# in nature. There are two places where scripting can be done, on the client-side and on the server-side.

Client-side Scripting and Server-side Scripting

Client-side scripting is coding emitted into the source html page for the browser to use to perform some tasks. Typically, it is used to validate user data entry prior to posting the results back to the server. This avoids many round trips of messages.

For example, the customer must enter their name, address, city, state, zip code, and email address on your form. A poor way to do it would be to send the collection of data straight back to the server when the user clicks Submit. What if they forgot to enter their state code and their email address? The server discovers this and has to resend back the page with the partial information on it as well as appropriate error messages. This wastes valuable bandwidth and connections to the busy server. Instead, the server sends out client-side validation coding, often in the form of a JavaScript function that the client uses. Now when the user presses Submit, first the browser calls this validation coding. If it fails, that coding causes error messages to appear allowing the user to correct them. Only when the validation is successful, indicating all data appears correct, does the browser actually post the information back to the server.

Okay, in Pgm12aWeb, the user must make a choice, either in the list box or radio button list. Pressing the Submit button ought to fire an error if nothing has yet been selected, so let's add some client-side coding to deal with this possibility.

Here we run into a major change in design philosophy with the current version of C#. In straight ASP style coding, heavy usage is made of client-side functions sent by the server to the client embedded within the html coding. Such functions did all manner of client-side validation. However, designers also needed to redo all of that error checking on the server side when the page was finally sent by the client browser back to the server. Thus, in effect, the same error checking is done twice! In the old days, programmers had to code the same functions twice, once for the client side, once for the server side.

The new ASP.NET handles this situation with its validator widgets. Essentially, we drag a validator onto our form and tie it to one of the controls which must be validated for correct data in some manner. Then, we can specify that the validation be done both by the server when it receives the page back from the client and by the client before it sends the page back to the server.

This brings us to the key design models that can be followed: **inline code** and **code-behind**. With inline code, all of the coding to make the web page operational is in the single aspx file. While it is handy to keep everything in one place, on more complex web pages, this file becomes large and merges the display actions from the code that makes the actions work.

C# introduces a new approach, the code behind model, which separates the web page into two pieces. One is the aspx file with the HTML and control tags in it and a .cs code file with the source code to handle the operational aspects dictated by the controls, such as loading a database. This model provides a better organization of a web page by separating out the visual aspects from the programming logic to make the controls work as needed. I will be using the code behind model throughout. If you make one of the new web site, projectless, you have no choice but to use the code-behind model.

When you make a text box control in your aspx file,
```
<asp:TextBox id="name" Text="Hello World" runat="server" />
```
the compiler also places a hidden line in your code-behind cs file.
```
protected System.Web.UI.TextBox name;
```
Thus, in our cs file, we can access it as
```
name = "New name";
```
This is very convenient indeed for performing operations on the controls.

Further, you can even use the debugger and step through the web program's execution! However, the first time you run the debugger, Visual Studio notifies you that you will later on need to remove a debug line from the configuration file before you put it into production.

Web Forms and Page Processing

Unique to ASP.NET is the concept of Web Forms, the web pages that clients view in their browsers. With web forms, we can create an application much like we do with Windows forms, using the same control based interface. The idea is to enable web developers to create web applications rapidly with full features. Web applications run on the server which sends a web form to the client browser. Once the user has made their entries, the client needs to send the data back to the server for processing and perhaps storing in a database. This is called a **postback**. The client browser posts back to the server the page with its data or selections made by the user or when certain actions are taken by the user, such as a mouse hovering over a specific location. Once ASP.NET receives the page, it can then issue the server-side events to your code.

266

Web applications are stateless. Once the page is rendered by the server and sent off to the client browser, all web page objects and client specific information (stored in controls such as a text box) are destroyed! To get around this stateless affair, ASP.NET provides a view state mechanism which automatically embeds information about the page into a hidden field in the rendered HTML sent to the browser.

The simplest way to send data back to the server is to provide a "Submit" button. When the user clicks Submit, the browser collects all of the information and pastes it into a long string which is then POSTed back to the server via an HTTP POST command.

Suppose that we had three text boxes whose names were: FirstName, LastName, and State. When the submit action occurs, the browser sends back a string similar to this.

```
FirstName=Sam&LastName=Spade&State=IL
```

It sends named pairs, the control's name and its value.

In old ASP style, we could get at it this way.

```
var firstName = Request.Form["FirstName"];
```

In the new OOP fashion, we now have direct access to it.

```
string firstName = FirstName.Text;
```

This is a vast improvement. But it is even more amazing. If you had:

```
<asp:Label id=Welcome runat="server"/>
```

then you could also do this next.

```
Welcome.Text = "Welcome " + FirstName + " " + LastName;
```

and the welcome message can appear in the browser's window!

If this isn't fancy enough, the new web controls also have an **automatic postback** feature or property. The controls will fire events back to your server, such as changing a radio button or clicking a check box or making different listbox selection. When you set the automatic postback property to true, ASP.NET embeds a client-side **_doPostBack** function, whose task is to set some values about the event and submitting the form back to the server. This then changes a client-side event into a server-side event.

Another problem the ASP.NET solves for us deals with this stateless mess, data and settings get lost after every postback. It solves this with what is called a **View State**. Every time that a page is posed back, it recreates the page based on the initial state dictated by the aspx file. It then deserializes all of the view state information and updates all of the controls. It then embeds a hidden field with these new changes in it as it sends the page back to the client. Thus, the information is not lost any longer. This allows the server to free resources once it sends the page off to the client. When it is posted back, it is a simple matter to recreate it. This makes for a greater scalability to large, highly active web sites.

Where are we likely to put coding for postbacks? Let's look at the code-behind for the simple web site we've created in this chapter, Pgm12aWeb. In it's .cs file we have the following.

```
public partial class _Default : System.Web.UI.Page
{
    protected void Page_Load(object sender, EventArgs e)
    {

    }

}
```

When a browser posts a page back to us, a member bool is set, **IsPostBack**. Typically, we can respond this way.

```
public partial class _Default : System.Web.UI.Page
{
    protected void Page_Load(object sender, EventArgs e)
    {
    if (Page.IsPostBack) {
        // here we handle the client's post back to us
    }
    }

}
```

The sequence of actions for a page go as follows. The server receives a request for a page from the client browser. It then calls **Page_Load** to handle page initializations. Each item that has the runat="server" specified, it generates the HTML for the control, placing it into the resultant page eventually to be sent to the browser. Again, the **IsPostBack** is used. If the bool is false, then this is the first time the page is being created and databases may need to be opened and queried to fill up tables and such with the initial information. On postbacks, the server does not have to redo all this work, the data is saved in the view state, eliminating tons of server workload.

From here, it goes into a Validation phase, applying various validation rules to the controls. We will use them in the next sample. Once this is done, ASP.NET then fires off any and all events that have taken place since the last postback. Next, the page is rendered and sent off to the client browser. Finally, it enters the clean up phase. Here, the page objects still exists, but the HTML can't be changed, it has already been sent. The garbage collector goes into action, deleting objects that are no longer being referenced.

Here is the actual HTML code that ASP.NET sent to the browser. You can view this by choosing View-Source in your browser.

```
<!DOCTYPE html PUBLIC "-//W3C//DTD XHTML 1.0 Transitional//EN"
"http://www.w3.org/TR/xhtml1/DTD/xhtml1-transitional.dtd">
```

```
<html xmlns="http://www.w3.org/1999/xhtml">
<head><title> Test Ebook Page </title>
 <style type="text/css"> td{text-align:left}</style>
</head>
<body bgcolor="#99CCFF">
 <form name="form1" method="post" action="Default.aspx" id="form1">
 <div>
  <input type="hidden" name="__VIEWSTATE" id="__VIEWSTATE"
     value="/wEPDwUJMTEyMDI3NzMxZGTYzUzmKdDR8tNpo4gSMDneb1btcQ==" />
 </div>
 <div style="text-align: center;  font-size: x-large">
   <h1> Broquard eBooks Test Page</h1>
   <p>
     <img id="Image1" src="logo1s.jpg" style="border-width:0px;" />
   </p>
   <p style="color: #FF0000">Pick Your Ebook</p>
   <p>
            <table    id="RadioButtonList1"   align="center"   border="0"
style="background-color:Yellow;border-color:Black;border-width:2px;bor
der-style:Solid;">
     <tr>
               <td><input   id="RadioButtonList1_0"   type="radio"
name="RadioButtonList1" value="Cpp for Computer Science and Engineering"
/><label   for="RadioButtonList1_0">Cpp   for   Computer   Science   and
Engineering</label>
       </td>
     </tr>
     <tr>
         <td><input      id="RadioButtonList1_1"      type="radio"
name="RadioButtonList1"  value="Beginning  Data  Structures"  /><label
for="RadioButtonList1_1">Beginning Data Structures</label>
       </td>
     </tr>
     <tr>
         <td><input      id="RadioButtonList1_2"      type="radio"
name="RadioButtonList1"  value="Advanced  Data  Structures"  /><label
for="RadioButtonList1_2">Advanced Data Structures</label>
       </td>
     </tr>
     <tr>
         <td><input      id="RadioButtonList1_3"      type="radio"
name="RadioButtonList1"  value="Object  Oriented  Programming"  /><label
for="RadioButtonList1_3">Object Oriented Programming</label>
       </td>
     </tr>
     <tr>
         <td><input       id="RadioButtonList1_4"      type="radio"
name="RadioButtonList1"  value="Windows  MFC  Programming  I"  /><label
for="RadioButtonList1_4">Windows MFC Programming I</label>
       </td>
```

```
    </tr>
   </table>
  </p>
  <p>
    <select size="4" name="ListBox1" id="ListBox1">
    <option value="Cpp for Computer Science and Engineering">Cpp for
Computer Science and Engineering</option>
    <option    value="Beginning    Data    Structures">Beginning    Data
Structures</option>
    <option    value="Advanced    Data    Structures">Advanced    Data
Structures</option>
    <option    value="Object   Oriented    Programming">Object   Oriented
Programming</option>
    <option value="Windows MFC Programming I">Windows MFC Programming
I</option>
    </select>

  </p>
  <p>
   <input type="submit" name="Button1" value="Submit" id="Button1" />
  </p>
 </div>
 <div>
  <input type="hidden" name="__EVENTVALIDATION" id="__EVENTVALIDATION"
value="/wEWDQLO5/HpDALhzvb5DAK8vfAcAuT8ttYBAvjcl7YHAve6kNwPAveMotMNAqv
7t6YIAvaIscMEAq7J94kFArLp1ukDAr2P0YMLAoznisYG6EXOtkf+cH/ea63k3T7JrzbxB
tk=" />
 </div>
 </form>
</body>
</html>
```

You can see the hidden view state items that ASP.NET has installed to keep track of the values of the form. You can also see that it implemented the radio button list control as a table with each row being one of the radio button items.

The **Page** class which encapsulates a web page contains several useful functions and members. It contains a **Session** object which contains user-specific information that needs to persist between page requests. It contains name=value pairs and often contains the user name, user id, a shopping cart and so on.

The **Application** object contains global information, again in named pairs. One might store the company contact values here to be inserted into numerous pages.

The **Request** object represents the browser's request. Some useful members include **FilePath** which contains the real file path relative to the server for this page, and **QueryString**, which contains the query string sent from the browser.

The **Response** object contains the function **Redirect**, which can be used to transfer control to another page or site. It is a round trip message, instructing the client to request this new page. The new page title will then be displayed by the browser.

```
Response.Redirect ("SomeNewPage.aspx");
Response.Redirect ("Http:\\SomeNewSite");
```

The **Server** object has two useful functions. The **MapPath** function returns the physical file path that corresponds to a specified virtual file path on the server. This way, one can get a real path so that you can open files and input or write them to/from the server.

```
string path = Server.MapPath ("somefile.txt");
StreamReader r = new StreamReader (path);
```

The second function is **Transfer**, which transfers control to another page. This one is fast as it does not send any message to the client, only the new page. It has the quirk in that the browser will still be showing the previous page name and not this new one. Thus, if the user does a refresh, the wrong page will be requested by the browser.

```
Server.Transfer ("SomeNewPage.aspx");
```

Armed with these basics, we need to take a closer look at the controls and validators and how to use them effectively.

Programming Problems

None

Chapter 13—Web Controls

Now it's time to explore making a series of web pages using some of the web controls available to us. The next four figures illustrate Pgm13aWeb in operation in a browser. This application represents the start of an order system for an e-commerce site. The user enters the quantities of ebooks to purchase and their personal information. When the user clicks Submit, the form's data is sent to the next page, which in this case summarizes his or her selections and figures the total cost of the items purchased. Figure 13.1 shows the initial page.

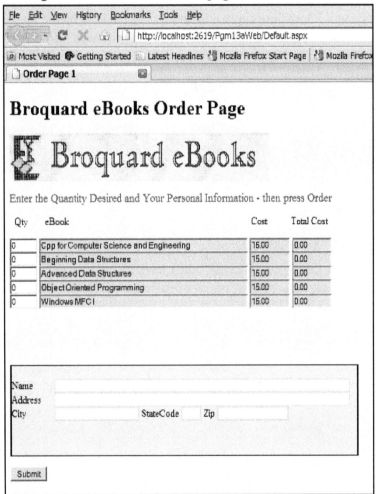

Figure 13.1 The Initial Order Page

As you look over the form, notice what kind of potential data entry errors could possibly occur. An invalid quantity, such as a letter, could be entered. The personal information could be omitted in whole or in part, such as forgetting the zip code. Figure 13.2 shows what happens if the user clicks on Submit without filling in any information at all.

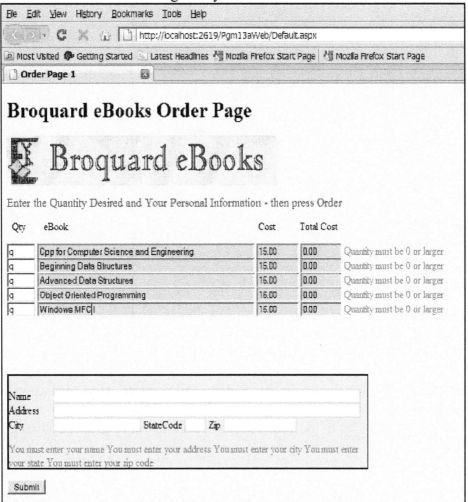

Figure 13.2 Clicking Submit with No Name and Letters for Quantity

Red error messages appear, alerting the user to omitted entries that must still be made and/or corrected.

Yet, there is still one additional possible problem. What if the user forgets to enter any quantity at all. That is, all the quantity fields are still zero? Again, this would be an error. Figure 13.3 shows what results when that happens. Another error message appears.

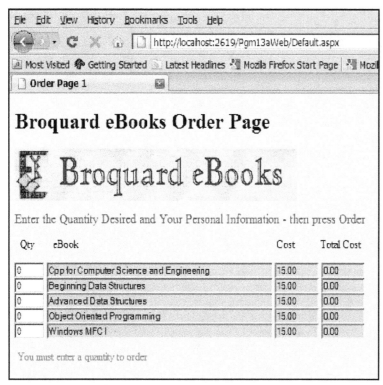

Figure 13.3 Failing to Enter Any Quantity Values

Okay, the user finally gets all of their personal information entered and makes valid entries for the quantities desired. Now when he or she presses the Submit button, all of the form's data is valid and the page can then be sent to the next web page to continue with the purchase. This next page is shown in Figure 13.4.

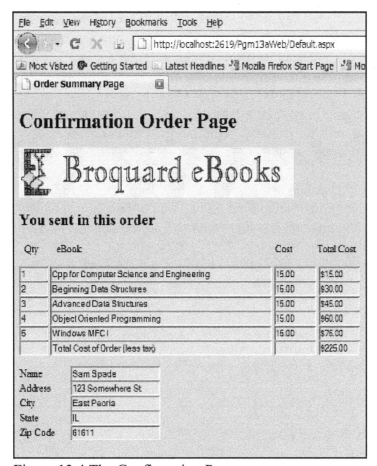

Figure 13.4 The Confirmation Page

Let's see how we can build this page. The starting point is the apparent table of five rows each with four columns

Simulating Tables the Easy Way

In straight HTML, tables were often used to layout data in rows and columns. Table handling can be fraught with difficulties, especially when disparate controls are places in the columns. While we now still have a Table widget that we can drag and use in our web pages, there is a vastly simpler, easier way to create them, the <div> sections.

One uses imbedded <div> sections. Each row is a separate <div> and the whole collection of five rows is placed into an outer <div>. Within a row, there are four text boxes. Three are marked read-only and their background color is greyed. The quantity text box is the only one in which the user will be allowed to enter data.

Further, within the browser, the tab key ought to only take the user to the quantity columns and not to the description, cost, and total cost columns. This is done by setting the **tabIndex** property. The five quantity text boxes have their **tabIndex** values arranged in order from 1 to 5. To prevent a control from being tabbed to by the user, set its **tabIndex** to -1.

Next, the widths of the columns need to be established. I used the **Width** property on each text box to set its width in pixels, as in Width="66px." Ignoring the Validators for now, we have in the source window the following thus far.

Please note the consistent indentation as I begin each new level. Code is far easier to read when you use a consistent indentation for each nested block. While the editor will highlight the ending tag when you select the beginning tag, it is lots easier to find erroneous tags when you can see the block structure of the coding.

```
<%@    Page    Language="C#"    AutoEventWireup="true"
CodeFile="Default.aspx.cs" Inherits="_Default" %>

<!DOCTYPE html PUBLIC "-//W3C//DTD XHTML 1.0 Transitional//EN"
"http://www.w3.org/TR/xhtml1/DTD/xhtml1-transitional.dtd">

<html xmlns="http://www.w3.org/1999/xhtml">
<head runat="server">
    <title>Order Page 1</title>
</head>
<body bgcolor="lightgoldenrodyellow">
 <form id="order1" runat="server" method="post" >
  <div >
   <h1>Broquard eBooks Order Page</h1>
   <img alt="logo1s.jpg" src="logo1s.jpg" />
  </div>
  <div>
   <p>
    <asp:Label ID="Label1" runat="server"
      Text="Enter the Quantity Desired and Your Personal Information - then
press Order"
             ForeColor="#3333CC" Font-Size="Large"></asp:Label>
   </p>
  </div>
  <div>
   <div style="font-size: medium">
    <p>
     <asp:Label ID="Label2" runat="server" Text="  Qty"
         Width="45px"></asp:Label>
     <asp:Label ID="Label3" runat="server"
        Text="   eBook" Width="357px"></asp:Label>
     <asp:Label ID="Label4" runat="server"
```

```
         Text="  Cost" Width="74px"></asp:Label>
      <asp:Label ID="Label5" runat="server"
         Text="Total Cost"></asp:Label>
     </p>
   </div>
   <div>
     <asp:TextBox id="Qty1" runat="server" Width="43px"
        tabIndex="1" Text="0" >0</asp:TextBox>
     <asp:TextBox ID="TextBox1" runat="server" readonly="True"
         Width="357px"
         Text="Cpp for Computer Science and Engineering"
         BackColor="#CCCCCC" TabIndex="-1"></asp:TextBox>
     <asp:TextBox ID="UCost1" runat="server" readonly="True"
         Text="15.00" BackColor="#CCCCCC" Width="66px"
         TabIndex="-1"></asp:TextBox>
     <asp:TextBox ID="TextBox3" Width="64px" runat="server"
         readonly="True" Text="0.00" BackColor="#CCCCCC"
         TabIndex="-1"></asp:TextBox>
     <asp:RangeValidator ID="RangeValidator1" runat="server"
           ControlToValidate="Qty1"
           ErrorMessage="Quantity must be 0 or larger"
           MaximumValue="9"
           MinimumValue="0"></asp:RangeValidator>
   </div>
   <div>
     <asp:TextBox id="Qty2" runat="server" Width="43px"
          tabIndex="1" Text="0" ></asp:TextBox>
     <asp:TextBox ID="TextBox4" Width="357px" runat="server"
         readonly="True"
         Text="Beginning Data Structures" BackColor="#CCCCCC"
         TabIndex="-1"></asp:TextBox>
     <asp:TextBox ID="UCost2" runat="server" readonly="True"
         Text="15.00" BackColor="#CCCCCC" Width="66px"
         TabIndex="-1"></asp:TextBox>
     <asp:TextBox ID="TextBox6" Width="64px" runat="server"
         readonly="True" Text="0.00" BackColor="#CCCCCC"
         TabIndex="-1"></asp:TextBox>
     <asp:RangeValidator ID="RangeValidator2" runat="server"
           ControlToValidate="Qty2"
           ErrorMessage="Quantity must be 0 or larger"
           MaximumValue="9"
           MinimumValue="0" Type="Integer"> </asp:RangeValidator>
   </div>
   <div>
     <asp:TextBox id="Qty3" runat="server" Width="43px"
          tabIndex="1" Text="0" ></asp:TextBox>
```

```
<asp:TextBox ID="TextBox7" runat="server" readonly="True"
    Width="357px"
  Text="Advanced Data Structures" BackColor="#CCCCCC"
    TabIndex="-1"></asp:TextBox>
<asp:TextBox ID="UCost3" runat="server" readonly="True"
    Text="15.00" BackColor="#CCCCCC" Width="66px"
    TabIndex="-1"></asp:TextBox>
<asp:TextBox ID="TextBox9" runat="server" readonly="True"
    Text="0.00" Width="64px" BackColor="#CCCCCC"
    TabIndex="-1"></asp:TextBox>
<asp:RangeValidator ID="RangeValidator3" runat="server"
    ControlToValidate="Qty3"
    ErrorMessage="Quantity must be 0 or larger"
    MaximumValue="9"
    MinimumValue="0" Type="Integer"></asp:RangeValidator>
</div>
<div>
 <asp:TextBox id="Qty4" runat="server" Width="43px"
    tabIndex="1" Text="0" ></asp:TextBox>
 <asp:TextBox ID="TextBox10" style="width: 357px;"
    runat="server" readonly="True"
    Text="Object Oriented Programming" BackColor="#CCCCCC"
    TabIndex="-1"></asp:TextBox>
 <asp:TextBox ID="UCost4" runat="server" readonly="True"
    Text="15.00" BackColor="#CCCCCC" Width="66px"
    TabIndex="-1"></asp:TextBox>
 <asp:TextBox ID="TextBox12" style="width: 64px;"
    runat="server" readonly="True" Text="0.00"
    BackColor="#CCCCCC" TabIndex="-1"></asp:TextBox>
 <asp:RangeValidator ID="RangeValidator4" runat="server"
    ControlToValidate="Qty4"
    ErrorMessage="Quantity must be 0 or larger"
    MaximumValue="9"
    MinimumValue="0" Type="Integer"</asp:RangeValidator>
</div>
<div>
 <asp:TextBox id="Qty5" runat="server" Width="43px"
    tabIndex="1" Text="0" ></asp:TextBox>
 <asp:TextBox ID="TextBox13" style="width: 357px;"
    runat="server" readonly="True"
    Text="Windows MFC I" BackColor="#CCCCCC"
    TabIndex="-1"></asp:TextBox>
 <asp:TextBox ID="UCost5" runat="server" readonly="True"
    Text="15.00" BackColor="#CCCCCC" Width="66px"
    TabIndex="-1"></asp:TextBox>
 <asp:TextBox ID="TextBox15" style="width: 64px;"
```

```
          runat="server" readonly="True" Text="0.00"
          BackColor="#CCCCCC" TabIndex="-1"></asp:TextBox>
    <asp:RangeValidator ID="RangeValidator5" runat="server"
          ControlToValidate="Qty5"
          ErrorMessage="Quantity must be 0 or larger"
          MaximumValue="9" MinimumValue="0" Type="Integer">
    </asp:RangeValidator>
  </div>
  <div>
    <p> <asp:Label ID="LabelErrorQuantity" runat="server"
          Text="You must enter a quantity to order"
          ForeColor="Red" Visible="False"></asp:Label></p>
    <p> </p>
  </div>
</div>
```

We'll come back to the validators in a bit. Now let's see how we can layout the personal information section. Here, I nested <div>'s. However, I first inserted a **Panel** widget. I set its width and height such that it contains all of the subsequent rows. Further, I set its **BackColor** to help group this collection of related data. By setting the **BorderStyle** and **BorderWidth** properties, a nice border outlines the whole panel. Then, within the main <div>, I added a subdivision for each row. Notice that I set the Width property in pixel units and kept the widths the same for the first three rows, name, address, and city.

```
<div>
  <asp:panel id="Panel1" style="height: 140px; width: 600px;"
      runat="server"
      BackColor="#C0FFFF" BorderStyle="Solid" BorderWidth="2px">
  <br />
  <div>
    <asp:Label id="Label6" runat="server"
        Width="70px"> Name</asp:Label>
    <asp:TextBox id="Name" tabIndex="6" runat="server"
        Width="510px" BorderStyle="Solid"></asp:TextBox>
  </div>
  <div>
    <asp:Label id="Label8" runat="server"
        Width="70px"> Address</asp:Label>
    <asp:TextBox id="Address" tabIndex="7" runat="server"
        Width="510px" BorderStyle="Double"></asp:TextBox>
  </div>
  <div>
    <asp:Label id="Label9" runat="server"
        Width="70px"> City</asp:Label>
    <asp:TextBox id="City" tabIndex="8" runat="server"
        BorderStyle="Solid"></asp:TextBox>
```

```
<asp:Label id="Label10"
    runat="server"> StateCode </asp:Label>
<asp:TextBox id="State" tabIndex="9" runat="server"
    Width="32px" BorderStyle="Solid"></asp:TextBox>
<asp:Label id="Label11" runat="server"> Zip </asp:Label>
<asp:TextBox id="Zip" tabIndex="10" runat="server"
    Width="120px" BorderStyle="Solid"></asp:TextBox>
<p>
 <asp:RequiredFieldValidator ID="RequiredFieldValidator1"
    runat="server" ControlToValidate="Name"
    ErrorMessage="You must enter your name">
    </asp:RequiredFieldValidator>
 <asp:RequiredFieldValidator ID="RequiredFieldValidator2"
    runat="server" ControlToValidate="Address"
    ErrorMessage="You must enter your address">
    </asp:RequiredFieldValidator>
 <asp:RequiredFieldValidator ID="RequiredFieldValidator3"
    runat="server" ControlToValidate="City"
    ErrorMessage="You must enter your city">
    </asp:RequiredFieldValidator>
 <asp:RequiredFieldValidator ID="RequiredFieldValidator4"
    runat="server" ControlToValidate="State"
    ErrorMessage="You must enter your state">
    </asp:RequiredFieldValidator>
 <asp:RequiredFieldValidator ID="RequiredFieldValidator5"
    runat="server" ControlToValidate="Zip"
    ErrorMessage="You must enter your zip code">
    </asp:RequiredFieldValidator>
 </p>
 </div>
 </asp:panel>
</div>
```

Finally, we need to add a Submit button. When pressed, the form will be sent back via a post operation. If the data entry is valid, control is then passed on to the next web page. I called both the ID and the button's text "Submit."

```
<div>
 <p>
  <asp:Button ID="Submit" runat="server" Text="Submit"
    onclick="OnClickSubmit" />
 </p>
 </div>
 </form>
</body>
</html>
```
Now, let's examine how we verify the form's data.

Validation of Form Data

This sample has several layers of data validation. C# provides several built-in data Validators. Two key ones are **RequiredFieldValidator** and **RangeValidator**. These are found under the Heading Validation on the tool box. When you drag one of these widgets onto the form, wherever you place it, that's where the error message will appear, if raises an error. The default color of the error message is red, but it can be changed as needed.

Let's examine the five **RangeValidators** first. Notice that I dragged them and placed each one after the Total Cost column on each row. That is, the quantity validator for a row is located as a "fifth column" in each row. That way, the user will have a visual clue as to which quantity the error is related.

```
<asp:RangeValidator ID="RangeValidator1" runat="server"
        ControlToValidate="Qty1"
        ErrorMessage="Quantity must be 0 or larger"
        MaximumValue="9"
        MinimumValue="0"></asp:RangeValidator>
```

First, you need to set the **ControlToValidate** property. When you click on it, a drop down box shows all of the known controls to which this could apply. Here, I selected Qty1. Next, the **ErrorMessage** property is set. This will be the error message shown in the Qty1 field fails the range check. Finally, set the two properties: **MinimumValue** and **MaximumValue**.

The Type property can be **Currency**, **Date**, **Double**, **Integer**, and **String**. The default is **String**. Notice a tiny detail. The Qty1 is using **String** type validation, while the other four are using **Integer** type. This impacts what the meaning of the min-max values imply. With **String**, valid entries include any string that lies between '0' and '9'. Hence, one can enter "222" for example. With the **Integer** type, the min-max values provide the range of acceptable integers. Thus, on the other four quantities, one can only enter values between 0 and 9. Entering 222 would raise a validation error. Try it.

```
<asp:RangeValidator ID="RangeValidator4" runat="server"
        ControlToValidate="Qty4"
        ErrorMessage="Quantity must be 0 or larger"
        MaximumValue="9"
        MinimumValue="0" Type="Integer"></asp:RangeValidator>
```

To check Date types, one could use the following to ensure the date entered was in January of 2009.

```
MaximumValue="01/01/2009"
MinimumValue="01/31/2009" Type="Date"
```

The **RequiredFieldValidator** flags an error if the Submit button is pressed and the field has no data in it.

```
<asp:RequiredFieldValidator ID="RequiredFieldValidator5"
    runat="server" ControlToValidate="Zip"
    ErrorMessage="You must enter your zip code">
    </asp:RequiredFieldValidator>
```

Again, one sets the **ControlToValidate** property to the text box which must have an entry in it. Then set the **ErrorMessage** to be shown if it has no entry in it. These are very easy controls to use. However, where are they going to be placed in our form? Wherever they are placed, that is where their messages will be shown, if the field has no entry.

I made the colored panel which houses the personal data section taller than it needed to be. To keep the first row from being too close to the very top of the panel, I inserted a </br> tag to cause a line break before the Name row. I added extra space in the panel's height so that the required field error messages would be shown in the bottom blank area of the panel.

I dragged the five validators and placed them below the City-State-Zip row, one after the other.

These validators handle all of the error situation except a failure to enter even one quantity, thus submitting an order of nothing, in effect. I want to trap this out on the client side and display a message to the effect that the user must enter some quantity. One trick is to use a label that displays the error message. We can programmatically cause any control to be either visible or invisible.

The last row in the series of book rows at the top contained just such a label.

```
<div>
 <p> <asp:Label ID="LabelErrorQuantity" runat="server"
       Text="You must enter a quantity to order"
       ForeColor="Red" Visible="False"></asp:Label></p>
 <p> </p>
</div>
```

Notice that initially its **Visible** property has been set to false. In our code behind section, if this error arises, we will reset the **Visible** property to true, causing the label to be displayed to the user. Thus, we can hide and show controls. But where do we do this checking?

Look again at the Submit button.

```
<asp:Button ID="Submit" runat="server" Text="Submit"
    onclick="OnClickSubmit" />
```

I added an event property that it responds to. Click on the lightening bolt in the properties to get to the various events to which a control can respond. Figure 13.5 shows the entry that I made.

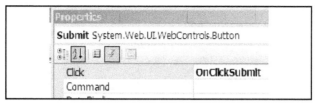

Figure 13.5 Responding to a Button Click

     I chose to call the new function OnClickSubmit. The editor then creates the function in our code behind file, the .cs file. Here is the entire .cs file, though we have a bit more to discuss about it. Examine the OnClickSubmit function.

```csharp
using System;
using System.Configuration;
using System.Data;
using System.Linq;
using System.Web;
using System.Web.Security;
using System.Web.UI;
using System.Web.UI.HtmlControls;
using System.Web.UI.WebControls;
using System.Web.UI.WebControls.WebParts;
using System.Xml.Linq;

public partial class _Default : System.Web.UI.Page
{
    protected bool isPageValid = false;

    protected void Page_Load(object sender, EventArgs e)
    {
        if (IsPostBack) {
            OnClickSubmit (this, null);
            if (isPageValid)
            {
                Server.Transfer("orderdone.aspx", true);
            }
        }
    }

    protected void OnClickSubmit(object sender, EventArgs e)
    {
        this.Validate();
        if (this.IsValid)
        {
            int total = 0;
            total = Int32.Parse(this.Qty1.Text) +
```

```
                          Int32.Parse(this.Qty2.Text) +
                          Int32.Parse(this.Qty3.Text) +
                          Int32.Parse(this.Qty4.Text) +
                          Int32.Parse(this.Qty5.Text);
            if (total == 0)
            {
                LabelErrorQuantity.Visible = true;
                isPageValid = false;
            }
            else
            {
                LabelErrorQuantity.Visible = false;
                isPageValid = true;
            }
        }
        else
        {
            LabelErrorQuantity.Visible = false;
            isPageValid = false;
        }
    }
}
}
```

First, I called the **Validate()** function of the web page. This causes all of the controls to be validated, firing off any range or required field error messages. Once that is done, the page property **IsValid**, a bool, is set. If **IsValid** is true, the page has no errors thus far. That is, all quantities are numerical and in range and the required fields have some entries in them. Only if the page data is valid at this point do I go ahead and see if at least one book was ordered.

Here is where ASP.NET shines. As long as we are still in our web page, all of the controls can be accessed in an OOP manner, totally unlike pure HTML or old ASP pages! `this.Qty1.Text` retrieves the string data from the text box. Since I called **Validate**, I know that these five quantity text boxes contain valid integers, thanks to the **RangeValidators**. There is no need for try-catch logic here. I can be confident that I can convert them.
```
Int32.Parse(this.Qty1.Text)
```

I add the five quantities together. If that total is zero, oops, the user forgot to select even one book to buy.
```
LabelErrorQuantity.Visible = true;
isPageValid = false;
```
I set the error message label's Visible property to true. At once, the label becomes visible. If the total is not zero, I set it back to being invisible once more.

The bool isPageValid I am using for another purpose. If no quantity has been entered, then the page is not yet valid and it is not ready to be sent back to the server and passed on to the next web page to continue the purchase process.

The **Page_Load** Function

When a web page has been requested, **Page_Load** is called to initialize controls. Usually, this is only done one time. Later on, whenever an attempt is made to submit the page, as well as other times, **Page_Load** is called again. This subsequent calling is know as posting back. A member bool **IsPostBack** keeps track of whether this is the initial page load or a subsequent post back. It is false during load time and true when it is a post back.

In this page, we need to respond to a post back. Why? Only if the page is valid and has at least one book quantity set do we then want to continue the purchase process by transferring control to the next web page in the process. I made a bool isPageValid and set it initially to false. Whenever **Page_Load** is called, if this is a post back event, then I check this bool. Only if everything is okay do I want to go on to the next page and continue the processing. Hence, I called OnClickSubmit directly, faking the two parameters which the function does not use in any way. This in turn sets the variable isPageValid to true or false.

If the page is valid, then I use the **Server.Transfer** function to pass this page on to the next web page in the process. I provided the name of the next aspx web page to load and passed true as well. The true tells ASP.NET to retain this page and its controls with their values a little longer so that I can access them from the next page, here orderdone.aspx.

```
protected void Page_Load(object sender, EventArgs e)
{
    if (IsPostBack) {
        OnClickSubmit (this, null);
        if (isPageValid)
        {
            Server.Transfer("orderdone.aspx", true);
        }
    }
}
```

Before we continue, notice one key point in all this coding. Within our web page, we can access our asp controls directly by name, using OOP methods! This is very convenient indeed, compared to old style ASP and HTML pages.

Client-side Coding

However, it is important to also see just what HTML the ASP.NET server actually created and sent to the browser. Chose the browser's View Source menu to examine it. Here is what was sent and what the browser is showing. I highlighted some key elements in boldface. Also, I cut out the repetitious coding for four of the main rows of ebooks.

There are two key points in this source. First, we know that a web page has no state. That is, when a page is posted, all data in the controls are lost. So how does ASP.NET remember what was in those controls? It does this by embedding hidden **ViewState** information within the form as it is created in **Page_Load**. Thus, when it is posted back, it retrieves that information and can restore all our OOP methods of dealing with the page. It does this automatically for us, greatly reducing the burden on our coding! This **ViewState** is the mechanism by which **Page_Load** can use its cached data to restore the page controls on a post back, which allows us to continue to use our OOP methods, directly accessing the controls. In ordinary HTML post backs, all of the initial state is gone. The **ViewState** cached data allows ASP.NET to restore them during post backs.

Second, data validation should be done on the client-side as well as on the server-side. It would slow the server down if the entire page had to be sent back just to get one control validated. Instead, client-side validation is done, duplicating what will be done on the server-side when the page actually goes back to the server. Yes, it must be done twice. The client get's a crack at validating the data. But the server also must make sure nothing happened to that data during transmission as well. Thus, the ASP.NET sends out client-side coding to deal with the data validation there. These sections begin with

```
<script type="text/javascript">
//<![CDATA[
```

Here is the abbreviated listing.

```
<!DOCTYPE    html    PUBLIC    "-//W3C//DTD    XHTML    1.0    Transitional//EN"
"http://www.w3.org/TR/xhtml1/DTD/xhtml1-transitional.dtd">

<html xmlns="http://www.w3.org/1999/xhtml">
<head><title>
        Order Page 1
</title></head>
<body bgcolor="lightgoldenrodyellow">
    <form    name="order1"    method="post"    action="Default.aspx"
onsubmit="javascript:return WebForm_OnSubmit();" id="order1">
<div>
<input type="hidden" name="__EVENTTARGET" id="__EVENTTARGET" value="" />
<input type="hidden" name="__EVENTARGUMENT" id="__EVENTARGUMENT" value="" />
<input    type="hidden"    name="__VIEWSTATE"    id="__VIEWSTATE"
value="/wEPDwUKLTk2MTI5MzQ5N2Rk6f/S1TDIa6o4WIApUFwsX4f3ELU=" />
</div>

<script type="text/javascript">
```

```
//<![CDATA[
var theForm = document.forms['order1'];
if (!theForm) {
    theForm = document.order1;
}
function __doPostBack(eventTarget, eventArgument) {
    if (!theForm.onsubmit || (theForm.onsubmit() != false)) {
        theForm.__EVENTTARGET.value = eventTarget;
        theForm.__EVENTARGUMENT.value = eventArgument;
        theForm.submit();
    }
}
//]]>

</script>


< s c r i p t
src="/Pgm13aWeb/WebResource.axd?d=1xsEHrRe_-pDlwPU7ZFW6Q2&amp;t=63343633026078
1250" type="text/javascript"></script>


< s c r i p t
src="/Pgm13aWeb/WebResource.axd?d=PekfP5JZvRUbwiPzz1UiWLvnAuvXehUV-3On1LESLBU1
&amp;t=633436330260781250" type="text/javascript"></script>
<script type="text/javascript">
//<![CDATA[
function WebForm_OnSubmit() {
if (typeof(ValidatorOnSubmit) == "function" && ValidatorOnSubmit() == false)
return false;
return true;
}
//]]>
</script>

  <div >
  <h1>Broquard eBooks Order Page</h1>

  <img alt="logo1s.jpg" src="logo1s.jpg" />
  </div>
  <div>
  <p>
   <span id="Label1" style="color:#3333CC;font-size:Large;">Enter the Quantity
Desired and Your Personal Information - then press Order</span>
  </p>
  </div>
  <div>

  <div style="font-size: medium">
   <p>
    <span id="Label2" style="display:inline-block;width:45px;"> Qty</span>
    <span id="Label3" style="display:inline-block;width:357px;">  eBook</span>
    <span id="Label4" style="display:inline-block;width:74px;"> Cost</span>
    <span id="Label5">Total Cost</span>
   </p>
```

```
    </div>
    <div>
        <input   name="Qty1"   type="text"   value="0"   id="Qty1"   tabindex="1"
style="width:43px;" />
      <input name="TextBox1" type="text" value="Cpp for Computer Science and
Engineering"   readonly="readonly"   id="TextBox1"   tabindex="-1"
style="background-color:#CCCCCC;width:357px;" />
        <input   name="UCost1"   type="text"   value="15.00"   readonly="readonly"
id="UCost1" tabindex="-1" style="background-color:#CCCCCC;width:66px;" />

        <input   name="TextBox3"   type="text"   value="0.00"   readonly="readonly"
id="TextBox3" tabindex="-1" style="background-color:#CCCCCC;width:64px;" />
    <span id="RangeValidator1" style="color:Red;visibility:hidden;">Quantity must
be 0 or larger</span>
    </div>
...
    <div>
    <p> </p>
    <p> </p>
    </div>
    </div>
    <div>
                        < d i v     i d = " P a n e l 1 "
style="background-color:#C0FFFF;border-width:2px;border-style:Solid;height:
140px; width: 600px;">

    <br />

    <div>
    <span id="Label6" style="display:inline-block;width:70px;"> Name</span>
                <input   name="Name"   type="text"   id="Name"   tabindex="6"
style="border-style:Solid;width:510px;" />
    </div>
    <div>
    <span id="Label8" style="display:inline-block;width:70px;"> Address</span>
            <input   name="Address"   type="text"   id="Address"   tabindex="7"
style="border-style:Double;width:510px;" />

    </div>
    <div>
    <span id="Label9" style="display:inline-block;width:70px;"> City</span>
                <input   name="City"   type="text"   id="City"   tabindex="8"
style="border-style:Solid;" />
    <span id="Label10"> StateCode </span>
                <input   name="State"   type="text"   id="State"   tabindex="9"
style="border-style:Solid;width:32px;" />
    <span id="Label11"> Zip </span>

                <input   name="Zip"   type="text"   id="Zip"   tabindex="10"
style="border-style:Solid;width:120px;" />
    <p>
    <span id="RequiredFieldValidator1" style="color:Red;visibility:hidden;">You
must enter your name</span>
    <span id="RequiredFieldValidator2" style="color:Red;visibility:hidden;">You
must enter your address</span>
    <span id="RequiredFieldValidator3" style="color:Red;visibility:hidden;">You
```

288

```
must enter your city</span>
    <span id="RequiredFieldValidator4" style="color:Red;visibility:hidden;">You
must enter your state</span>
    <span id="RequiredFieldValidator5" style="color:Red;visibility:hidden;">You
must enter your zip code</span>

    </p>
    </div>

</div>
  </div>
  <div>
  <p>
                <input     type="submit"     name="Submit"     value="Submit"
onclick="javascript:WebForm_DoPostBackWithOptions(new
WebForm_PostBackOptions(&quot;Submit&quot;,  &quot;&quot;,  true,  &quot;&quot;,
&quot;&quot;, false, false))" id="Submit" />
    </p>
    </div>


<script type="text/javascript">
//<![CDATA[
var Page_Validators =  new Array(document.getElementById("RangeValidator1"),
document.getElementById("RangeValidator2"),
document.getElementById("RangeValidator3"),
document.getElementById("RangeValidator4"),
document.getElementById("RangeValidator5"),
document.getElementById("RequiredFieldValidator1"),
document.getElementById("RequiredFieldValidator2"),
document.getElementById("RequiredFieldValidator3"),
document.getElementById("RequiredFieldValidator4"),
document.getElementById("RequiredFieldValidator5"));
//]]>
</script>

<script type="text/javascript">
//<![CDATA[
var RangeValidator1 = document.all ? document.all["RangeValidator1"]  :
document.getElementById("RangeValidator1");
RangeValidator1.controltovalidate = "Qty1";
RangeValidator1.errormessage = "Quantity must be 0 or larger";
RangeValidator1.evaluationfunction = "RangeValidatorEvaluateIsValid";
RangeValidator1.maximumvalue = "9";
RangeValidator1.minimumvalue = "0";
...
var    RequiredFieldValidator1    =    document.all    ?
document.all["RequiredFieldValidator1"]    :
document.getElementById("RequiredFieldValidator1");
RequiredFieldValidator1.controltovalidate = "Name";
RequiredFieldValidator1.errormessage = "You must enter your name";
RequiredFieldValidator1.evaluationfunction    =
"RequiredFieldValidatorEvaluateIsValid";
RequiredFieldValidator1.initialvalue = "";
```

289

```
...
//]]>
</script>

<div>

        <input    type="hidden"    name="__EVENTVALIDATION"    id="__EVENTVALIDATION"
value="/wEWGwLd+qnqBgKMgeTKBQLs0bLrBgLEiKeVDQLs0Yq1BQKMgdDvDALs0e58AsSIo5UNAuz
RxsYPAoyBvJQEAuzR2qEIAsSIn5UNAuzRkpIBAoyBqLkLAqnU7OEDAsSIu5UNAqvU7OEDAoyB1N4CA
qzU7OEDAsSIt5UNAq7U7OEDApu59B0Cy6HS4AgCo4a41wgCrdrO1AgC0OH0bAK8w4S2BJJMFVtJ0OC
IhhGjcD7TKOzZFY97" />
</div>

<script type="text/javascript">
<!--
var Page_ValidationActive = false;
if (typeof(ValidatorOnLoad) == "function") {
    ValidatorOnLoad();
}

function ValidatorOnSubmit() {
    if (Page_ValidationActive) {
        return ValidatorCommonOnSubmit();
    }
    else {
        return true;
    }
}
// -->
</script>
        </form>

</body>
</html>
```

Notice the submit process on the client-side:
```
function __doPostBack(eventTarget, eventArgument) {
    if (!theForm.onsubmit || (theForm.onsubmit() != false)) {
```
When Submit is pressed, the client first checks to see if there is any onsubmit function on the client side. If not, it posts the page. Usually, this function is there, so it calls it. These type functions return true or false. If it returns false, the page is not ready to be posted back to the server and it does not. Usually error message now appear. Only if the onsubmit function returns true does it actually do the post back to the server.

Transferring Data Between Pages

Next, we must handle the passing of information from page to page. Here is where the stateless web pages pose an even greater problem. Just how can we transfer data from one page to the next? There are several ways to do this. One is the Query String approach and the other is to access the previous page's form control's values.

Often in searches on a site, the search criteria is passed via query strings. One might see something like this in the URL requesting a new page.

http://www.broquard-ebooks.com/find.asp?s=cpp+mfc

This is telling the server to launch the find.asp page and to set up a query string called s whose value is the string "cpp+mfc." The query string comes after the ? in the URL. If there are more than one query string, they are separated by an &.

The query string is limited to string values only and have to contain characters that are valid in a URL. The limitations are several. Limited information can be passed. Second, the data being passed is exposed to the world. There is no security at all. Anyone can see the information being passed.

To request a new page and send it some query strings, we must do it manually.

```
Response.Redirect("nextpage.aspx?s=cpp+mfc&bid="        +
    number.ToString());
```

In nextpage.aspx, we can get at these two by using the **Request** object.

```
string parms = Request.QueryString["s"];
string bids = Request.QueryString["bid"];
```

Accessing the previous page's form controls is another matter. The ASP.NET main method is called **cross-page posting**. When a page is posted back and you transfer control to a different page, you can send the current state of all the previous page's controls along with it. Such is stored in the object **Request.Form**.

Method 1 Using Server.Transfer

From anywhere within your web page, you can transfer control to a different page by using the **Server.Transfer** function. If you want the previous page's controls available, pass true for the second parameter. This is what I did in Pgm13aWeb.

```
Server.Transfer("orderdone.aspx", true);
```

A side effect of this method is that the browser does not know that it has gone to a new page and does not show the new URL in its address box. While in fact the browser is showing the orderdone.aspx page, it still shows the default.aspx in its address box. However, Firefox will show the name of the new page in the tab of the window. Most importantly, if the user presses the browser's back button, they will be taken back to the default.aspx page as we would hope.

Before we look at the vitally important coding to retrieve the previous page data, let's see the visual side of this next page. Figure 13.6 shows the design view of the many text box controls. Some will have to be filled with the data from the previous page. Further, we will need to calculate the total cost of each book and accumulate the grand total as well.

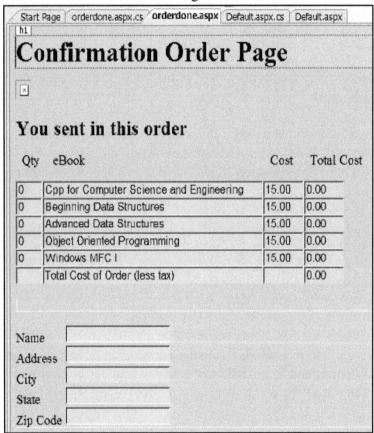

Figure 13.6 The Design View Showing the Text Boxes

Again, I used nested <div>'s to lay out the apparent table rows. Here is a snippet of the design coding. I boldfaced some of the key text box id's that we need to fill with either the previous page's data or our calculated results.

```
<div>
  <h1>Confirmation Order Page</h1>
  <img alt="logo1s.jpg" src="logo1s.jpg" />
</div>
<div>
  <h2>You sent in this order</h2>
```

```
 </div>
 <div>
  <div style="font-size: medium">
   <p>
    <asp:Label ID="Label2"  runat="server"
     Text="  Qty" Width="45px"></asp:Label>
    <asp:Label ID="Label3" runat="server"
      Text="   eBook" Width="357px"></asp:Label>
    <asp:Label ID="Label4" runat="server"
      Text="  Cost" Width="74px"></asp:Label>
    <asp:Label ID="Label5" runat="server"
      Text="Total Cost"></asp:Label>
   </p>
  </div>
  <div>
   <asp:TextBox id="Qty1" runat="server" Width="43px"
        tabIndex="-1" Text="0" readonly="True"
        BackColor="#CCCCCC">0</asp:TextBox>
   <asp:TextBox ID="TextBox1" runat="server" readonly="True"
        Width="357px"
        Text="Cpp for Computer Science and Engineering"
        BackColor="#CCCCCC"
        TabIndex="-1"></asp:TextBox>
   <asp:TextBox ID="TextBox2" runat="server" readonly="True"
        Text="15.00"
        BackColor="#CCCCCC" Width="66px"
        TabIndex="-1"></asp:TextBox>
   <asp:TextBox ID="TCost1" Width="64px" runat="server"
        readonly="True"
        Text="0.00" BackColor="#CCCCCC"
        TabIndex="-1"></asp:TextBox>
  </div>
...
  <div>
   <asp:TextBox id="TextBox3" runat="server" Width="43px"
     tabIndex="-1" Text=" "
     readonly="True" BackColor="#CCCCCC"></asp:TextBox>
   <asp:TextBox ID="TextBox6" style="width: 357px;"
     runat="server" readonly="True"
     Text="Total Cost of Order (less tax)" BackColor="#CCCCCC"
     TabIndex="-1"></asp:TextBox>
   <asp:TextBox ID="TextBox9" runat="server" readonly="True"
     Text=" " BackColor="#CCCCCC" Width="66px"
     TabIndex="-1"></asp:TextBox>
   <asp:TextBox ID="GrandTotal" style="width: 64px;"
     runat="server" readonly="True" Text="0.00"
```

```
      BackColor="#CCCCCC" TabIndex="-1"></asp:TextBox>
  </div>
 </div>
 <div>
  <p> </p>
 </div>
 <div>
  <div>
   <asp:Label ID="Label1" runat="server" Width="80px"
      Text="Name"></asp:Label>
   <asp:TextBox ID="Name" runat="server" readonly="True"
      Text=" " BackColor="#CCCCCC" TabIndex="-1"></asp:TextBox>
  </div>
...
```

Okay now that we know what the text box controls that must be filled are called, let's see how we access the previous page's controls. Since a control could possibly have a series of return values, as in a multiple selection listbox, we must use an array of strings. The function **GetValues** returns an array of string results stored in the control. With a text box, there is only one string, so it would be at subscript 0.

```
     string[] s = Request.Form.GetValues("Qty1");
     qty1 = Int32.Parse(s[0]);
```

In **Page_Load**, we must initialize our new page's controls, based upon what was sent to us from the previous page. This initialization should only be done once, as the page is initially loaded. Again, use the bool **IsPostBack** to check. If it is false, this is the time to load our new page's controls once. However, there is nothing to keep a mischievous user from entering in the browser's URL line the address of this page! In this case, there is no previous page and would be considered an error or an attempt to hack into the site. The simple choice is to redirect the browser to the initial page whose controls are to be sent to this one, namely default.aspx in this case.

Thus, I wrap a **try-catch** block around the retrieval of the various previous page's controls. If the catch triggers, I merely redirect the browser to the real starting page in this series. Here is the coding in orderdone.aspx.cs, the code behind page. It begins by defining variables to hold the various values from the previous page.

```
using System;
using System.Collections;
using System.Configuration;
using System.Data;
using System.Linq;
using System.Web;
using System.Web.Security;
using System.Web.UI;
using System.Web.UI.HtmlControls;
```

```csharp
using System.Web.UI.WebControls;
using System.Web.UI.WebControls.WebParts;
using System.Xml.Linq;

public partial class orderdone : System.Web.UI.Page
{
    protected int qty1, qty2, qty3, qty4, qty5;
    protected double cost1, cost2, cost3, cost4, cost5;
    protected string name, address, city, state, zip;

    protected void Page_Load(object sender, EventArgs e)
    {
        if (!IsPostBack)
        {
            try
            {
                string[] s = Request.Form.GetValues("Qty1");
                qty1 = Int32.Parse(s[0]);
                s = Request.Form.GetValues("Qty2");
                qty2 = Int32.Parse(s[0]);
                s = Request.Form.GetValues("Qty3");
                qty3 = Int32.Parse(s[0]);
                s = Request.Form.GetValues("Qty4");
                qty4 = Int32.Parse(s[0]);
                s = Request.Form.GetValues("Qty5");
                qty5 = Int32.Parse(s[0]);

                s = Request.Form.GetValues("UCost1");
                cost1 = Double.Parse(s[0]);
                s = Request.Form.GetValues("UCost2");
                cost2 = Double.Parse(s[0]);
                s = Request.Form.GetValues("UCost3");
                cost3 = Double.Parse(s[0]);
                s = Request.Form.GetValues("UCost4");
                cost4 = Double.Parse(s[0]);
                s = Request.Form.GetValues("UCost5");
                cost5 = Double.Parse(s[0]);

                s = Request.Form.GetValues("Name");
                name = s[0];
                s = Request.Form.GetValues("Address");
                address = s[0];
                s = Request.Form.GetValues("City");
                city = s[0];
                s = Request.Form.GetValues("State");
                state = s[0];
```

```
s = Request.Form.GetValues("Zip");
zip = s[0];
```

Down to this point, I am merely gathering the data from the previous page, putting the numerical ones into numerical fields for calculation purposes. Next, I must calculate the total cost of each ordered book, accumulate the grand total, and insert the quantities into the respective text boxes on our new page. Notice that I format into dollars the total cost of each book, if any of that kind is to be purchased.

```
double grandTotal = 0;
Qty1.Text = qty1.ToString();
if (qty1 != 0)
{
    double t = qty1 * cost1;
    grandTotal += t;
    TCost1.Text = String.Format("{0,6:C}", t);
}
Qty2.Text = qty2.ToString();
if (qty2 != 0)
{
    double t = qty2 * cost2;
    grandTotal += t;
    TCost2.Text = String.Format("{0,6:C}", t);
}
Qty3.Text = qty3.ToString();
if (qty3 != 0)
{
    double t = qty3 * cost3;
    grandTotal += t;
    TCost3.Text = String.Format("{0,6:C}", t);
}
Qty4.Text = qty4.ToString();
if (qty4 != 0)
{
    double t = qty4 * cost4;
    grandTotal += t;
    TCost4.Text = String.Format("{0,6:C}", t);
}
Qty5.Text = qty5.ToString();
if (qty5 != 0)
{
    double t = qty5 * cost5;
    grandTotal += t;
    TCost5.Text = String.Format("{0,6:C}", t);
}
```

```
        GrandTotal.Text = String.Format("{0,6:C}", grandTotal);
```

Now, I store the personal information directly into the new text boxes.

```
            Name.Text = name;
            Address.Text = address;
            City.Text = city;
            State.Text = state;
            Zip.Text = zip;
        }

        catch
        {
            Response.Redirect("default.aspx");
        }


    }
  }
}
```

Notice that if there are any errors, specifically if anyone tries to bypass the previous page, coming to this page directly, the **Response.Redirect** function forces them back to the initial order page. Of course, this page is really a dead end. There is no submit button to continue the purchase process.

Method 2 Using **PostBackUrl** on a Submit Button

On all button type controls, one property is the **PostBackUrl**. If you set this to the next page, when the user clicks on the button, automatically this page will be posted to this new page with all controls retaining their current values, ready for the new page to retrieve them. Again, this is a cross page post. The new URL to this page does show up in the browser's address box, unlike Method 1.

This style does not go through our **Page_Load** function, but heads off directly to the new page, assuming the validators do not mark the page as invalid. Translation: we will not have an opportunity to verify that the user has even selected one ebook! They could make an order of nothing! Thus, we need a different approach, Pgm13bWeb shows it.

Well, this requires some redesign on our part. In fact, this gives us an opportunity to correct a slight missing action in Pgm12aWeb. Did you notice that when you entered a quantity, the total cost of those ebooks was not calculated until control was transferred to the final web page? In reality, when the user enters a number in the quantity column, we ought to calculate the total cost of those books and also display the total cost of this order, the grand total.

297

To make this happen, we will need to respond to the text being changed in the quantity text boxes, posting back to our cs file so that we can do the calculations required. On each quantity text box, I added the following properties: **AutoPostBack** as true and **TextChanged** event set to OnQty1Changed. Since we will need to reset the total cost of those ebooks, I changed the names of the fourth column of text boxes to TCost1, etc. Then, I added a sixth row to the table which holds the total cost of the order. Here is the first row, Qty1, and the new added row. I boldfaced the property changes. Also, examine the **RangeValidator** for the total cost of the order.

```
  <div>
    <asp:TextBox id="Qty1" runat="server" Width="43px"
        tabIndex="1" Text="0"
        ontextchanged="OnQty1Changed" AutoPostBack="True"
        ></asp:TextBox>
    <asp:TextBox ID="TextBox1" runat="server" readonly="True"
            Width="357px"
            Text="Cpp for Computer Science and Engineering"
            BackColor="#CCCCCC"
            TabIndex="-1"></asp:TextBox>
    <asp:TextBox ID="UCost1" runat="server" readonly="True"
            Text="15.00"
            BackColor="#CCCCCC" Width="66px"
            TabIndex="-1"></asp:TextBox>
    <asp:TextBox ID="TCost1" Width="64px" runat="server"
            readonly="True"
            Text="0.00" BackColor="#CCCCCC"
            TabIndex="-1"></asp:TextBox>
    <asp:RangeValidator ID="RangeValidator1" runat="server"
            ControlToValidate="Qty1"
            ErrorMessage="Quantity must be 0 or larger"
            MaximumValue="9"
            MinimumValue="0"></asp:RangeValidator>
  </div>
...
  <div>
    <asp:TextBox id="TextBox2" runat="server" Width="43px"
        TabIndex="-1" Text=" "
        BackColor="#CCCCCC" readonly="True" ></asp:TextBox>
    <asp:TextBox ID="TextBox5" style="width: 357px;"
        runat="server" readonly="True"
        Text=" Total Cost of Order" BackColor="#CCCCCC"
        TabIndex="-1"></asp:TextBox>
    <asp:TextBox ID="TextBox8" runat="server" readonly="True"
            Text=" "
            BackColor="#CCCCCC" Width="66px"
            TabIndex="-1"></asp:TextBox>
    <asp:TextBox ID="TotCost" style="width: 64px;" runat="server"
```

```
         Text="0.00" BackColor="#CCCCCC" TabIndex="20"
         readonly="True"
         AutoPostBack="True" ontextchanged="OnFixTotCost">
         </asp:TextBox>
   <p> 
    <asp:RangeValidator ID="RangeValidator6" runat="server"
            ControlToValidate="TotCost"
            ErrorMessage="You must enter a quantity to order"
            MaximumValue="9999.00" MinimumValue="15.00"
            Type="Double"></asp:RangeValidator>
   </p>
   <p> </p>
  </div>
...
  <div>
   <p>
    <asp:Button ID="Submit" runat="server" Text="Submit"
            PostBackUrl="orderdone.aspx" />
   </p>
  </div>
```

Notice that I added a **RangeValidator** for the TotCost text box, which contains the total cost of the order. Even though it is read only, in the event that it was not read only, I show how you can add an **ontextchanged** property calling OnFixTotCost, which will put the correct data back into the control. To test this effect, change the text box TotCost to not read only and try it. Enter some quantities and then change the total cost on the sixth line. As you pull away, it automatically recalculates the correct value.

Now let's look at the minimal code behind in the cs file. Since the coding is nearly identical for the five quantities, I show only the first one. **Page_Load** does nothing now, it is being bypassed by the cross page posting.

```
protected void Page_Load(object sender, EventArgs e)
{

}

protected void OnQty1Changed(object sender, EventArgs e)
{
    int qty1 = 0;
    double cost1 = 0;
    try
    {
        qty1 = Int32.Parse(Qty1.Text);
        cost1 = Double.Parse(UCost1.Text);
```

299

```
        }
      catch (SystemException) {
        ;
      }
      Qty1.Text = qty1.ToString();
      double t = qty1 * cost1;
      TCost1.Text = String.Format("{0,6:F}", t);
      CalcGrandTotal();
    }
```

Notice that if the text in Qty1 is not an integer, the validator message appears. The try-catch catches. It. Since I set qty1 to 0, if the data is bad, qty1 still is 0. I then reset the text to the right quantity. If it was valid, no harm done. If the user had entered a letter, the letter is now replaced with a 0 and the error message disappears. I then calculate the new cost and place it nicely formatted into the TCost1 text box. Now that the quantity has changed, the grand total must be re-figured.

```
    protected void CalcGrandTotal ()
    {
    double cost1 = 0, cost2 = 0, cost3 = 0, cost4 = 0, cost5 = 0;
      try
      {
          cost1 = Double.Parse(TCost1.Text);
          cost2 = Double.Parse(TCost2.Text);
          cost3 = Double.Parse(TCost3.Text);
          cost4 = Double.Parse(TCost4.Text);
          cost5 = Double.Parse(TCost5.Text);
      }
      catch (SystemException) {
       TotCost.Text = "0";
      }

      double grandTotal = cost1 + cost2 + cost3 + cost4 + cost5;
      TotCost.Text = String.Format("{0,6:F}", grandTotal);
    }

    protected void OnFixTotCost(object sender, EventArgs e)
    {
        CalcGrandTotal();
    }
```

Additional Methods of Accessing the Previous Page's Controls

Nothing changes in the order summary page. We could use the very same OrderDone.aspx file that was in Pgm13aWeb. Recall this method of getting at the previous page's controls was:

```
string[] s = Request.Form.GetValues("Qty1");
qty1 = Int32.Parse(s[0]);
```

However, there are two additional OOP methods that can be used. Both methods cannot access private or protected data members of the previous page class. Hence, you must provide **public** read only properties for the objects that you wish to expose to subsequent pages. Thus, I added into the OrderPage1.aspx.cs file the following public properties, designed for our convenience, returning the numerical values where needed.

```
public int IQty1 { get { return Int32.Parse(Qty1.Text); } }
public int IQty2 { get { return Int32.Parse(Qty2.Text); } }
public int IQty3 { get { return Int32.Parse(Qty3.Text); } }
public int IQty4 { get { return Int32.Parse(Qty4.Text); } }
public int IQty5 { get { return Int32.Parse(Qty5.Text); } }

public double DUCost1 { get { return Double.Parse(UCost1.Text); } }
public double DUCost2 { get { return Double.Parse(UCost2.Text); } }
public double DUCost3 { get { return Double.Parse(UCost3.Text); } }
public double DUCost4 { get { return Double.Parse(UCost4.Text); } }
public double DUCost5 { get { return Double.Parse(UCost5.Text); } }

public string SName    { get { return Name.Text; } }
public string SAddress { get { return Address.Text; } }
public string SCity    { get { return City.Text; } }
public string SState   { get { return State.Text; } }
public string SZip     { get { return Zip.Text; } }
```

With these setup in our source page, now we can provide an OOP approach to the previous page's controls. There are two ways this can be done.

Method A: Using an @**PreviousPageType** Directive

In the target page, the OrderDone.aspx file, add the following at the top, just below the DOCTYPE directive:

```
<!DOCTYPE html PUBLIC ....>
<%@ PreviousPageType VirtualPath="OrderPage1.aspx" %>
```

In it specify the aspx file of the sending page, that is, the previous page.

This then typecasts the normal member, **PreviousPage**, from its base class to the actual derived class, OrderPage1, in this case. Now you can call the public properties by using **PreviousPage**.

```
string ss = PreviousPage.SName;
```

Method B: Typecast the **PreviousPage** into an OrderPage1 Class

Typically, before you typecast **PreviousPage**, you want to make sure that it is valid. You can access basic information of the **Page** class as shown in string s.

```
if (PreviousPage != null) {
 if (PreviousPage.IsValid) {
      string   s   =   "You   came   from   a   page   titled   "   +
PreviousPage.Header.Title;
```

With the **PreviousPage** in a good state, you do the type case as follows and then use the new reference variable, prevPage, to access the public properties.

```
OrderPage1 prevPage = PreviousPage as OrderPage1;
string sss = prevPage.SName;
```

Here is the OrderDone.aspx.cs file. Notice how these OOP properties make it a breeze to access the previous page's controls.

```
public partial class OrderDone : System.Web.UI.Page
{

    protected int qty1, qty2, qty3, qty4, qty5;
    protected double cost1, cost2, cost3, cost4, cost5;
    protected string name, address, city, state, zip;

    protected void Page_Load(object sender, EventArgs e)
    {
        if (!IsPostBack && PreviousPage != null &&
            PreviousPage.IsValid)
        {

           string s = "You came from a page titled " +
                        PreviousPage.Header.Title;
           OrderPage1 prevPage = PreviousPage as OrderPage1;
           // following lines just for fun
           string ss = PreviousPage.SName;
           string sss = prevPage.SAddress;

           try {
               qty1 = prevPage.IQty1;
```

```
qty2 = prevPage.IQty2;
qty3 = prevPage.IQty3;
qty4 = prevPage.IQty4;
qty5 = prevPage.IQty5;

cost1 = prevPage.DUCost1;
cost2 = prevPage.DUCost2;
cost3 = prevPage.DUCost3;
cost4 = prevPage.DUCost4;
cost5 = prevPage.DUCost5;

name = prevPage.SName;
address = prevPage.SAddress;
city = prevPage.SCity;
state = prevPage.SState;
zip = prevPage.SZip;

double grandTotal = 0;
Qty1.Text = qty1.ToString();
if (qty1 != 0) {
   double t = qty1 * cost1;
   grandTotal += t;
   TCost1.Text = String.Format("{0,6:C}", t);
 }

 Qty2.Text = qty2.ToString();
 if (qty2 != 0) {
   double t = qty2 * cost2;
   grandTotal += t;
   TCost2.Text = String.Format("{0,6:C}", t);
 }

 Qty3.Text = qty3.ToString();
 if (qty3 != 0) {
   double t = qty3 * cost3;
   grandTotal += t;
   TCost3.Text = String.Format("{0,6:C}", t);
 }

 Qty4.Text = qty4.ToString();
 if (qty4 != 0) {
   double t = qty4 * cost4;
   grandTotal += t;
   TCost4.Text = String.Format("{0,6:C}", t);
 }
```

```
                Qty5.Text = qty5.ToString();
                if (qty5 != 0) {
                    double t = qty5 * cost5;
                    grandTotal += t;
                    TCost5.Text = String.Format("{0,6:C}", t);
                }

        GrandTotal.Text = String.Format("{0,6:C}", grandTotal);

                Name.Text = name;
                Address.Text = address;
                City.Text = city;
                State.Text = state;
                Zip.Text = zip;
            }

            catch
            {
                    Response.Redirect("OrderPage1.aspx");
            }


        }
    }
}
```

The next two figures, 13.7 and 13.8, show this web application in action.

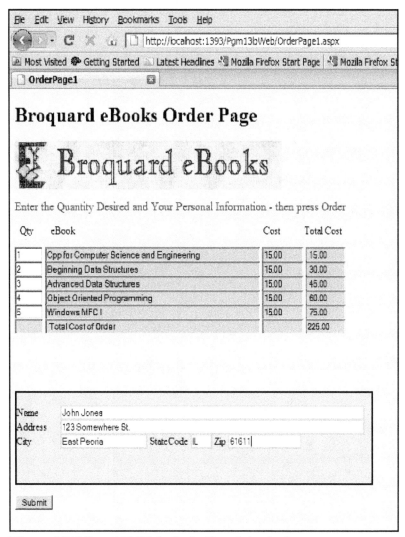

Figure 13.7 Pgm13bWeb OrderPage1 in Action

Figure 13.8 Pgm13bWeb Order Done Page

Programming Problems

None

Chapter 14—Web Sites and Databases

Many web sites make heavy use of server databases. Two web controls make working with databases easy: the **DetailsView** and the **GridView**. The **GridView** allows both editing and deleting records, while the **DetailsView** additionally allows adding or inserting records. With these two controls, working with databases on the web becomes very easy, so easy in fact, that we will be writing zero lines of code!

Pgm14aWeb illustrates both of these two controls. The key difference, functionally, is the **DetailsView** is required if an Add or Insert operation is needed. Both handled editing and deleting records. The top control in this program is the **GridView** of the Customer table from the Purchase.mdb Access database. The database was first copied into the **App_Data** subfolder of Pgm14aWeb. Figure 14.1 shows the web application running.

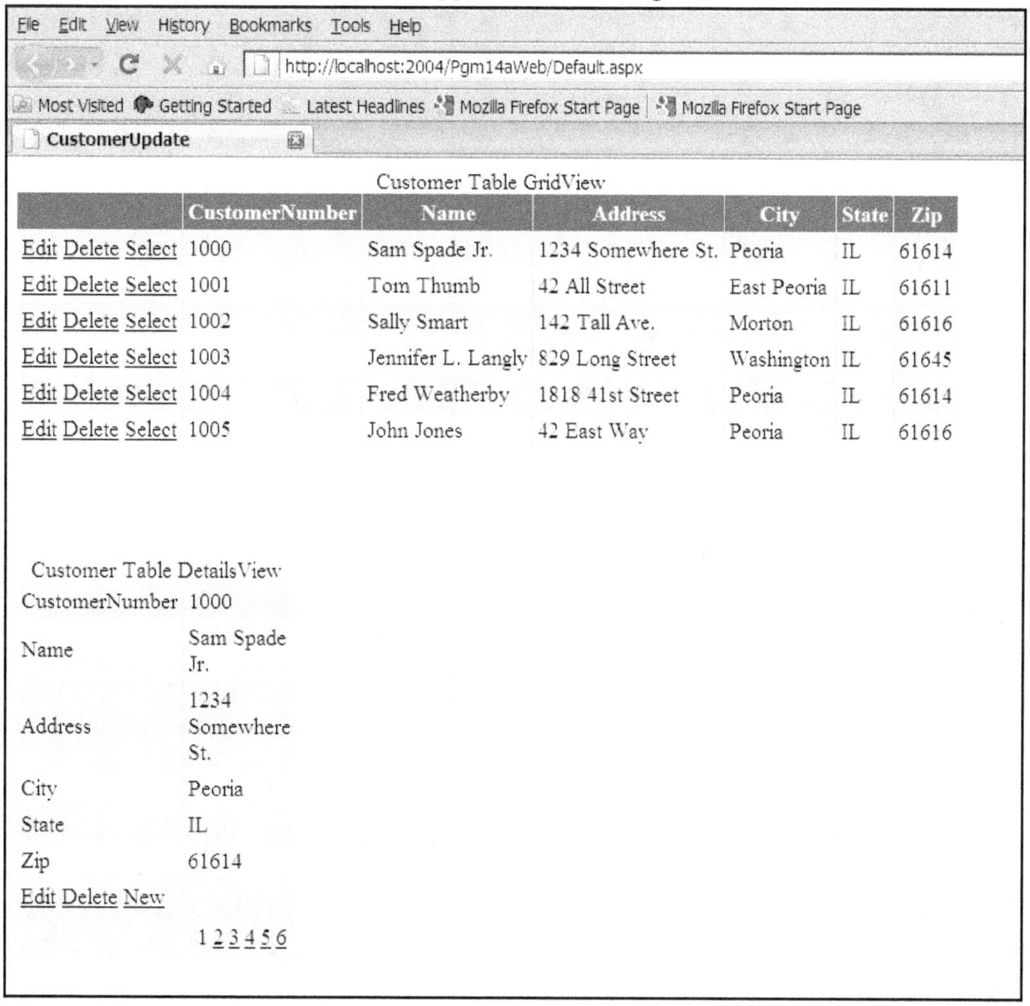

Figure 14.1 Pgm14aWeb in Operation

Let's examine the **GridView** first. Notice that the control allows one to provide Edit, Delete, and Select links. These are created using the AutoGeneratexxxButton properties as shown below in Figure 14.2. Clicking on these carries out the indicated action. The control has a number of color options which I set. Of course, after dragging the **GridView** icon from the tool box and dropping it on the form, the first action is to select the database to be used, here the Customer Table from the Purchase.mdb.

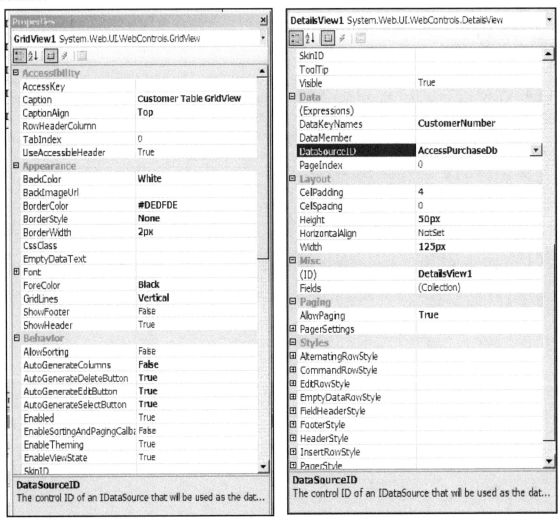

Figure 14.2 Some GridView Properties

First, I created the new web project. Then, I copied the Purchase.mdb file into the App_Data folder. Now drag the **GridView** control onto the form and start the connection process, Figure 14.1. One flaw I noticed is that when I went to choose the Purchase.mdb file, the dialog simply did not show it in the App_Data folder, Figure 14.2. I closed the project and then reopened it and now the dialog saw the file and I could continue setting up the connection.

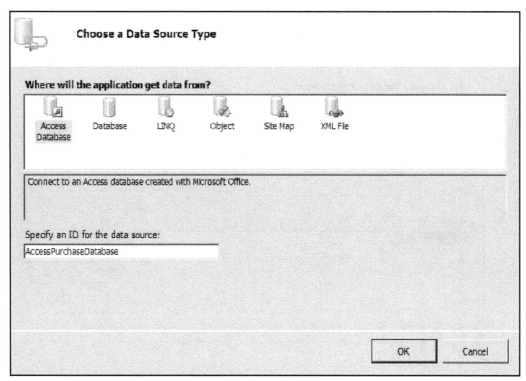

Figure 14.4 Choose a Data Source

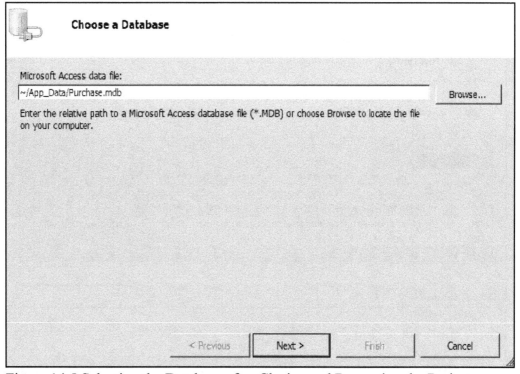

Figure 14.5 Selecting the Database after Closing and Reopening the Project

The next step in the construction process is to build the SQL statement, Figure 14.6. Here, I checked the * box, saying I want all fields and it created the SELECT statement as shown. It then allows you to test the retrieval, Figure 14.7.

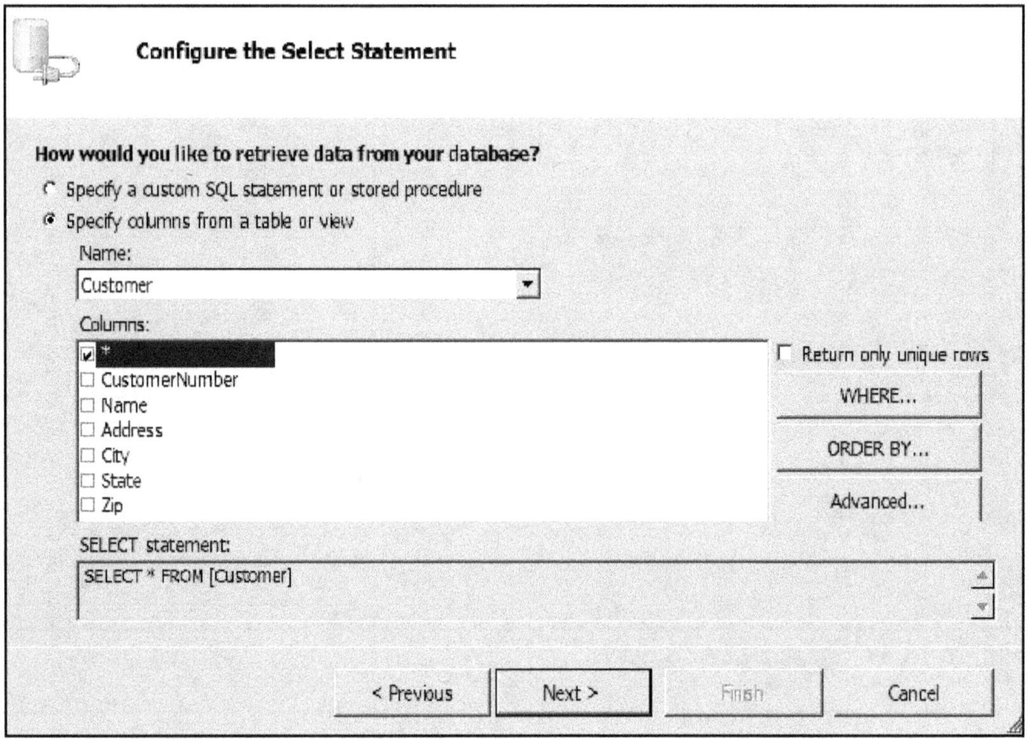

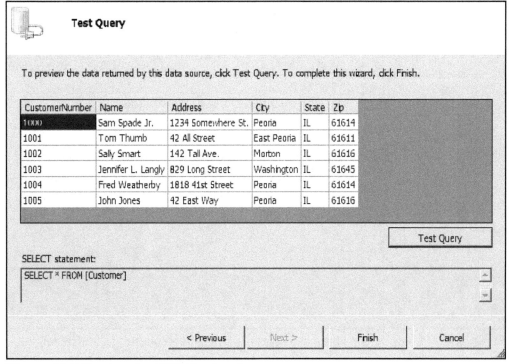

Figure 14.6 Building the Select Statement

Figure 14.7 Testing the SQL Retrieval 310

Finally, I ran the application to see what it would look like in the browser thus far, Figure 14.8.

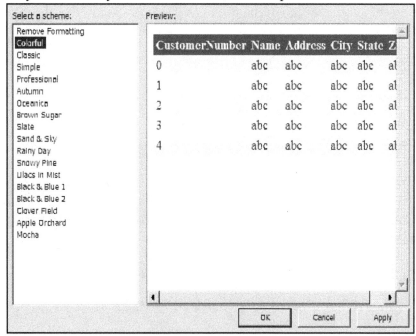

Figure 14.8 First Test Execution

Now that it appears correctly, I then began adjusting the other cosmetic properties, such as caption, colors, and so on. Make sure that the AutoGeneratexxxxButtons get enabled so that edits and deletes are easily done.

Under the tiny arrow at the top of the **GridView**, one selection is called AutoFormat, Figure 14.9. Here you can easily set a colorful scheme that pleases.

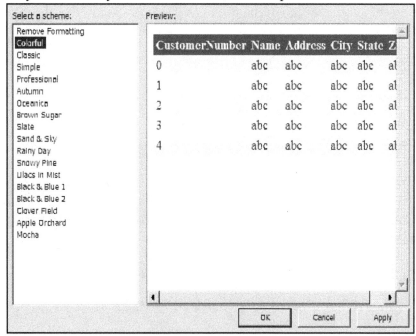

Figure 14.9 Auto Formatting the GridView

The next step is to drag a **DetailsView** from the tool box onto the form and connect it also to the same Purchase.mdb and the Customer table as well. With it, we can also add or insert new records. After making the connection, from the tiny **DetailsView** Task button drop down menu, I set the Enable Paging property which then provides the mechanism to move from record to record. I also set the four AutoGeneratexxxButtons so that we could add, edit, and delete records from here as well.

Viola, we have a fully working web program and have not yet written one line of code! Figure 14.10 shows the Design View of Pgm14aWeb.

Default.aspx.cs	**Default.aspx**	Start Page

div

Customer Table GridView

	CustomerNumber	Name	Address	City	State	Zip
Edit Delete Select	Databound	Databound	Databound	Databound	Databound	Databound
Edit Delete Select	Databound	Databound	Databound	Databound	Databound	Databound
Edit Delete Select	Databound	Databound	Databound	Databound	Databound	Databound
Edit Delete Select	Databound	Databound	Databound	Databound	Databound	Databound
Edit Delete Select	Databound	Databound	Databound	Databound	Databound	Databound

AccessDataSource - AccessPurchaseDb

Customer Table DetailsView

CustomerNumber	Databound
Name	Databound
Address	Databound
City	Databound
State	Databound
Zip	Databound

Design | Split | Source | <html> <body> <form#form1> <div>

Figure 14.10 The Design View

To run this one, you will need to click on the little arrow at the top of the control and in the popdown menu, chose Configure Data Source. Point it to the Purchase.mdb file in the App_Data subfolder. Then, rebuild the web.

Programming Problems

Problem 14-1—A Web Feedback Database Application

Construct a Web application using my provided Access database, feedback.mdb. The web form contains a text box for the person's name and one for their email address. A set of radio buttons allow the user to select which book on which he or she is providing feedback. For the titles use those I had in the sample Web applications or add your own. Finally, provide a multi-line text box for their feedback.

When they press the Submit button, first ensure that all text boxes contain something. For extra credit, try to validate the form of the email address. If a field has been omitted, display an error message. If all fields contain something, then add that information to the feedback data base. After adding the data to the database, then display "thank you" message below the Submit button.

Turn in a screen shots showing the application working and a screen shot of the resultant access database record. Note: make the Web Project first, then copy the feedback.mdb file into the project's App_Data folder. Then, close and reopen the project and Visual Studio should be able to find the database.

Problem 14-2—A Feedback Viewer

Make a project and copy the feedback.mdb file into the App_Data folder. Close and reopen the web project. Use Access to add six records of data to the database. Next, construct a Viewer web application that allows the user to view the data. Use any method desired. The only requirement is that the user is able to select in some manner the record that he or she desires to view.

Chapter 15—Miscellaneous Topics

The System Registry

Let's explore the System Registry a bit. The Registry (system.dat and user.dat—one user.dat for each user; user0.dat, user1.dat, etc) is organized into six major groups, known as HKEY_nnn. HKEY is a handle to a key—a key can be thought of as a "folder" and a handle is an unsigned int subscript into a table of values, that is, a subscript. These six top keys have many subkeys (subfolders). Eventually, one gets to the actual values being stored in a "folder." The six top most keys are

HKEY_CLASSES_ROOT—ties file extensions to programs and "classes"
HKEY_CURRENT_USER—info about the current user, their profile and settings
HKEY_LOCAL_MACHINE—this computer's hardware and software setup and
settings
HKEY_USERS—info on all users
HKEY_CURRENT_CONFIG—current setup info
HKEY_DYN_DATA—recreated each time system is booted, temp stuff is here

The actual data stored—such as the last file used—is stored as pairs of values.
```
value=data
```
such as
```
LastUsedFile=C:\Prod\work.txt
```

The Registry functions are in the following file.
using Microsoft.Win32;

Per Microsoft, the **Registry Class** "provides the set of standard root keys found in the registry on machines running Windows. The Registry is a storage facility for information about applications, users, and default system settings. For example, applications can use the Registry for storing information that needs to be preserved once the application is closed, and access that same information when the application is reloaded. For instance, you can store color preferences, screen locations, or the size of the window. You can control this for each user by storing the information in a different location in the Registry."

"The base (root) **RegistryKey** instances that are exposed by **Registry** delineate the basic storage mechanism for subkeys and values in the Registry. The keys are all readonly since the Registry depends on their existence. The keys exposed by **Registry** are:

CurrentUser—Stores information about user preferences.

LocalMachine—Stores configuration information for the local machine.

ClassesRoot—Stores information about types (and classes) and their properties.

314

Users—Stores information about the default user configuration.

PerformanceData—Stores performance information for software components.

CurrentConfig—Stores non-user-specific hardware information.

DynData—Stores dynamic data.

Once you have identified the root key under which you wish to store/retrieve information from the Registry, you can use the **RegistryKey** class to add or remove subkeys, and manipulate the values for a given key."

One of the most commonly used key for application software is located in the Local Machine key under the Software subkey. Frequently, the data stored there is organized by company name subkeys.

Typically we then want to open a specific one by generating a new **RegistryKey** which can be either readonly or read-writeable (true as the second parameter). Here is a typical startup sequence we might use after **InitializeComponents**().

```
RegistryKey companyKey = Registry.LocalMachine.OpenSubKey (
                    "Software\\Broquard Consulting", true);
if (companyKey == null) { // not existing yet, so make it
  companyKey = Registry.LocalMachine.CreateSubKey (
                    "Software\\Broquard Consulting");
  companyKey.Close ();
}
RegistryKey appKey = Registry.LocalMachine.OpenSubKey (
  "Software\\Broquard Consulting\\WindowsApplication06", true);
if (appKey == null) { // not existing yet, so make it
  appKey = Registry.LocalMachine.CreateSubKey (
      "Software\\Broquard Consulting\\WindowsApplication06");
  appKey.Close ();
}
```

These then build the folders in which we can to retrieve and store our values and their associated data. We use **GetValue** or **SetValue** functions.

```
appKey.SetValue ("LastFile", "This is a test.txt");
appKey.SetValue ("OurNumber", 42);
```

However the **GetValue** is overloaded.

```
appKey.GetValue ("LastFile");
```

returns the setting for LastFile, or null if it is not there. Whereas,

```
appKey.GetValue ("OurNumber", 42);
```

returns the setting of OutNumber or the value 42 if it is not there. We must typecast the returned object value into what we are expecting, (string), (int) and so on.

Typically, strings and DWORDs (unsigned int or 32bit values) are stored in the registry.

So with just this much information, we can load and store our key information in the Registry.

```
appKey = Registry.LocalMachine.OpenSubKey (
  "Software\\Broquard Consulting\\WindowsApplication06", true);
string last = (string) appKey.GetValue ("LastFile");
int num = (int) appKey.GetValue ("OurNumber");
appKey.Close ();
textBoxNumber.Text = "" + num;
textBoxLastFile.Text = last;
```

Here our two text boxes are filled from the Registry settings.

Figure 15.1 shows the Registry Editor examining our newly added Registry values.

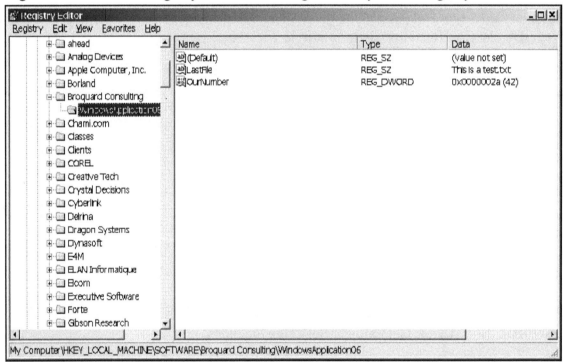

Figure 15.1 Using Reg Edit to Examine Values Placed into the System Registry

Attributes

These are notations (annotations) placed on elements of source: **class**, **members (data and functions)**, and **parameters**, for example. They can be used at run time for various purposes, including providing alternate runtime behavior, version information, organizational information by the designer, and so on. This includes just about any use that one wishes to make of this information, such as: how to associate a set of member variables of a class with the fields of a web page? Or where in the Registry and under what key do we retrieve or store a field? This information can now be stored in a set of attributes of the class and queried by the web page coding. An attribute is a generic means to associate information with your C# defined types.

C# provides some pre-built attributes and also allows you to create your own custom attribute class! They are stored with the metadata of the element and can be retrieved at runtime using a method known as reflection. For example, C# uses a conditional attribute to control whether or not to insert debugging function calls.

```
class MyClass {
 [Conditional("DEBUG")]
 public void ValidateData () {
}
```

In our current application, let's say that our company is creating a series of applications that all work together. Thus, some information is to be shared between applications and this info is to be stored in the registry. What hive? What Key? What value name? While we could diligently code this info into each and every program, if we later decided to change it, we'd have a mess trying to update it in all the applications. So let's make an attribute class to handle this communication for us.

With the application selected, I right clicked on it and chose "Add New Item and then selected "class" and entered **RegistryKeysAttribute.cs**. Then, I changed all namespace statements everywhere to `Broquard_Consulting_App_Group` so that all applications share the same namespace.

I derived the RegistryKeysAttribute class from the **Attribute** base class. If we use Attribute as the last part of our class name, when we use the [] notation, we can omit using the class qualifier because the compiler then assumes this class qualifier. The class defines the two needed properties: the subkey and the value name. Given this pair, we can then retrieve and set Registry values.

```
namespace Broquard_Consulting_App_Group
{
    public class RegistryKeysAttribute : Attribute
    {
        // by using Attribute as the last part of our class name,
        // when we use it in [ ], we can omit it - compiler assumes it

        protected String appKey; // subkey where the values are stored
```

317

```
        protected String valueName; // value=data string name to use

        public RegistryKeysAttribute(String appKey, String valueName)
        {
            this.appKey = appKey;
            this.valueName = valueName;
        }

        public String AppKey
        {
            get { return appKey; }
            set { appKey = value; }
        }

        public String ValueName
        {
            get { return valueName; }
            set { valueName = value; }
        }
    }
}
```

So we now have an attribute class which can store the application key and the item's value name to be used.

Now back in the actual application class, I added the attribute [] values this way to three data members of our class. I also show the data members whose values will be stored and retrieved from the system Registry.

```
        [RegistryKeys("Pgm15aWindows", "LastFile")]
        public String lastFile;

        [RegistryKeys("Pgm15aWindows", "OurNumber")]
        public int ourNumber;

        [RegistryKeys("Pgm15aWindows", "BkColor")]
        public Color bkColor;
```

Notice that since I ended the class name with "Attribute" the compiler assumed this and allowed me to code just **RegistryKeys** for short. Here the ctor requires two strings, the **appKey** and the **valueName**. These are provided as two positional parameters to the attribute ctor. Positional parameters are assigned then just as they would be if this were a "function call."

Alternatively, one can use named parameters. But if there are a mix of positional and named parameters, the positional ones must come first. It could have been coded this way.

```
    [RegistryKeys("Pgm15aWindows", ValueName="LastFile")]
    private String lastFile;

    [RegistryKeys(AppKey="Pgm15aWindows", ValueName="OurNumber")]
```

```
private String ourNumber;
```

Now how do we use the attributes at runtime? This is done by querying or reflection. Reflection allows you dynamically at runtime to determine the characteristics for an application. The .NET reflection APIs iterate through the metadata. The attributes can be on a class, on member functions and on member data.

```
using System.Reflection;
```

There are several different ways to iterate through the attributes depending on the circumstances.

1. specifying the **namespace** and the **class**
```
Type t = Type.GetType ("Broquard_Consulting_App_Group.Form1");
```

2. just a **class**
```
Type t = typeof (MyClass);
foreach (Attribute a in t.GetCustomAttributes()) {
 MyAttribute my = a as MyAttribute;
 if (my != null) {
  // we have one attribute
 }
}
```
where MyClass is coded
```
class MyClassAttribute : Attribute {
```

3. **member function**
```
Type t = Type.GetType ("MyClass");
foreach (MethodInfo m in t.GetCustomAttributes()) {
 foreach (Attribute a in m.GetCustomAttributes()) {
  if (a is MyAttribute) {
   // we have one attribute
  }
 }
}
```
where we have coded
```
[MyAttribute]
public void SumFunction () {
```

4. **data member**
```
Type t = Type.GetType ("MyClass");
foreach (FieldInfo m in t.GetFields()) {
 foreach (Attribute a in m.GetCustomAttributes()) {
  MyAttribute my = a as MyAttribute;
  if (my != null) {
   // we have one
  }
```

319

```
  }
 }
```
where we have coded
```
[MyAttribute]
public String mydataitem;
```

   In this application, we can create a get Registry values function this way. Our objective is to retrieve a last used filename, a last used number, and a last color used as three RGB values.
```
public void GetRegistryValues() {
 RegistryKey appKey;
 Type t = Type.GetType("Broquard_Consulting_App_Group.Form1");
 foreach (FieldInfo fi in t.GetFields()){
  foreach (Attribute a in fi.GetCustomAttributes(true)) {
   String s = a.ToString();
   RegistryKeysAttribute r = a as RegistryKeysAttribute;
   if (r != null) {
    if (fi.Name.CompareTo("lastFile") == 0) {
     appKey = Registry.LocalMachine.OpenSubKey(
                "Software\\Broquard Consulting\\" + r.AppKey, true);
     if (appKey != null) {
      lastFile = (string)appKey.GetValue(r.ValueName);
      appKey.Close();
      textBoxLastFile.Text = lastFile;
     }
    }
    else if (fi.Name.CompareTo("ourNumber") == 0) {
     appKey = Registry.LocalMachine.OpenSubKey(
                "Software\\Broquard Consulting\\" + r.AppKey, true);
     if (appKey != null) {
      ourNumber = (int)appKey.GetValue(r.ValueName);
      appKey.Close();
      textBoxNumber.Text = "" + ourNumber;
     }
    }
    else if (fi.Name.CompareTo("bkColor") == 0) {
     appKey = Registry.LocalMachine.OpenSubKey(
                "Software\\Broquard Consulting\\" + r.AppKey, true);
     if (appKey != null) {
      String color = (string)appKey.GetValue(r.ValueName);
      if (color == null) continue;
      appKey.Close();
      SetColors(color);
     }
    }
   }
  }
 }
}
```

Using Colors

C# encapsulates color in a **Color** class. When you examine the class members, notice that there are a huge number of predefined color values you can use directly. However, the class provides an easy way for you to set any custom color by providing the red, green, and blue components, RGB, which can have a value from 0 to 255. The function is called **FromArgb** that is passed three integers for red, green and blue intensities. By using a form's property, **BackColor**, we can set our form to any desired background **Color** value.

Suppose that we also want to store the background color the application should use in the Registry. While we could store the three colors values, r g b, it is easier to store it as a single string. Let's place a colon as a separator between these three values. For example, if we wanted to store a grey color, the registry string could be 210:210:210.

To make a simple user interface to change color values, we can use three text boxes for the red, green and blue components. (Naturally, this would more likely be in a dialog box launched from a choose background color menu item.) We need to provide functions to respond to the changes in these text boxes and reflect that new color as the user enters the numbers. Thus, we can use the **TextChanged** event: OnRedChanged, OnGreenChanged and OnBlueChanged. Since we are going to store an instance of Color and not the individual red,green,blue integers, the simplest approach to use is have all three of these events call the same function, SetColor. This function must retrieve all three text values, use try-catch logic to convert them into integers, verify they are in range, and if all is okay, construct a Color instance and set the background color to this new value so that changes are reflected in real-time.

Here is what the Pgm15aWindows looks like when running.

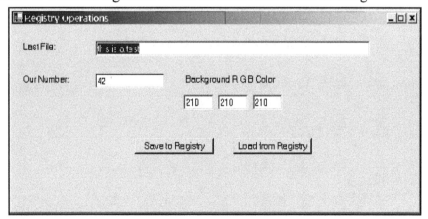

Figure 15.2 Pgm15aWindows in Operation

And here is what the registry looks like after we have saved the settings.

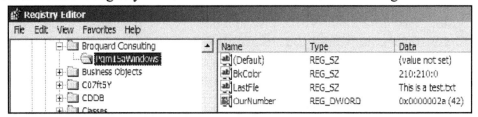

Figure 15.3 The Registry After Running Pgm15aWindows

Here is the complete coding.

```csharp
using System;
using System.Collections.Generic;
using System.ComponentModel;
using System.Data;
using System.Drawing;
using System.Linq;
using System.Text;
using System.Windows.Forms;

using Microsoft.Win32;
using System.Reflection;

namespace Broquard_Consulting_App_Group {
 public partial class Form1 : Form {
  public Form1() {
   InitializeComponent();
   InitialLoad();
  }

  [RegistryKeys("Pgm15aWindows", "LastFile")]
  public String lastFile;

  [RegistryKeys("Pgm15aWindows", "OurNumber")]
  public int ourNumber;

  [RegistryKeys("Pgm15aWindows", "BkColor")]
  public Color bkColor;

  private void InitialLoad(){
   RegistryKey companyKey = Registry.LocalMachine.OpenSubKey(
                        "Software\\Broquard Consulting", true);
   if (companyKey == null) {
    companyKey = Registry.LocalMachine.CreateSubKey(
                                 "Software\\Broquard Consulting");
    companyKey.Close();
   }
```

```
RegistryKey appKey = Registry.LocalMachine.OpenSubKey(
            "Software\\Broquard Consulting\\Pgm15aWindows", true);
if (appKey == null){
 appKey = Registry.LocalMachine.CreateSubKey(
                "Software\\Broquard Consulting\\Pgm15aWindows");
 appKey.SetValue("LastFile", "This is a test.txt");
 appKey.SetValue("OurNumber", 42);
 appKey.Close();
}
appKey = Registry.LocalMachine.OpenSubKey(
            "Software\\Broquard Consulting\\Pgm15aWindows", true);
string last = (string)appKey.GetValue("LastFile");
int num = (int)appKey.GetValue("OurNumber");
appKey.Close();
textBoxNumber.Text = "" + num;
textBoxLastFile.Text = last;

bkColor = Color.FromArgb(210, 210, 210);
this.BackColor = bkColor;
textBoxRed.Text = "210";
textBoxGreen.Text = "210";
textBoxBlue.Text = "210";

GetRegistryValues();
}

private void OnSaveToRegistry(object sender, EventArgs e) {
 SetRegistryValues();
}

private void OnLoadFromRegistry(object sender, EventArgs e) {
 GetRegistryValues();
}

public void SetRegistryValues() {
 lastFile = textBoxLastFile.Text;
 try {
  ourNumber = Int32.Parse(textBoxNumber.Text);
 }
 catch (Exception) {
  ourNumber = 0;
 }
 RegistryKey appKey;
 Type t = Type.GetType("Broquard_Consulting_App_Group.Form1");
 foreach (FieldInfo fi in t.GetFields()) {
  foreach (Attribute a in fi.GetCustomAttributes(true)) {
   String s = a.ToString();
   RegistryKeysAttribute r = a as RegistryKeysAttribute;
   if (r != null) {
    if (fi.Name.CompareTo("lastFile") == 0) {
```

```
        appKey = Registry.LocalMachine.OpenSubKey(
                "Software\\Broquard Consulting\\" + r.AppKey, true);
      if (appKey != null) {
       appKey.SetValue(r.ValueName, lastFile);
       appKey.Close();
      }
    }
    else if (fi.Name.CompareTo("ourNumber") == 0){
      appKey = Registry.LocalMachine.OpenSubKey(
                "Software\\Broquard Consulting\\" + r.AppKey, true);
      if (appKey != null) {
       appKey.SetValue(r.ValueName, ourNumber);
       appKey.Close();
      }
    }
    else if (fi.Name.CompareTo("bkColor") == 0) {
      appKey = Registry.LocalMachine.OpenSubKey(
                "Software\\Broquard Consulting\\" + r.AppKey, true);
      if (appKey != null) {
       String color = textBoxRed.Text + ":" + textBoxGreen.Text + ":"
                     + textBoxBlue.Text;
       appKey.SetValue(r.ValueName, color);
       appKey.Close();
      }
    }
   }
  }
 }
}

public void GetRegistryValues() {
 RegistryKey appKey;
 Type t = Type.GetType("Broquard_Consulting_App_Group.Form1");
 foreach (FieldInfo fi in t.GetFields()) {
  foreach (Attribute a in fi.GetCustomAttributes(true)) {
   String s = a.ToString();
   RegistryKeysAttribute r = a as RegistryKeysAttribute;
   if (r != null) {
    if (fi.Name.CompareTo("lastFile") == 0) {
      appKey = Registry.LocalMachine.OpenSubKey(
                "Software\\Broquard Consulting\\" + r.AppKey, true);
      if (appKey != null) {
       lastFile = (string)appKey.GetValue(r.ValueName);
       appKey.Close();
       textBoxLastFile.Text = lastFile;
      }
    }
    else if (fi.Name.CompareTo("ourNumber") == 0) {
      appKey = Registry.LocalMachine.OpenSubKey(
                "Software\\Broquard Consulting\\" + r.AppKey, true);
```

```
      if (appKey != null) {
       ourNumber = (int)appKey.GetValue(r.ValueName);
       appKey.Close();
       textBoxNumber.Text = "" + ourNumber;
      }
     }
     else if (fi.Name.CompareTo("bkColor") == 0) {
      appKey = Registry.LocalMachine.OpenSubKey(
              "Software\\Broquard Consulting\\" + r.AppKey, true);
      if (appKey != null) {
       String color = (string)appKey.GetValue(r.ValueName);
       if (color == null) continue;
       appKey.Close();
       SetColors(color);
      }
     }
    }
   }
  }
}

private void SetColors(String color) {
 String sr, sg, sb;
 int end = color.IndexOf(":", 0);
 sr = color.Substring(0, end);
 int start = end + 1;
 end = color.IndexOf(":", start);
 sg = color.Substring(start, end - start);
 sb = color.Substring(end + 1);
 int r, g, b;
 try {
  r = Int32.Parse(sr);
 }
 catch (Exception) {
  r = 0;
 }
 try {
  g = Int32.Parse(sg);
 }
 catch (Exception) {
  g = 0;
 }
 try {
  b = Int32.Parse(sb);
 }
 catch (Exception) {
  b = 0;
 }
 if (r > 255) r = 255;
 else if (r < 0) r = 0;
```

```
 if (g > 255) g = 255;
 else if (g < 0) g = 0;
 if (b > 255) b = 255;
 else if (b < 0) b = 0;
 textBoxRed.Text = "" + r;
 textBoxGreen.Text = "" + g;
 textBoxBlue.Text = "" + b;
 bkColor = Color.FromArgb(r, g, b);
 this.BackColor = bkColor;
}

private void OnRedChanged(object sender, System.EventArgs e) {
 SetColor();
}

private void OnGreenChanged(object sender, System.EventArgs e) {
 SetColor();
}

private void OnBlueChanged(object sender, System.EventArgs e) {
 SetColor();
}

private void SetColor(){
 int r, g, b;
 try {
  r = Int32.Parse(textBoxRed.Text);
 }
 catch (Exception) {
  return;
 }
 try {
  g = Int32.Parse(textBoxGreen.Text);
 }
 catch (Exception) {
  return;
 }
 try {
  b = Int32.Parse(textBoxBlue.Text);
 }
 catch (Exception) {
  return;
 }
 if (r > 255) {
  r = 255;
  textBoxRed.Text = "255";
 }
 else if (r < 0) {
  r = 0;
  textBoxRed.Text = "0";
```

```
    }
    if (g > 255) {
     g = 255;
     textBoxGreen.Text = "255";
    }
    else if (g < 0) {
     g = 0;
     textBoxGreen.Text = "0";
    }
    if (b > 255) {
     b = 255;
     textBoxBlue.Text = "255";
    }
    else if (b < 0) {
     b = 0;
     textBoxBlue.Text = "0";
    }
    bkColor = Color.FromArgb(r, g, b);
    this.BackColor = bkColor;
   }
 }
}
```

Programming Problems

None

Chapter 16—Dlls and Deployment Code—Assemblies

Making DLLs—Class Library

When you want to deploy your solutions, often times you merely want to market your components as add-ons instead of an application program. In this situation, you make a new project, choosing **Class Library** as the project type.

I am purposely keeping the actual class coding trivial so that we can concentrate on the mechanics. Here is the class library I intend to market, a multi-roots finder.

```csharp
using System;
using System.Collections.Generic;
using System.Linq;
using System.Text;

namespace MultiRootsLibrary
{
    public class MultiRoots
    {
        public MultiRoots()
        {
        }

        public static double FindRoot(double number, double root)
        {
            return Math.Pow(number, root);
        }
    }
}
```

When this solution is built, it generates Pgm16aClassLibrary.dll in the Bin\Release subfolder.

However, I also edited the AssemblyInfo.cs file to provide business and copyright information.

```csharp
[assembly: AssemblyTitle("MultiRootsLibrary")]
[assembly: AssemblyDescription("MultiRoots Finder Collection")]
[assembly: AssemblyConfiguration("")]
[assembly: AssemblyCompany("Broquard Consulting")]
[assembly: AssemblyProduct("Math Helper")]
[assembly: AssemblyCopyright("2009 by Broquard Consulting")]
[assembly: AssemblyTrademark("")]
```

```
[assembly: AssemblyCulture("")]
```

Next to use our fancy package or dll, we build another project, Pgm16bClassLibraryClient. Here is the Pgm16bClassLibraryClient cs file that then wants to make use of our dll. Notice the use of the using statement to avoid having to further qualify the function call.

```
using System;
using System.Collections.Generic;
using System.Linq;
using System.Text;
using MultiRootsLibrary;

namespace Pgm16bClassLibraryClient
{
    class Class1
    {
        static void Main(string[] args)
        {
            double x = 100;
            double p = .5;
            double ansr;
            ansr = MultiRoots.FindRoot(x, p);
            Console.WriteLine("" + ansr);
        }
    }
}
```

Of course, when it compiles, the compiler cannot find the MultiRoots.FindRoot function.

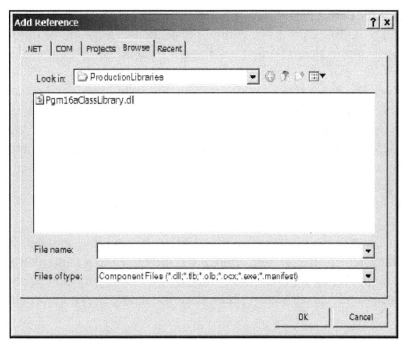

Figure 16.1 Adding a Reference to a DLL

However, in order to use the dll, we need add a reference to it. Normally, one would put these into some kind of production library. In this case, I made a folder called ProductionLibraries and copied the dll into it. Choose Project—Add Reference. Click on the Browse tab and then navigate to this folder and select the dll, as shown in Figure 16.1.

Rebuild and when the program runs, it now produces a line saying 10, the square root of 100. This is the basic idea of assemblies.

Assemblies

Assemblies make up the building blocks of the .NET Framework, forming the fundamental unit of deployment, version control, reuse, and security permissions. By definition, "An assembly provides the common language runtime with the information it needs to be aware of type implementations." The assembly is the collection of types and resources that make up the application logical unit. The runtime platform does not see a type outside the context of an assembly.

The simplest assembly is a single file loaded into a single application domain. This simple assembly cannot be referenced by other assemblies outside the folder it is in. No version checking is done on it either because it is the smallest unit of work. To install such an application, just make a directory for it and place the files in it. To uninstall such an, delete the directory where it resides.

However, if you are going to market a package or wish to have some coding shared between applications, in other words some common routines, then we need a multifile approach. Here we see the benefits of code reuse, bu providing a library of commonly needed objects and/or functions that can be shared between various applications. Sometimes these are called code libraries.

A multifile assembly can be either several code modules and resource files working together or it can be an assembly that is shared across multiple applications. Usually, a shared assembly must have a strong name and can be deployed in the global assembly cache. The idea of a strong name is this. Suppose you wish to deploy MultiRoots to the entire world. How can you guarantee that our chosen names are not going to conflict with other packages from other vendors? Further, how can the user guarantee that our release modules have not been altered?
This is done by making use of a strong name which is very unique.

An assembly's name impacts the assembly's scope and use by multiple applications. In the simplest case, assemblies intended for use by one application only require a name that is unique within the application. The moment that we cross that boundary by desiring to share with multiple applications we must sign our assemblies with strong names using standard public key cryptography.

Note: "The runtime treats assembly names as case-insensitive when binding to an assembly, but preserves whatever case is used in an assembly name."

A strong name consists of a public key and a digital signature in addition to the simple text assembly name. It is generated over an assembly file using a corresponding private key. (The assembly file contains the assembly manifest, which contains the names and hashes of all the files that make up the assembly.) Signing an assembly with a strong name allows the assembly to be deployed in the global assembly cache.

Each computer where the common language runtime is installed has a machine-wide code cache called the global assembly cache. The global assembly cache stores assemblies specifically designated to be shared by several applications on the computer.

If you put an assembly in the global assembly cache, the common language runtime requires that the file name of the assembly match the assembly name (not including the file name extension, such as .exe or .dll). For example, if the file name of an assembly is myAssembly.dll, the assembly name must be myAssembly. Private assemblies deployed only in the root application directory can have an assembly name that is different from the file name.

The runtime does not consider the file name when determining an assembly's identity. The assembly identity, made up of the assembly name, version, culture, and strong name, must be clear to the runtime.

An assembly's location determines whether the common language runtime can locate it when referenced and can also determine whether the assembly can be shared with other assemblies. You can deploy an assembly in the following locations.

1. The application's directory or subdirectories. This is the most common location for deploying an assembly. The subdirectories of an application's root directory can be based on language or culture. If an assembly has information in the culture attribute, it must be in a subdirectory under the application directory with that culture's name.

2. The global assembly cache. This is a machine-wide code cache that is installed wherever the common language runtime is installed. In most cases, if you intend to share an assembly with multiple applications, you should deploy it into the global assembly cache.

3. On an FTTP server. An assembly deployed on an FTTP server must have a strong name; you point to the assembly in the codebase section of the application's configuration file.

Assembly Manifest Contents

The first four items—the assembly name, version number, culture, and strong name information—make up the assembly's identity.

Information	Description
Assembly name	A text string specifying the assembly's name.
Version number	A major and minor version number, and a revision and build number. The common language runtime uses these numbers to enforce version policy.
Culture	Information on the culture or language that the assembly supports. This information should be used only to designate an assembly as a satellite assembly containing culture- or language-specific information. (An assembly with culture information is automatically assumed to be a satellite assembly.)
Strong name information	The public key from the publisher if the assembly has been given a strong name.
List of all files in the assembly	A hash of each file contained in the assembly and a file name. Note that all files that make up the assembly must be in the same directory as the file containing the assembly manifest.
Type reference information	Information used by the runtime to map a type reference to the file that contains its declaration and implementation. This is used for types that are exported from the assembly.
Information on referenced assemblies	A list of other assemblies that are statically referenced by the assembly. Each reference includes the dependent assembly's name, assembly metadata (version, culture, operating system, and so on), and public key, if the assembly is strong named.

You can add or change some information in the assembly manifest by using assembly attributes in your code. You can change version information and informational attributes, including Trademark, Copyright, Product, Company, and Informational Version.

The pair, Pgm15aClassLibrary and Pgm15bClassLibraryClient, illustrate the simplest approach. It has the draw back that no strong name is used and it cannot be placed in global assembly cache. There is no protection for the user if it gets clobbered or overwritten, that is, there is no security.

Deployment Methods

There are several ways to put your application into production. Let us examine some of these.

Private Assemblies

This is the simplest method. One makes a production folder and copies all of the exe and dll files into this folder. This is illustrated in the samples folder called Pgm16bClassLibDeployment1. I copied the dll and exe here. If you double click the exe in the Explorer, the program launches and runs. However, look fast, as soon as it displays the answer, the window closes.

Sometimes, you may wish to place the many dlls in a subfolder beneath the client exe application. This is illustrated in Pgm16bClassLibDeployment2. Here I made a subfolder called MyClasses and placed the dll in this folder. The client exe is in the main folder above this one. If you try to run it now, it fails. Why? When the framework looks for the dll, it does not probe any subfolders beneath the one in which the exe is located, not automatically, that is.

By using a configuration file, we can instruct the framework to look in the MyClasses subfolder. I used Notepad to generate the config file. Sometimes, you can create the config file from the project within Visual Studio .NET. The file is in XML format and is case sensitive. The file name must be the same name as the exe but with .config appended to it. Here is the Pgm16bClassLibraryClient.exe.config file.

```
<configuration>
 <runtime>
  <assemblyBinding xmlns="urn:schemas-microsoft-com:asm.v1">
   <probing privatePath="MyClasses"/>
  </assemblyBinding>
 </runtime>
</configuration>
```

The key line is the probing one. If you have more than one folder to search, add a semicolon and blank after each one. For example,

```
<probing privatePath="MyClasses; MyClasses\More; MyWork"/>
```

With the config file added, now the application will once more run perfectly. Shared assemblies, that is, assemblies that are going to be used in several applications requires a bit more work to get them deployed.

Making a Strong Name DLL

Next, ClassLibrary3 project is the same as version 1, it is the MultiRoots dll. However, it is now given a strong name. In the AssemblyInfo.cs file, I coded the following:

```
[assembly: AssemblyTitle("MultiRoots")]
[assembly: AssemblyDescription("A MultiRoots Application Package")]
[assembly: AssemblyConfiguration("")]
[assembly: AssemblyCompany("Broquard Consulting")]
[assembly: AssemblyProduct("MultiRoots")]
[assembly: AssemblyCopyright("Copyright ©  2009")]
[assembly: AssemblyTrademark("")]
[assembly: AssemblyCulture("")]
```

Next, we must make the strong key. This is done using the sn.exe SDK utility program. I used Explorer to do a search for the file and then ran the utility. Here is the DOS screen of the run. Note that it made the two files in the folder where sn.exe is located. I then copied them into the Samples folder. Here, keypair.snk is our new strong name file. To build a strong name, we must use the .NET Sdk DOS program **sn**. (ie. StrongName.exe)

```
C:\>cd "\program files\microsoft visual studio 8\sdk\v2.0\bin"
C:\Program Files\Microsoft Visual Studio 8\SDK\v2.0\Bin>sn -k keypair.snk
Microsoft (R) .NET Framework Strong Name Utility   Version
2.0.50727.42
Copyright (c) Microsoft Corporation.  All rights reserved.
Key pair written to keypair.snk
```

Once the key is built, it consists of a private and public use portions. We need to give our customers the public key portion. So we use the sn utility to extract the public portion:

```
C:\Program Files\Microsoft Visual Studio 8\SDK\v2.0\Bin>sn -p keypair.snk public
.snk
Microsoft (R) .NET Framework Strong Name Utility   Version
2.0.50727.42
Copyright (c) Microsoft Corporation.  All rights reserved.

Public key written to public.snk
```

Finally, if you want to dynamically load a dll when needed and not make it a part of the application proper, the load function requires a "text" format of the public key called a token. Again, the sm utility can give us this number this way.

```
C:\Program Files\Microsoft Visual Studio 8\SDK\v2.0\Bin>sn -tp public.snk
Microsoft (R) .NET Framework Strong Name Utility   Version
2.0.50727.42
Copyright (c) Microsoft Corporation.  All rights reserved.
Public key is
00240000048000009400000006020000002400005253413100040000010001003
```

```
f7b5445ae4487
bf6f370df945c12ea4e1d9c7cb9594ea88c0c5483c097940fa69af672b8422e52
a86f3496afab6
88c200cfe3dd0433a520521d26260ed9ca9bed7b1a971c3f48c9b8ccc1ef7a929
c7a1ad71720ec
1e0e7fab476ec3cf84c31ec0502a7353666b62374d482f0eaa2fa80d379bc517e
10c8f137c62c4
17222bbf
```

```
Public key token is 9575c20fd54cb2c7
C:\Program Files\Microsoft Visual Studio 8\SDK\v2.0\Bin>
```

Next, I built the Pgm16cClassLib cs file similar to the previous one.

```
namespace MultiRootsLibrary {
    public class MultiRoots       {
        public MultiRoots() { }
        public static double FindRoot(double number, double root)
        {
            return Math.Pow(number, root);
        }
    }
}
```

To add the strong key, right click on the project, choose properties. Select Signing and browse for the key file. This is shown in Figure 16.2. Build the project.

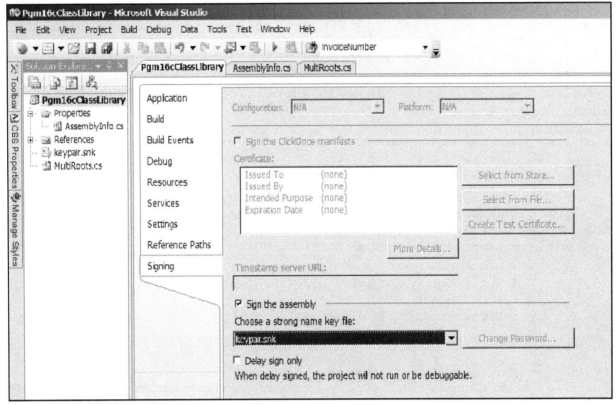

Figure 16.2 Installing the Strong Key File

Making the Pgm16dClassLibClient with Strong Key Assembly

Next, I built Pgm14dClassLibClient much as before, only I will use the strong named version of the MultiRoots. However, we must put the public key into the same folder as the release dll so that it can find it. In our cs file, we must specify the key file to use, shown in bold. I also right clicked on References and chose Add Reference, browsed to the dll and selected it.

```csharp
using System;
using System.Collections.Generic;
using System.Linq;
using System.Text;
using System.Reflection;
using MultiRootsLibrary;
[assembly: AssemblyKeyFileAttribute(@"keypair.snk")]

namespace Pgm16dClassLibraryClient {
 class Class1  {
  static void Main(string[] args) {
   double x = 100;
```

```
    double p = .5;
    double ansr;
    ansr = MultiRoots.FindRoot (x, p);
    Console.WriteLine ("" + ansr);
  }
 }
}
```

Dynamically Loading a Needed DLL at Run Time

Sometimes, one might want to load in the dll at runtime when it is needed and explicitly find the function that one wishes to call. Notice that now there is no using for the ClassLibrary3 namespace and no Assembly directive. Copy the strong key pair and the dll into the bin\debug or release folder of the project. However, you still must add or insert a Reference to the dll.

```
using System;
using System.Collections.Generic;
using System.Linq;
using System.Text;
using System.Reflection;

namespace Pgm16eClassLibraryClient {
 class Class1  {
  static void Main(string[] args)          {
   double x = 100;
   double p = .5;
   double ansr;
   Assembly a =
        Assembly.Load("Pgm16cClassLibrary,Version=1.0.0.0,"
            "Culture=neutral,PublicKeyToken=9575c20fd54cb2c7");
   Module m = a.GetModule("Pgm16cClassLibrary.dll");
   Type t = m.GetType("MultiRootsLibrary.MultiRoots");
   object[] parms = new object [2];
   parms[0] = x;
   parms[1] = p;
   ansr = (double) (t.InvokeMember ("FindRoot",
            BindingFlags.Public | BindingFlags.InvokeMethod |
            BindingFlags.Static, null, null, parms));
   Console.WriteLine ("" + ansr);
  }
 }
}
```

The first step is to load the dll of the right version. That is, we need to load in the strong keyed assembly. Make and instance of **Assembly** and call the static **Load** function. Notice that the Load function takes the version and the text public key to use.

Given the loaded assembly, from it, we need to find the module known as Pgm16cClassLibrary.dll. This is done using the member function **GetModule**.

From the module, we get the type of class desired using **GetType**. Here, I am looking for the MultiRootsLibrary namespace and within it the class called MultiRoots.

Given the type, we can use it to invoke various functions using the **InvokeMember** function which returns an object which can be typecasted back to that it was, a double. Of course, many functions require one or more parameters, so they are passed as an array of objects. This is the really clumsy part, the construction of a parameter list.

However, we are now dynamically loading and calling our dll without having it hardcoded into our assembly. This gives us more flexibility at runtime.

The Global Assembly Cache

The global cache is located in the windows subfolder called Assembly. Use the Explorer to view it. Right clicking brings up an item's properties. Here is where all of the production .Net libraries are found, along with many other third party libraries.

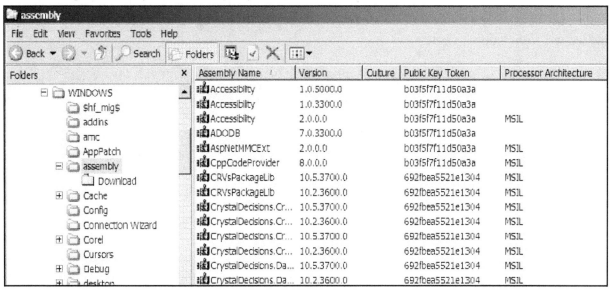

Figure 16.3 Exploring the Assembly Global Cache

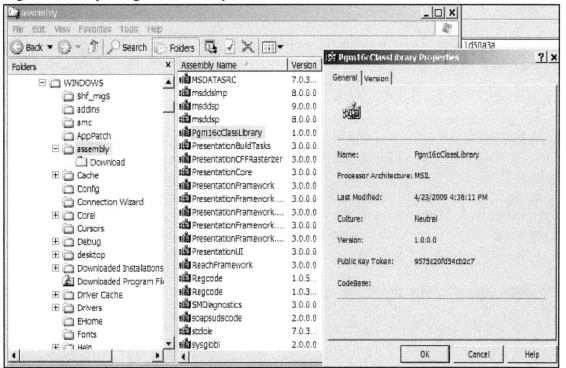

Figure 16.4 After Dragging the DLL into the Global Cache and Displaying Properties

To install our package to the cache, drag the strongly named dll from release folder of Pgm16cClassLibrary into the Assembly folder. Windows adds it to the global cache. I then right clicked and displayed its properties as shown in the above Figure 16.4.

Note only strong named assemblies can be placed in the global cache. While you can easily drag and drop into the global cache on your computer, this isn't practical when you want to market your dlls. The preferred method for production work is to use the Microsoft Windows Installer, which we will examine shortly.

Now we need to test the use of the dll in the global cache. Pgm16fClassLibraryClient has the exact same coding as Pgm16eClassLibraryClient in its cs file. However, there is nor reference to that dll in the project solution. Further, there is no dll or public key files in the executable folder either. The needed dll is found automatically by the compiler in the global cache. Remember, if you want to actually execute Pgm16fClassLibraryClient, you will have to drag the release dll from Pgm16cClassLibrary into your machine's global cache.

Deployment Methods Continued

1. If the application is a simple one, you can simply copy the exe and distribute it by all the usual methods, such as zipping, copying, and so on. The user puts it in their desired folder and runs it. If it is a web application, just ftp all the files to the desired folder and run it.

2. If you need registry settings or items in the global cache, then you have to use the Microsoft Window Installer.

Distributing a Windows Forms application using the Windows Installer allows you to leverage both the Installer and Windows Application Management. You can also advertise the application's availability, publish the application, use the **Add/Remove Programs** option in Control Panel to install or remove the application, and easily repair the application, if necessary.

Microsoft Windows Installer can install and manage common language runtime assemblies. According to Microsoft, "Developers of Windows Installer packages can install assemblies to the global assembly cache or to a location that is isolated for a particular application. This improved capability to isolate applications is an important part of the .NET Framework."

"Windows Installer has the following features that support common language runtime assemblies:
Installation, repair, or removal of assemblies in the global assembly cache.
Installation, repair, or removal of assemblies in private locations designated for particular applications.

Rollback of unsuccessful installations, repairs, or removals of assemblies.
Install-on-demand of strong-named assemblies in the global assembly cache.
Install-on-demand of assemblies in private locations designated for particular applications.
Patching of assemblies.
Advertisement of shortcuts that point to assemblies.

Authors of Windows Installer packages can use these features by populating the MsiAssembly and MsiAssemblyName tables."

How Windows Installer 2.0 Works with Assemblies

Windows Installer treats an assembly built with the .NET Framework as a single Windows Installer component. All the files that constitute an assembly must be contained by a single Windows Installer component that is listed in the component table of the Installer.

According to Microsoft, "Windows Installer installs assemblies into the global assembly cache using the Microsoft .NET Framework. When installing assemblies into the global assembly cache, the Installer does not use the same directory structure and file versioning rules that it uses to install regular Windows Installer components. Assemblies are added and removed from the global assembly cache as a unit; that is, the files that constitute an assembly are always installed or removed together."

"Windows Installer uses a two-step transactional process to install products containing assemblies, which enables the installer to roll back unsuccessful installations.

"When Removing Assemblies from the Global Assembly Cache, Windows Installer determines whether to remove an assembly based on a client list that it keeps independent of the assembly. Windows Installer keeps one pin bit that represents all Windows Installer clients of the assembly. The assembly maintains one pin bit for each client. The Installer pins the assembly for the first Windows Installer client and unpins the assembly when the last Windows Installer client is removed. The file is then deleted from the global assembly cache."

Setup For Pgm16aWindows (Pgm08aWindows revisited)

I took our purchase records program (Pgm08aWindows) and chose to make an install for it.

Make a new project called Pgm16gSetup. For the project type, near the bottom of the Project Types on the left, select Other Project Types and then Set Up and Deployment. Choose in the right pane Setup Project. This is shown in Figure 16.5.

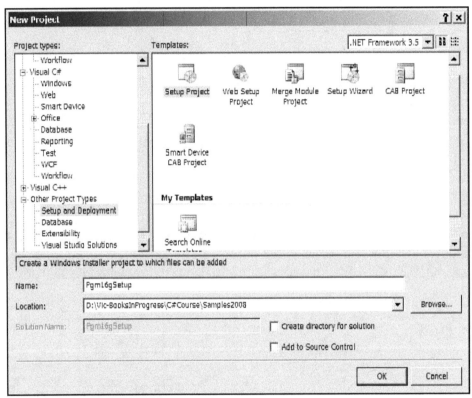

Figure 16.5 Creating a Setup Project

When you click OK, the empty setup project is built, as shown below in Figure 16.6

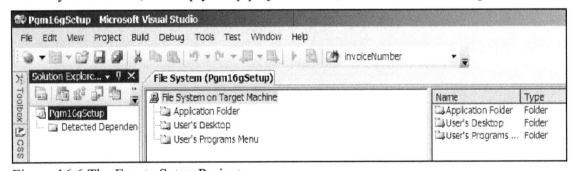

Figure 16.6 The Empty Setup Project

Next, can click on Application Folder and right click and choose Add File and point it to the exe file and the database file. Figure 16.7 shows what it looks like after I added the exe and the sales dat file.

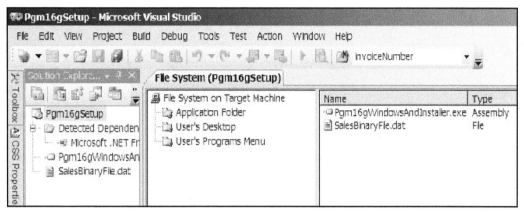

Figure 16.7 After Adding the Exe and the Dat file to the Application Folder

Next, right click on the icon Application Folder and chose Properties. Set the destination folder where you want the application to be installed. Figure 16.8 shows what I used.

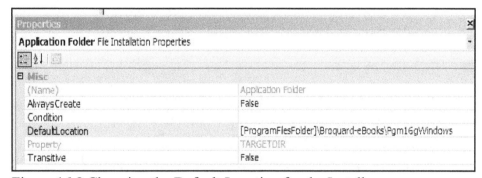

Figure 16.8 Changing the Default Location for the Install

Now build the project. When it is done, in the Release folder there are two versions, the standalone setup.exe and the Pgm16gSetup.msi installer. Either one can be used. Double click one of these to launch the installer.

When it runs the first time, Figure 16.10, the default folder is shown, but the user can change it. Figure 16.9 shows its folder in Program Files. When it runs after the first time, Figure 16.12, the user is given the option of Repair or Remove the application.

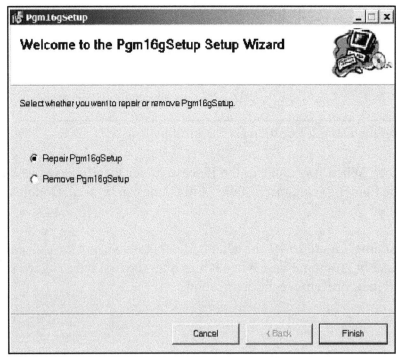

Figure 16.10 Running the Installer the First Time

Figure 16.11 Running the Installer a Second Time

You can do much more with this, including conditional actions in response to user selections and do on. Search help for Deployment.

The End.